A decade after the publication of what has become a cult guidebook to understanding, **Richard Saul Wurman,** *in this expanded & updated volume, gives clarity to confusion with new maps for navigating through a stream of bytes that leaves us inundated with data but*

INFORMATION**ANXIETY**2

starved for the tools & patterns that give them meaning. In reality there has not been an information explosion, but rather an explosion of non-information, or data that simply doesn't inform. DISCARD

with additional research & writing by Loring Leifer & David Sume
Karen Whitehouse, editor & Michael J. Nolan, information designer

INFORMATION**ANXIETY 2**

International Standard Book Number: 0-7897-2410-3

Library of Congress Catalog Card Number: 00-100600

Printed in the United States of America

First Printing: November, 2000

01   00   99   4   3   2   1

Trademarks
All terms mentioned in this book that are known to be trademarks or service marks have been appropriately capitalized. Que cannot attest to the accuracy of this information. Use of a term in this book should not be regarded as affecting the validity of any trademark or service mark.

Warning and Disclaimer
Every effort has been made to make this book as complete and as accurate as possible, but no warranty or fitness is implied. The information provided is on an "as is" basis. The author(s) and the publisher shall have neither liability nor responsibility to any person or entity with respect to any loss or damages arising from the information contained in this book.

Indexing by Aamir Burki and Lisa Wilson

Proofreading by Marta Partington

Cover production design by Aren Howell

201 W. 103rd Street
Indianapolis, Indiana 46290

Dedicated to Tony, Vanessa, Reven,
Ling & Joshua my children

INFORMATION ANXIETY IN THE INTERNET AGE

Since *Information Anxiety* was published in 1989, the sky has not fallen. We still use centuries-old languages to communicate, and we do not speak in the zeroes and ones of binary language. Humans have shaped computers more than they have shaped us. If the reverse were the case, we all would be memorizing Unix commands.

ANXIETY2

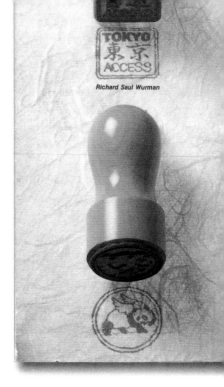

Richard Saul Wurman

INFORMATION**ANXIETY2**

ANXIETY2

INFORMATION**ANXIETY2**

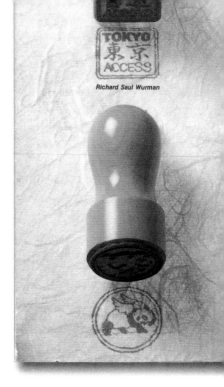

Richard Saul Wurman

THE BUSINESS OF UNDERSTANDING

2

When I came up with the concept and the name information architecture in 1975, I thought everybody would join in and call themselves information architects. But nobody did—until now. Suddenly, it's become an ubiquitous term. Of course, as is the case with any ubiquitous label, there are some information architects who legitimately meet the definition of the term, but there are lots who don't.

Writers and graphic designers seem preoccupied with stylistic and aesthetic conerns rather than making information understandable to the public.

The key to understanding is realizing that all accounts are subjective.

Trying to wade through information without a sense of its structure is like going to the Library of Congress and aimlessly combing the shelves for a particular book.

Information can only be organized by location, alphabet, time, category, or hierarchy.

Each distinct vantage point and each mode of organization creates a different structure of information.

Negative space—the silence between friends, breaks between meetings, space between buildings—is full of the opportunity for understanding. We learn through context, through what surrounds, informs, and opposes an idea. Consider doing something the wrong way and you'll often find a new or better way.

The best way to accomplish any endeavor is to determine its essential purpose. For every problem, there are many *hows* but only one *what*. The *what* should precede proposed solutions.

LAND MINES IN THE UNDERSTANDING FIELD

S ince the advent of the Industrial Age, we have increased our use of a terrific word: *more*. It really worked for everything. When our roads became crowded, we built more roads. When our cities became unsafe, we hired more police officers, ordered more police cars, and built more prisons.

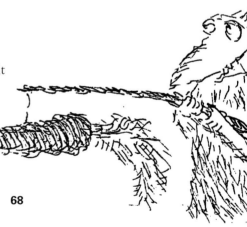

AN AGE OF CONNECTIONS: INTEGRATED MESSAGES

What do escalators, bananas, bathroom stalls, and chair backs at movie theatres have in common? They are all new media for marketing. Advertising messages have become so pervasive that the world surface area without them is disappearing faster than the rain forest in South America.

THE STRUCTURE OF CONVERSATION

This page is like a conversation. The quotes in the margins are like a "let-me-put-this-another-way" feature of conversations. You hear a voice when you read it. Like a conversation, the page explores asides and anecdotes and trails off to distractions. It has diversions; it stops and starts. It makes leaps, and one thought doesn't always link to another in a linear fashion.

TALK IS DEEP

6

The industrial design critic **Ralph Caplan** was talking to a woman who was trying to explain something to him. "I know what I want to say, but I just can't put it into words," she told him. Puzzled, Caplan asked her, "Can you tell me what form it is in now?"

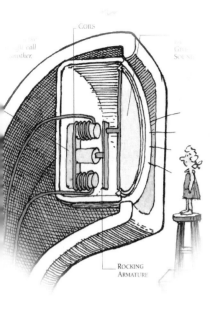

7
THERE IS ALWAYS A QUESTION

There is a Danish proverb that the one who is afraid of asking questions is ashamed of learning.

FINDING THINGS

Most things can be found in context with a map. A map provides people with the means to share in the perceptions of others. It is a pattern made understandable; it is a rigorous, accountable form that follows implicit principles, rules, and measures.

Major U.S. Interstates, West-East

BEYOND PERSONALITIES

O ur work environment is still far from paradise: mistakes abound, work needs to be redone, and people operate with different understandings of the same project. If our personalities were the only difficulty we had to surmount in the office, working wouldn't be such a dirty word.

9

improving…

needs adjustment

needs fixing

problematic

bad

Very Bad

Terrible

HORRIBLE

CATASTROPHIC!

10 EMPOWERMENT: THE WORD OF THE NEW CENTURY

Empowerment is what enables employees to go beyond the instructions they are given. Empowerment means to give rights and responsibilities to employees by giving them a say in their work as well as in company business in general. It recognizes and rewards their input. It is a movement designed to nurture human resources and replace the manager-as-warden mentality with the manager-as-aide-to-action approach.

INSTRUCTIONS: THE DRIVER OF CONVERSATION

E very successful communication is really an instruction in disguise—from love letters to company brochures.

12

TALKING ON THE JOB: SEEING INSTRUCTIONS IN THE CONTEXT OF WORK

What makes work so bad? Most executives imagine their employees complaining they don't get paid enough, their office partitions aren't high enough, their bosses aren't nice enough, and too much is expected of them. But at the top of most employees' gripe lists are problems in communication—not understanding what is expected of them, feeling excluded from important information, working under people who give vague and confusing instructions. When employees see their superiors as their main roadblock to getting their jobs done, the culprits are likely to be irrational or incompetent instruction-givers.

EDUCATION IS TO LEARNING AS TOUR GROUPS ARE TO ADVENTURE

Contrary to Voltaire's Dr. Pangloss, we are not living in the best of all possible worlds. Not only are we overwhelmed by the sheer amount of information, most of us are also hampered by an education that inadequately trains us to process it.

LEARNING IS REMEMBERING
WHAT YOU'RE INTERESTED IN

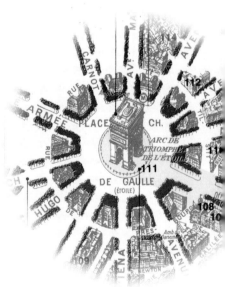

Learning can be seen as the acquisition of information, but before it can take place, there must be interest; interest permeates all endeavors and precedes learning. In order to acquire and remember new knowledge, it must stimulate your curiosity in some way.

YOU ONLY LEARN THINGS RELATIVE TO SOMETHING YOU UNDERSTAND

The origin of the word Eureka is attributed to **Archimedes** on discovering the principle of specific gravity. As the story goes, he was sitting in the bathtub and, as the water ran over him, the idea came to him, and he shouted, "Eureka, I understand!"

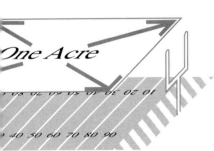

One Acre

HAILING, FAILING, AND STILL SAILING

16

The winds of Puget Sound twisted, contorted, and destroyed the Tacoma Narrows Bridge, but also prompted urgent and exacting aerodynamic research that ultimately benefited all forms of steel construction. Beauvais Cathedral was built to the limit of the technology in its day, and it collapsed, but succeeding cathedrals made use of its failure.

17 DESIGNING YOUR LIFE

I was originally trained as an architect and my mentor was and is **Louis Kahn**. In 1959, I graduated first in my class in the School of Architecture at the University of Pennsylvania—then the best school in the country. I was the fair-haired boy, a protégé of the great Louis Kahn. Anything was possible. Even though Lou Kahn died years ago, he still lives with me every day.

INTRODUCTION

I'll begin with a couple of literary references that have always had a connection for me with navigating information: **Robert Graves** and *The Waking Dream*, and **Proust** and his *Remembrance of Things Past*. The concept of the waking dream has always fascinated me. I also believe we consist of our memories. I hold an image of myself at 65 that I consist of 67 inches of memory.

It was **Muriel Cooper**, however, in her final work at the Visual Language Workshop at the MIT Media Lab, whose prototype demonstrations made the dream of flying through information of one's own choice real for me.

A revolution will occur in gaming. We've evolved from Pong to Sega and Nintendo, to Sony PlayStation, now to PlayStation2 and the Microsoft X-Box. The intriguing development will be a change in demographics, as these machines and their software—now directed primarily at males of ages 10-18—will extend to both females and males from 18–80. While the interfaces evolve, the software will move beyond violent games to business gaming, problem solving and decision-making, vicarious travel, and ultimately to flying through information—perhaps all human knowledge. What began with simple games will result in the most powerful tool for learning, strategic decisions, and navigation (virtual or real) invented to date.

However, beyond any technology, what we have to remember when dealing with information, is that it all comes down to having the right attitude. We have to give ourselves permission to seek out and accept only that information which applies to our interests with a heavy focus on interest connections. Nodes of connection opportunities at each thoughtful breath. When we accumulate and organize information around our interests, and consequently reject the vast majority of the overwhelming onslaught of raw data and understand the differentiation between data and information, we will be able to learn what we desire to know so that we can design our lives.

Learning is remembering what we're interested in.

Memory is what we are ultimately made of. That memory needs an organization that comes from our personal vision—eyes with thoughtful filtering lenses, ears with our own frequency, and finally, brains of Velcro tuned to our personal interest connections.

1 INFORMATION ANXIETY IN THE INTERNET AGE

Since *Information Anxiety* was published in 1989, the sky has not fallen. We still use centuries-old languages to communicate, and we do not speak in the zeroes and ones of binary language. Humans have shaped computers more than they have shaped us. If the reverse were the case, we all would be memorizing Unix commands.

The Web world hasn't replaced print. The magazine industry is healthier than ever. Advertising dollars are at all time highs because the dot-coms have sought traditional ways to buy eyeballs.

Contrary to the Luddites, the Digital Age hasn't mechanized humanity and isolated people in a sterile world of machines. Rather, it has expanded our sense of community. Now people with like interests can get together around the world to share their passions in chat rooms. People with like diseases can share information. Every issue has its proponents who can band together through technology.

The Pew Internet & American Life Project included a study that found 26 million Americans have used email to start communicating regularly with a family member with whom they had had little previous contact. That hardly suggests a loss of community or family bonds.

"Multitudes have found a nearly forgotten friendship suddenly made intimate again, because of email," says **Adam Gopnik** in an article in *The New Yorker*.

…for me email has been as welcome as the afternoon post must have been to the women of 18th century England, when heavy, cream-colored envelopes would arrive on a tray, notes from dear friends whom you had perhaps seen only two hours before, but who had had further thoughts about the conversation, and wanted to follow up.

– Adair Lara,
San Francisco Chronicle
(1/20/00)

The Internet has transcended barriers of wealth and class, ethnicity, and age. A neighbor's child who attended Johns Hopkins University was given an impossible physics problem to solve. During the course of his research, he began a correspondence with a Nobel physicist in Europe. The 19-year-old youth couldn't have dreamed of making this kind of acquaintance just 15 years ago.

There may be a falling out in certain industries, but by and large, most new technologies make a place for themselves without pushing old ones out of the nest. Who even threatens the paperless office anymore? Sure, DVD will replace videotapes, but this is a modification not a melee. Broadcast and print media now regularly refer readers to Web sites for more information. Cross-pollination is the norm.

Accompanying the explosion of information has come an explosion of means to handle the increased information. Take data storage, for example. Today a tape cartridge can store 10 gigabytes of information or 10,000 times more information than the 1-megabyte tapes available in 1960. In 1987, floppy disks could store 720 kilobytes; today they store 120 megabytes, more than 100 times more.

With the explosion of information available on the Internet has come the birth of new industries such as data mining and knowledge management which make use of information gained. Data-mining programs developed by companies like Digital Archeology, Informix, Integral Solutions (ISL), Oracle, and SAS are the hottest products of the hour.

According to **Larry Hawes**, a Delphi Group analyst, the combined software-license revenue for programs specializing in information-management tasks like text search and retrieval was $48 million in 1996. By the end of 2000, the figure will be an estimated $604 million.

Much energy is being wasted on the perceived confrontation between new media and old media, between the old world of storefronts and the new world of Web sites. Upstarts like to insist that they will destroy the oldstarts, but this rarely happens. They are much more likely to merge than annihilate. Just look at AOL and Time Warner.

The Internet will certainly alter our lifestyles and change the way we do business, but it will not change the business we do. New millennium man will not live by software alone. The bulk of our everyday lives will still be devoted to acquiring the "hard" products required to satisfy "old economy" human needs: food, shelter, clothing, transportation, etc.

– *The Trends Journal* (Spring 2000)

Technology has given us more places to store things, which means more ways to lose things.

– Jan Jasper, time expert

If we cannot survive all the information that we're going to develop, we're in real trouble. Because no one is going to stop writing books. No one is going to stop creating information.

– Brian Lamb, founder, chairman, sometime anchor of C-Span

More evidence of merging can be found in interactive movies like *Running Time*, a new Internet thriller about a sexy London bicycle courier that lets viewers vote on outcomes after each five-minute episode. The movie drew 1.5 million hits in its first few weeks, and producers are now toying with the idea of putting the episodes together for general release in movie theaters.

"I really think this is the way [filmmaking is going] to go," says **Gareth Miller**, one of the *Running Time* actors. "It won't be long before Hollywood is doing this," according to a Reuters article (6/14/00).

Soon our microwaves might turn into banks. At NCR's Knowledge Lab in London, they already have. Engineers created a "Microwave Bank," a fully-functioning microwave oven with a computer screen on the front door. A touchscreen lets users send email, pay bills, access their bank accounts, and heat up their leftovers. "The context for everything we do is the networked economy, and the central purpose of networks is to establish and maintain relationships," says **Stephen Emmott**, the Lab's director. The idea is to reach the non-computer-using consumer with invisible computers embedded in useful devices.

We are proving that we can handle increased information channels. We can easily switch between our morning paper and surfing for financial news. Yes, we all have increased appetites and can cross platforms. We can naturally make decisions with little trauma about when to send an email or make a phone call, when to send a package or a fax. These aren't overwhelming decisions.

THE AGE OF ALSO

Our culture is obsessed with absolutes—a phenomenon manifest in many different areas. Who is the best and the brightest? Who is the fastest? Who are the 400 richest? What are the top 10? These distinctions may make for amusing magazine covers, but they have little to do with the way we live. We live in an Age of Also, of adapting to alternatives.

Each new technology that comes along is touted as the best that will replace the rest. However, most predictions haven't come to pass, and each technology seems to get added to the rest. The computer was supposed to make paper obsolete; it has done just the opposite.

The newest of new things will not reroute the circuitry of fundamental economic and human forces.

– *The Trends Journal* (Spring 2000)

The Age of Also means that on a daily basis I get faxes. I also get email, I also get snail mail, also many phone calls, I also receive CD-ROMs and DVDs. Packages come in daily by priority mail, Fedex, Fedex Ground, Airborne, UPS and DHL.

I also get much of my information from magazines and three daily newspapers. We live in the Age of Also. For the next decade, there will not be a single best way to receive information, rather a choice. Certainly, there will be a falling out between all the options, some growing in usage and some diminishing.

Computers have been a bigger boon to the paper business than the Gutenberg press. The ability of computer printers to crank out paper, and copiers to copy has us drowning in it. Videos were supposed to turn out the lights on movies, but there are more movies than ever.

- **Prediction:** Computers will result in the "paperless office."

  Reality: Paper-handling has become a number one office problem.

- **Prediction:** Television and home videos will be the death of the movie industry.

  Reality: More films are being produced than ever before, and they are making more money.

- **Prediction:** Faxes will replace phone calls.

  Reality: Many people now make a phone call just to tell someone they are going to send a fax. Then they call again to find out if the person has received it.

- **Prediction:** Printing books will become an archaic process.

  Reality: There's nothing low-tech about printing a book. Every single aspect is high-tech. Books are created and typeset on the computer, files are transmitted electronically, and plates are created from computer-generated film.

- **Prediction:** E-books will replace books as we know them.

  Reality: There is an explosion of e-book publication and availability; however the Law of Also will apply—there will be more books and more e-books.

- **Prediction:** Games devices like the PlayStation 2 and the X-Box will replace the PC.

  Reality: This could happen. If combined with voice control, it could happen even faster. There were not many horses in New York City after 1920.

- **Prediction:** Email will replace phone calls.

  Reality: Yes, email often stands in for phone conversations, but wireless phones have made it possible to phone people anywhere. So phones have expanded their territory. However in an email you lose tone of voice and context, so more emails will result in more phone calls.

The symptoms of a Technologically Intoxicated Zone are:

1. We favor the quick fix, from religion to nutrition.

2. We fear and worship technology.

3. We blur the distinction between real and fake.

4. We accept violence as normal.

5. We love technology as a toy.

We live our lives distanced and distracted.

— John Naisbitt, *High Tech High Touch: Technology and Our Search for Meaning*

Traditional forms of entertainment still are holding strong. Whether old-fashioned TV game shows, familiar movie epics or fresh-faced pop stars, our favorite ways of entertaining ourselves are still making money and drawing people in. And it's happening while dot-com growing pains are everywhere: e-commerce sites are fighting to survive, consumers are balking at download times, and Wall Street is demanding more results.

— Ann Oldenburg, "In a Wired World, Multimedia is the Message," *USAToday*, (8/23/00)

■ **Prediction:** Upstart dot-coms will replace old-line retailers.

Reality: The dot-coms, as a whole, are probably not doing as well as a group of bricks-and-mortar companies that have entered the world of e-commerce, using age-old marketing precepts—like putting a face on the product. Of course, there will be an inevitable blur between dot-coms and their predecessors.

We live with alternative versions, ersatz and originals, all in multiple copies. Personalized news services will not replace newspapers and magazines. Scanning articles isn't the same as flipping through a newspaper or magazine. With a news service, you can't tear out an article, nor happen upon the article you didn't know you were looking for. And, you can't cover as much territory as quickly as you can with a real newspaper or magazine. Many have claimed that newspapers are dead. However, they are still the cheapest, most efficient way to get in-depth news on a daily basis.

A weekday edition of *The New York Times* contains more information than the average person was likely to come across in a lifetime in 17th-century England.

Most of the dire forecasts made at the birth of new technologies have failed to materialize. The "new" gets incorporated, and the "old" adapts.

When *Information Anxiety* first appeared, it broke the mold. It was a Chatty-Cathy, non-academic book. It was loosely organized, and there were diversions on every page that included pretty much anything we felt like adding. Since then, hundreds of books have come out with marginalia. The success of the book gave others permission to write non-linear tomes that didn't fit the orthodox concept of a book at that time. Since then marginalia and diversions have become more the norm than the exception. Readers have easily adjusted to having multiple typographic elements on every page, moving between text and diagrams.

If you want to see how much more sophisticated you've become, try watching *Gone with the Wind*. The dialogue is unbearable. Our palettes are more refined. We expect more of movies, ads, and the news. (Only **Shakespeare** has been unchangeable.)

BIT LITERACY by Mark Hurst

Information anxiety is more important today than ever, thanks to the arrival of the bit. The tiniest one- or zero-pulse of digital data, the bit will affect our lives as much as the atom. Ten years ago, Americans may have felt some anxiety over the magazines and newspapers piling up at home, but today the anxiety is increasing as bits appear in all areas of our lives. Email, Web sites, e-newsletters, chat rooms, email, instant messages, and more email—all of these streams of bits can interrupt us, and keep us engaged, anywhere and anytime. Devices made to hold these bits are springing up, too: PDAs and cell phones bring us the bits when we're away from our PC.

For those who own a PC or a PDA, there is little escape from the bits. Even when we turn off the device, the bits pile up quietly, ready to flood us with anxiety when we return to the device. If anything, an escape from the bits can be dangerous. Take a week-long vacation without email, and upon return, a bloated inbox welcomes us back to work with seven times more bits.

And this is still *early* in the current explosion of digital information. One research study recently predicted that, within a few years, the number of emails we each receive every day will increase to *forty* times its current volume. That's a lot of bits demanding our attention—just from email. It's likely that still other devices and other bitstreams will threaten the typical American with exponentially more information anxiety.

"Bit literacy is an awareness of bits: what bits are, how they affect our lives, and how we can survive in a society permeated by bits."

The problem of near-infinite bits, however, does have a solution. The solution is what I call "bit literacy." Bit literacy is an awareness of bits: what bits are, how they affect our lives, and how we can survive in a society permeated by bits. With that awareness, bit literate people are able to *control* the bits, and not be *controlled by* the bits, that are becoming central to our lives and jobs.

All of bit literacy can be distilled into a simple philosophy that allows people to regain their life, free from information anxiety, while still living in the bits. Here is the four-word philosophy:

Let the bits go.

That's right, let the bits go. Don't acquire them. Don't try to acquire them, and don't worry about acquiring them, since the bits will come to you. The bits touch our lives at so many points that it's impossible to escape them, and it's insane to try to acquire *all* of them. Instead, being bit literate means constantly working on *letting go* of as many of the bits as we can. Bit literacy allows us to clear a path of emptiness through the jungle of bits that surround and distract us; the emptiness allows us to see.

Here's a real-life example. Recently I visited a Web site where visitors can sign up to receive email

newsletters, published by respected companies, on any number of topics. Internet news, sports commentary, entertainment gossip—all of these were available to me at the click of a button. I could get *all* of this information, delivered to my email inbox weekly…for free! And unlike subscriptions to paper magazines, these bits wouldn't clutter my apartment or need recycling. (I didn't sign up; I was there to unsubscribe from a newsletter.) So, one might reasonably ask, what's the problem with getting some potentially valuable or entertaining bits, if they don't clutter my living space, don't weigh me down, and don't cost a penny?

The problem is that the bits are different from paper-based information. Bits are more engaging, more immediate, more personal, and more abundant than other types of information. In the middle of lunch with a friend, we're interrupted by bits—perhaps a stock quote—and we instinctively reach for our PDAs to see what it is. Or we sit down to "read through some email" and blow through two hours like it was twenty minutes. Like the magazines and other anxiety-producing information, the bits call for our attention—but the bits call more loudly, more sweetly, more frequently, and in more areas of our lives.

These radically different qualities of bits mean that we must engage bits in a radically different way. Bit literacy is radical about letting the bits go. We can't let all the bits go—we must engage them first, and inevitably save the few most important bits—but our *default* behavior must be to let the bits go, rather than acquire and save them.

Here are some ways you can let the bits go: Keep your email inbox empty, by deleting your emails after saving the few that you *must* retain for later reference. Restrict the interruptions you allow on your cell phone and PDA, so that the interruptions that do come through are the important ones. And certainly don't open up any new bitstream—a newsletter, a ticker, or any other ongoing feed—unless it's vitally important. Instead, concentrate on letting go of the bits that find their way to you; the few remaining bits will be all the more valuable to you as a result.

I'd like to emphasize that last sentence: When a person becomes bit literate, what remains after all the letting go is *valuable*. I equate that with *meaningful*. Because—and here's the kicker— the bits by themselves aren't meaningful. Bits are just pointers to meaning, just containers of thoughts, just phantom images of the real item. The meaning is what

lies behind the bits, what *drives* the bits. In their super-abundant quantities, swarming and over- whelming our consciousness, bits obscure the very meaning that created them. It's only after clearing out a path of emptiness that we can arrive at the meaning *behind* the bits.

This is true bit literacy. Going through the bits by letting them go, then arriving at the meaning *behind* the bits. A common example is the employee's email inbox that fills up with email from numerous projects. The real issue isn't the number of emails coming in, but rather the number of projects that the em- ployee is assigned. The meaning of the bits is not the bits them- selves, but what they point to— that is, the employee needs to commit to fewer projects

Bit literacy is uniquely suited to this moment in history. We have never needed bit literacy before, because the bits were never so numerous or engaging. Ten years ago we engaged bits through a "user interface" on a "personal com- puter." But the bits were bottled up, not very engaging, and couldn't touch us except when we sat in front of the screen. And there were so few bits that we could give each bit the individual attention it called for. Today, and much more so in a few years, the bits reach us even

when we leave the computer screen. On every street corner, in every restaurant, in every house, while we eat, while we sleep, the bits pile up. And they call for us.

To have a chance to survive the infinite bits in the future, we'll need a lot of bit literacy: in our behavior (letting go of bits), in our beliefs (searching for the meaning behind the bits), and in our technology— with simpler tools granting us control over the bits, and working with bits in their simplest formats. And as we shift to becoming not just consumers but *creators* of bits, the discipline of bit literacy will show us how to *create* bits differently: mindfully, meaningfully, and with an acceptance of their essential emptiness.

Mark Hurst
(mark@creativegood.com) is the founder and president of Creative Good, an Internet consulting firm.

"…the bits call for our attention—but the bits call more loudly, more sweetly, more frequently, and in more areas of our lives."

THE RISE OF THE PROSUMER

We've all become prosumers: consumers and producers of content. Because we can independently access previously unavailable information, many of us are more empowered, more involved in researching the pros and cons of the various decisions we have to make about all aspects of our lives and work, rather than relying on experts. We don't want to know just the ingredients in mayonnaise, we want to know where the eggs were laid, what the chickens were fed, and what affects the preservatives will have on our health.

We've become more suspicious. We understand that much of the information that we get is biased by its sources. Lawyers make more money by slowing down the process. A surgeon makes more money when he operates. Real estate agents make commissions by selling you the most expensive house. Your car mechanic wants to find something wrong with your car. Your stock broker doesn't just have your portfolio in mind when he/she encourages you to churn stock.

The ability to collect information has inspired a newfound hunger for sources of information based on our own interests. That's why you see the growth in the medical information industry. Prosumers are clamoring for hospitals to release data on surgical outcomes by doctor so they can make informed choices and assess their own chances of surviving a procedure. How many patients survive open–heart surgery at Hospital A versus Hospital B? The information exists, but it hasn't been made accessible or understandable yet.

I look at the food label as the model for what should be on computers and electronic equipment. How much storage does this machine have? How long will it take to get it running? What are the other machines with which it is compatible? That is all part of responding to prosumers.

The Internet has become so large so fast that sophisticated search engines are just scratching the surface of the Web's vast information reservoir....The 41-page research paper, prepared by a South Dakota company (BrightPlanet) that has developed new software to plumb the Internet's depth, estimates the World Wide Web is 500 times larger than the maps provided by popular search engines like Yahoo!, AltaVista and Google.com.

– Michael Liedtke
"Study: Internet Bigger Than We Think,"
Associated Press, (7/27/00)

ALTERATIONS ON THE INFORMATION LANDSCAPE

More sophisticated audiences aren't the only changes in the landscape. Information was once a sought after and treasured commodity like a fine wine. Now, it's regarded more like crabgrass, something to be kept at bay. When *Information Anxiety* was published, the cry was less data, more information. More than a dozen years of exploding quantities of information have elevated us to a higher level. How can we find what we want and tune the rest out?

Living in an Information Age has profoundly altered our lives, and those who fail to recognize that the rules of information design are changing will find themselves left behind. Businesses clamoring for an audience find that it's harder to be heard.

When content streams 24 hours a day from multiple channels, the rules of navigation change. Designers need to rethink how they can make the journey more meaningful. This book is about how humans navigate down the path to understanding and what information designers can do to make the trip more compelling.

The way that information is presented in these different channels has yet to be fully explored, so you have both opportunity and catastrophe. The opportunity is that there is so much information; the catastrophe is that 99 percent of it isn't meaningful or understandable.

PLUGGED IN OR PLUGGED UP?

The Internet world is still adjusting to the new channels of communication. Search engines are still crude, navigation cumbersome, and ways to find what you want are primitive, but an industry of information shapers is rising. No one had ever heard of an information architect in 1987. Now a search of Google turns up 6,270 listings under that term.

Those who shape information for the masses—the media, marketers, designers, writers, information architects—do need to rethink the way information is delivered to the masses because people's information appetites are much more refined.

Where we once went to great lengths to find information—like walking from one town to the next, we were concerned with not having enough information; now we're more concerned with winnowing down the amount, even avoiding the constant barrage. We seem more concerned with getting less information than more, focusing on slowing down the avalanche of information instead of how to procure more.

America's best-known documentary filmmaker, Ken Burns, who spends years creating a single film, is concerned about a sort of mass attention deficit disorder. "When you're bombarded with so many images—not just television, but all around—you really speed up. You need so much, so quickly—food, impressions, everything—that the opposite has begun to happen: Instead of enriching ourselves, as you might imagine you would if you get more of something, we've actually created a kind of poverty. And that poverty, first and foremost, can be measured in a loss of attention."

– William F. Mitchell, *e-topia*

That changes the rules for people who want to be heard, for businesses that want to reach customers.

WARP-SPEED RULES

Here's what successful designers and communicators will have to master in the new connected world:

Information is not enough. Many companies have no clear purpose in releasing numbing mountains of information and, as such, much of it is wasted. Just pumping your market or audience full of information is meaningless.

Organization is as important as content. Finding, winnowing, sorting, organizing, and imprinting the information takes priority over creating it. After all, the Library of Congress wouldn't be of much value if all the books were piled randomly on the floor. The way information is presented and organized becomes as important as the content. New fields like bioinformatics are cropping up to explore how to store and use information, not just collect it.

The Electronic Messaging Association estimates this year 108 million email users will receive over 7 trillion email messages—about 65,000 each if you're counting.

Your market is the world. We now have the technology to bring customers from all over the world to your doorstep 24 hours a day. Independent of your business size or location, anyone in the world can visit your store at any time of the night or day. One click of a button, and you've captured them. The Internet has made the world everyone's target market. One click and a guy in Singapore can be in your shop in Salinas. Of course, the conundrum of doing business in an Age of Information is that the technologies that bring the customers to your doorstep spirit them away just as easily. One click and you've lost them, maybe forever.

If you can't integrate, you can't operate. The mantra in today's work world is less information, more integration. It's not enough to design a perfect software program. The market wants to know how well it will work with other programs. This forces software developers to do more compatibility testing and puts pressure on them to adopt specification standards. The Internet has connected every aspect of our lives, so we have been indoctrinated by a vision of total communications, not just among humans but also among our appliances from toasters to PDAs. We want them all connected, so that information can be synched and perpetually updated. The devices of our lives are being integrated into all of our environments: our homes, our offices, even our cars.

An article in *Business Week* (4/10/00) claimed that sales of in-car navigation systems in Japan will hit 2.5 million by 2001. And these aren't primitive GPS systems either. Toyota's Monet system displays "almost-real-time" views of traffic conditions at major intersections, enabling you to decide way ahead of time if that's the best route. In the European market, DaimlerChrysler's new Mercedes S-class sedans automatically notify the nearest police station in the event of an accident, and the company is working on a system that will provide hospitals with the driver's medical details if necessary. Meanwhile, BMW is experimenting with voice-based Web browsers on a dashboard screen. General Motors showed an infotainment system at the 2000 New York Auto Show. The Virtual Advisor from OnStar reads stock quotes, sends email, and turns on the radio—all with voice commands.

Cars are becoming more like computers, while computers are becoming more like cars in that they are making it easier for us to get where we want to go. Integration allows that.

Size really doesn't count. Success and size once promised clout. You could buy the best location, the best advertising spots, and the most glamorous store. A store at 57th and Fifth Avenue in New York will get more traffic than one in Sanford, Manitoba, but only in the bricks-and-mortar world. Those with the deep pockets could scream louder, pay higher agency fees, and guarantee more eyeballs. The new click world now exists alongside the old brick world. In the click world, a 16-year old in Tecumseh, Iowa, can have a Web site that competes in traffic with *The Wall Street Journal.*

It's not the what, but the how. In the Old World economy, companies differentiated themselves by what they sold, not by how they sold it. They touted their products as the "best shoes in Paris, or the fastest cars on the road." With the expansion in purchasing channels, the *how* becomes more important than the what. Consumers will choose the most advantageous purchasing experience. Exclusivity of merchandise has become as antiquated as doilies on a chair.

Envision being able to access email, the Internet, and your home security system during your commute. Using voice activation, the ICES in-vehicle computer is designed to keep drivers connected to the world. ICES is powered by Intel Architecture microprocessors and uses the Microsoft Windows CE operating system.

Because ICES uses verbal commands, drivers can safely check email, schedules, look up phone numbers, and make calls without taking their hands off the steering wheel or their eyes off the road. As an added safety feature, the computer screen is blocked out when the vehicle is in motion. Industry analysts estimate that the worldwide market for in-vehicle multimedia computers that rely on speech recognition will top $1 billion by 2005.

– Marketing information from Visteon Web site

"Online, you don't differentiate yourself by what you sell. You have to differentiate yourself by *how* you sell—by the experiences that you create around finding, trying, and purchasing. In the actual world, providing a bad experience is damaging. But people will keep going to the same supermarket, because it's on the way home. On the Web, a bad customer experience can be fatal," says **Jeffrey F. Rayport**, a professor at the Harvard Business School and executive director of Marketspace Center in Cambridge, Massachusetts, in an article in *Net Company*, a special publication of *Fast Company* (Fall 1999). According to a Forrester Research study, 70 percent of all Internet shopping carts are abandoned.

The Web is not the answer to all problems. "The vision of the Internet as a medium for the open sharing of information will fade as it becomes more difficult and more time-consuming to distinguish between meaningful and irrelevant facts. Indeed, as reliable data, news, and research become harder and more costly to secure, we will become more proprietary about content," says **Richard Worzel**, author of *The Next 20 Years of Your Life* and *The Only Secure Job: Changing from Employee to Entrepreneur.*

All of us have had Internet experiences where we realized down the road that another channel would have been quicker to solve our problem.

For example, a member of a national chain of health clubs went to the chain's Web site to seek information about her membership renewal. Under the account information, she found everything but the cost of her membership. She found how to add a family member or how to add automatic withdrawal to pay for her membership. Then to compound her frustration, the site promised to respond to her email question within 7 to 10 working days. Had she called the organization's 800 number, it would have taken 7 to 10 minutes.

The highest-tech choice isn't always the most efficient, although sometimes the dazzle blinds us to more dowdy, but perhaps speedier solutions, like the good old-fashioned reference librarian. Those librarians find information for a living. If you need to know how much wood a woodchuck can chuck, you can likely get an answer from a librarian before you've dialed up your Internet connections.

We were conducting another talk tonight at the Cambridge Public Library in Boston. A musty old place (and lovely too for its old world charm); upon entering I got an immediate flashback to grammar school when I would have to hunt through the endless rows of card catalogs to find anything in the always incomprehensible—at least to me—Dewey Decimal system. It was the first time in a long time that I had thought of doing that and I quickly realized it was something I would never, ever probably do again.

The reason? The ease of finding a giant trove of information in the endless stacks of the Internet. One can grouse all you want about how hard it is to find things online, but it is a giant step forward from the old days when it was much more of a hit-or-miss proposition.

– Kara Swisher, author *AOL.com*
"at Random" interview

The nation's public and academic libraries answer over seven million questions a week, according to *The Bookmark,* a newsletter published by the University of Missouri-Kansas City Friends of the Library. Standing single file, the line of questioners would stretch from Boston to San Francisco. Academic librarians answer 112 million reference questions a year. That's three times the number of people who attend college football games.

THE INTERNET IS THE GREAT EQUALIZER

A 16-year old is equal to an institution. The right information is equal to the wrong information.

Access to information was once highly controlled. You had to have enough money to afford a book and an education, as well as time enough to read. Now anyone can acquire information.

If information is the product of the Digital Age, then the Internet is the transportation vehicle. That means more misinformation. The wrong information can be transmitted just as easily as the right information. The push of one button can send erroneous information about you around the world.

The Internet is exploding with empty dazzle, sites that direct you to non-existent links, send you down fruitless paths, and generally don't help you get where you want to go. Some even make it nearly impossible to get there. Several studies have found that somewhere between 60 and 80 percent of people searching for information on the Web failed to find what they were looking for.

In March of 2000, Vividence—a company that evaluates Web sites from visitor opinions—sent 800 people to two popular job hunting sites and asked them to complete several tasks. When asked to find a specific job listing, only 25 percent found the correct listing on one site, while on the other site, only 36 percent succeeded.

Another task was to post a resume that would be hidden to the user's current employer. On the first site, only 19 percent succeeded and 58 percent incorrectly posted their resumes. The other site was more employee-friendly: 63 percent were able to post their resumes and keep them hidden from their current employers, while 28 percent could not. The rest quit trying.

The Web is information at your fingertips but also information overload: it's a storehouse of information so vast that it can often overwhelm. It's spending an hour getting information that you could have gotten on the phone in no time at all. In my life the Web has proven invaluable, like when I helped a friend sort through potential cervical cancer treatments, but it's also meant yet more junk mail in my life, cyberscams, and porn, porn, porn ("nude dancers LIVE in your browser!"). It's busy signals and servers down, and the stresses and the thumb-twiddling frustrations and aggravations of pages that take too much time to download. We as a society were already feeling overworked and burned out when along came the Web, yet another breakthrough that makes life feel more like a perpetual run on a treadmill turned up high. Palm Pilots, pagers, laptops: Why is it that every invention, from the microwave to the fax machine to email to the cell phone, makes our lives more hectic rather than less?

– Gary Rivlin, author *The Plot to Get Bill Gates,* "at Random" interview

Then 80 percent tried to conduct a transaction and failed, not only losing revenue for the site, but also potentially endangering their own jobs. Moreover, the people who failed had no idea they were making a mistake. How many job seekers had their bosses find their resumes?

THE NON-INFORMATION EXPLOSION

People still have anxiety about how to assimilate a body of knowledge that is expanding by the nanosecond. It's full of misinformation and mayhem.

Information anxiety is produced by the ever-widening gap between what we understand and what we think we should understand. Information anxiety is the black hole between data and knowledge. It happens when information doesn't tell us what we want to know.

Our relationship to information isn't the only source of information anxiety. We are also made anxious by the fact that other people often control our access to information. We are dependent on those who design information, on the news editors and producers who decide what news we will receive, and by decision-makers in the public and private sector who can restrict the flow of information. We are also made anxious by other people's expectations of what we should know, be they company presidents, peers, or even parents.

My family used to discuss current events around the dinner table. My father would ask us questions. If we answered one incorrectly, we had to leave the table and go find the correct answer. I experienced my first case of information anxiety, had my first intimation that information would be a driving force in my life, and swore I'd learn ways to find it—faster.

Almost everyone suffers moments of frustration with a manual that refuses to divulge the secret to operating a digital video camera, or struggling with a map that bears no relation to reality.

It can happen at a cocktail party when someone mentions the name Allan Bloom and the only person you know by that name is your dentist. It also can manifest as a chronic malaise, a pervasive fear that we are about to be overwhelmed by the very material we need to master in order to function in this world.

We are bombarded with material from the media, from colleagues, from cocktail party conversation, all of which is delivered in the form of what we have been taught to think of as information. We are like a thirsty person who has been condemned to use a thimble to drink from a fire hydrant. The sheer volume of available information and the manner in which it is often delivered render much of it useless to us.

FORMS OF INFORMATION ANXIETY by Nathan Shedroff

Information overload is a term often discussed in this last decade but seldom explained or explored —much like the condition itself implies. In my opinion, it isn't even a real condition, but an obscured attempt at understanding the emotions, frustrations, and bewilderment many of us often feel. It is this condition that is worthy of discussion as it is a true information *anxiety*, as Richard has appropriately observed and named. Since people cannot really digest more that they are inherently able to (just like with drinking water or eating), it isn't really possible to overload one's brain with too much information. Indeed, it is still unclear how much excess, unused capacity, we have for the storage and processing of data in our heads, but it is generally understood that there is plenty. Instead, what does affect us on both mental and emotional levels—some things even with physical results—is the anxiety we feel trying to keep up with the world around us,

"Information anxiety can have many forms… What makes this worse is that the data is not just passive, but actively inserting itself into our environment, our attentions."

beginning with the cultural assumption that we are supposed to keep up.

We have been given few resources with which to deal with the common, though mistaken, idea in society that the more we know, the better-off we are, and the better a person we can be. Only the strongest individuals can break the cultural forces of this unspoken requirement of post-1900 citizenship.

Information anxiety can have many forms, only the first of which is the frustration with the inability to "keep up" with the amount of data present in our life. What makes this worse is that the data is not just passive, but actively inserting itself into our environ-

ment, our attentions. Whether in the form of advertising or gesture, data is much more prevalent and attention-demanding than simply laying in books waiting to be opened. To compound this, as a society, we've made the mistake of commonly confusing data with information, indistinguishing the raw commodities that are the building blocks of meaning with meaning itself (the true meaning of the word, *information*).

A second form of anxiety is more subtle and less conscious to us. It is a frustration with the quality of what we encounter—especially what passes as *news*. We have built whole cultures and institutions around the rapid, even instantaneous, delivery of data labeled as important and worthy of vast amounts of our time, yet it serves almost no importance in our lives except to lord the speed and depth of trivia over others ("Didn't you see what happened in the market today? You *didn't*?"). Unfortunately, because we've been sold a need to be up-to-date and constantly "informed," we've forgotten that the speed at which news is delivered and the depth of trivial detail does not substitute for quality. This quantity over quality shift in our culture has created an even deeper need for truly informing experiences—for insight, the most precious form of information.

Insight is information that is not only new to us but transforming of our thoughts, not just helpful or informing about the subject matter, but applicable to our concerns, our lives, and other subject matter. It is the highest form of understanding that can be directly shared from one person to another. It is the most valuable substance in the world and it is difficult to come by, because we are so busy filling our minds and attentions with news and trivia that there is no time to see, let alone appreciate the need for true understanding.

This is a grave situation.

A third form of information anxiety is the guilt associated with not being "better informed," of not being able to keep up with the amount of data masquerading as information. By definition, since there is so much more data produced in the world than any one person can encounter, it is impossible to know everything (despite how many people act). Therefore, we are all at risk of feeling incapable in a society that tells us that knowing everything is more important than understanding it. Only those with tremendous self-confidence can survive under such conditions, much like a teenager in high school not being interested in the "popular" sports, music, or other activities.

Fourth (and probably not lastly), there is a dangerous hubris that develops for "knowing things first." I'm sure everyone has experienced a friend, relative, colleague—even a stranger—use a tone of surprised indignation at discovering something considered "important" that we didn't yet know. In most cases, they are only interested in the details—often sordid at that—and not the meaning. For example, I have rarely met someone that felt superior over me for not yet

knowing some insightful process (as these are usually valued so highly that it is assumed that they are *not* easy to understand). Instead, I have often been met with an attitude of superiority for not knowing something in the news that happened on the other side of the world, or in an area over which I have no control, despite the fact that it had no relation to my life, nor added insight to my own personal understanding.

Now, I'm not trying to argue that news isn't important and that there are not pieces of data—even information—that many people should know and be informed about. But, to me, this amount of information is a mere fraction of the total and still well under what is assumed by us collectively as important to know.

Ultimately, information anxiety is about how we personally relate to the data around us. It is a personal mission.

Nathan Shedroff
Experience Designer
(nathan@nathan.com)

"This quantity over quality shift in our culture has created an even deeper need for truly informing experiences—for insight, the most precious form of information"

THE GREATEST TEACHING IS PERMISSION-GIVING

Where *Information Anxiety* was a guide for the overloaded, *Information Anxiety 2* is a handbook for those who shape information. It's about Velcro, memory, and interest. It's about how to give people permission.

The greatest teaching you can do is permission-giving, to allow others to get in touch with themselves. The architect **Louis Kahn** was that kind of teacher for me. He allowed me to be more of me. I was talking to his son, **Nathaniel Kahn**, who is making a film about his father by talking to a lot of people. I said to him that I have observed on the Biography Channel that when everyone says the same thing about a person, where there is absolute agreement, the person is usually totally boring. The people who inspire conflicting opinions are the most interesting. When one person characterizes someone as funny, another says serious, one says stupid, another says smart— that's someone you want to know. Louis was different with everyone. That is a measure of his importance.

Permission-giving is a powerful notion. At my **TED** (Technology, Entertainment, Design) conferences I give permission to the audience to love equally what appears to be silly jugglers juggling as much as a brilliant scientist telling us about nanobots. Everything is interesting. Everything can be focused. Everything shouldn't be strictly and immediately practical.

CLARIFICATION, NOT SIMPLIFICATION

Most of us are growing apprehensive about our inability to deal with, understand, manipulate, or comprehend the epidemic of data that increasingly dominates our lives. Where once, during the Age of Industry, the world was ruled by natural resources, it is now run on information, and while resources are finite, information seems to be infinite.

Information is power, a world currency upon which fortunes are made and lost. And we are in a frenzy to acquire it, firm in the belief that more information means more power.

However, just the opposite is proving to be the case. The glut has begun to obscure the radical distinctions between data and information, between facts and knowledge. Our perception channels are short-circuiting. We have a limited capacity to transmit and process images, which means that our perception of the world is inevitably distorted in that it is selective; we cannot assimilate everything. The more images with which we are confronted, the more our view of the world is likely to be distorted.

Take the news as an example. Anyone who has ever played the children's game where you are given a few seconds to look at a tray of objects and then must recount all of the items on the tray, knows that the less time you have and the more objects on the tray, the more likely you are to recall things that weren't there and forget things that were there.

The amount of news we are expected to ingest every day hampers our ability to perceive in much the same way. Not only are we more likely to make errors of perception, but the more time we

> Bertrand Russell declared that in case he met God, he would say to Him, "Sir, you did not give us enough information." I would add to that, "All the same, Sir, I'm not persuaded that we did the best we could with the information we had. Toward the end there, we had tons of information."
>
> – Kurt Vonnegut, *Palm Sunday*

THE **TED** CONFERENCE

*"I decided to have a party to celebrate the idea of **TED**... the merging and converging of technology, entertainment, and design."*

In the early 1980s it was clear to me that there was an exciting series of parallel occurrences:

- The most interesting conversations I had on airplanes, trains, boats, and at meetings were with people in the technology business, the entertainment industry, and design professions.

- There was a focus in these groups of a hopeful creativity that didn't occur anyplace else.

- As a result of this positive and creative energy, these three career paths were attracting the very best of the graduates from universities.

- The remarkable observation was that these three human endeavors had become one.

I decided to have a party to celebrate the idea of **TED**, which is the acronym representing the merging and converging of technology, entertainment, and design. Along with Harry Marks, the eminent computer graphics maven, and Frank Stanton, the former President of CBS, Inc., we decided to hold a meeting to give credibility to what seemed an obvious idea to us. That was the first **TED** Conference, held in February 1984 in Monterey, California.

We had a difficult time filling the room because, although it seemed obvious to us, it wasn't obvious to others. We had gotten some extraordinary people to speak. Nicholas Negroponte had just

established the Media Lab at MIT. From IBM came Benoit Mandelbrot and Richard Voss who had recently given birth to fractal geometry. My hero. Stewart Brand of *The Whole Earth Catalog,* was there. Michael Schulhof of Sony handed out little shiny discs, but nobody in the audience knew what they were, since nobody owned a CD player yet. Herbie Hancock put on an amazing performance and left the next morning to get the first of his many Grammys. Bob Abel gave us a preview of his seminal multimedia project on Columbus. We had a group of people from a new newspaper, *USA Today,* that many in the audience said would not survive. As a wonderful kind of bookend, John Naisbitt gave mega-talks at the beginning and end with a grand predictive perspective.

The Conference was wonderful. We didn't fill the room but the word on the street was terrific, and we spend with reports of disparate events, the less time we have to understand the "whys and wherefores" behind them, to see relationships between them, and to understand the present in the context of history. Instead, we are lulled by a stream of surface facts; we are made numb, passive, and unreceptive by a surfeit of data that we lack the time and the resources to turn into valuable information.

Therefore, the great Information Age is really an explosion of non–information; it is an explosion of data. To deal with the increasing onslaught of data, it is imperative to distinguish between the two; information is that which leads to understanding. Everyone needs a personal measure with which to define information. What constitutes information to one person may be data to another. If it doesn't make sense to you, it doesn't qualify.

each went back to our respective careers. Several years later, in response to numerous requests by many people who had been at **TED**, Harry Marks and I agreed to try it again.

In 1988 we began planning the **TED**2 Conference which took place in early 1990, again in Monterey. This time we had no trouble filling the room, and in fact, we turned away hundreds of people. The program was again remarkable.

TED3 was my first solo adventure two years later in 1992. And this time because of the amount of conversation that occurred and the difficulties we had with over-subscription, I decided not to do a poster, a press release, or a brochure. The anti-marketing worked, and the conference sold out six months in advance and 1,000 people were turned away.

The next year, I put on **TED**4 in Kobe Japan, in partnership with Dentsu. It was attended by 700 people; 450 Japanese and 250 from the rest of the world. **TED**4 was a complex and spirited event of cross-cultural idea exchange. What clarity was lost in language translation was more than made up in the tumultuous embrace of many cultures.

Since then, **TED** has occurred in Monterey each February. Because of registration pressures, we've added simulcast rooms. I continue to program the meeting for myself,

to learn about the things I'm interested in, and we continue to turn people away who want to join me.

Besides **TED**4 in Kobe, I've held two **TED**s on the communication of medical information in Charleston SC. I also held a **TED** on learning in New York. Most recently, in partnership with Moses Znaimer of CityTV, we put on a Canadian **TED** called **TED**City in Toronto in June 2000.

I often refer to **TED** as the dinner party I always wanted to have, but couldn't.

"The anti-marketing worked and the conference sold out six months in advance and 1,000 people were turned away."

In the landmark 1982 treatise, *The Mathematical Theory of Communication*, authors **Claude Shannon** and **Warren Weaver** allow for that distinction by defining information as that which "reduces uncertainty."

Paul Kaufman, an information theorist, claims, "our society has an image of information which, although alluring, is ultimately counter-productive." Kaufman calls for creating a new image of information that departs from the current view that confuses the capacity to transmit raw signals with the capacity to create meaningful messages.

"In our television commercials, information leaps around offices on laser beams of colored light. This is the kind of information that engineers are rightly proud of: pulses and signals zipping along through optical fibers, rather indifferent to the meaning of it all. However, to use information productively, (toward some valued end or purpose), people must know what they are doing and why."

ORDER DOESN'T EQUAL UNDERSTANDING

I think there is a debilitating misconception that the shortest way from Point A to Point B is the best way and that order is the solution to all problems—that is, if we could just deliver information in a more orderly fashion, we could make it more understandable.

Order is no guarantee of understanding. Sometimes, just the opposite is true. The traditional format for guidebooks calls for chapters divided into neat categories—restaurants, museums, hotels, stories, each with its own chapter. In the *Access* guidebooks, all are jumbled together. They are divided by neighborhoods. This is the way that cities are laid out and experienced. My guidebooks are an attempt to mirror cities, to capture the fabric of urban life. Cities don't come in chapters with restaurants in one section and museums in another; their order is organic, sometimes confusing, and never alphabetic. To really experience a city, you have to acknowledge confusion.

To entertain the radical idea that understanding might involve accepting chaos threatens the foundations of our existence. Confusion is anti-American; it flies in the face of benevolent efficiency—that outstanding Puritanical virtue. To admit to anything that suggests chaos is subversive. Sometimes, however, subversion is the way to understanding, and understanding is the cure for information anxiety.

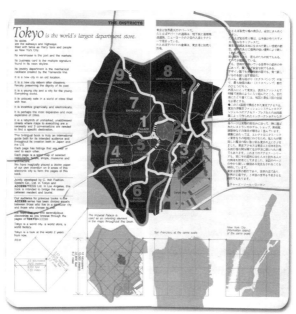

Cover and spread, *Tokyo Access.*

ACCESS IS THE ANTIDOTE TO ANXIETY

Access has a range of meanings that are all related to making things usable and understandable. If you are in a wheelchair, it represents ramps, elevators, and special toilets. Access signifies the ability to do what everybody else can do and to make use of what everybody else can use; access means the liberty to take advantage of resources.

Accessibility is the breeze through the window of interest.

I am concerned with public access to experience and to use information in giving people new ways to look at their environment and their lives. In fact, I regard myself as a teacher about physical and emotional experience, one who now communicates via a printed page that has been stretched to new applications. And, as a teacher, I want to test my ideas about how people learn to decode experience, especially experience that relies on visual understanding—shape, color, and relationships between objects and empty space.

In developing guidebooks, I've employed some principles that are applicable to the study of information-at-large and to reducing its anxiety-production factor in particular. Perhaps the three principles closest to my heart—and the most radical—are learning

The concept of access is so central to my work that I named one of my companies ACCESSPRESS Ltd. The diverse guidebooks that I have designed open doors of understanding to cities, jobs, sports, and medicine. I am an expert on none of these subjects, which makes me the appropriate author. Why? My expertise is my ignorance. Because I ask the obvious questions—the ones that everyone else is afraid to ask because they are so obvious.

I've found there is a relationship between creating books that make cities accessible to creating books that make medicine, finances, and sports understandable. In each case, accessibility is made possible by the discovery of a structure—the simplest correct form of organization—unique to a specific subject that allows readers to find what interests them and feel no guilt about ignoring what does not.

to accept your ignorance, paying more attention to the question than to the answer, and never being afraid to go in an opposite direction to find a solution.

Just as this book was going to press, a fascinating study on information anxiety was released, authored by Hal Varian and Peter Lyman of UC Berkeley: http://www.sims.berkeley.edu/how-much-info.

I've applied these principles in this book in its content and in its form. The emphasis is on learning how to ask questions. Where I don't know, I've asked someone else, thus throughout the pages are conversations I've had with people in various arenas of the information field. The traditional book form has been broken to insert marginalia, stories, and diagrams inspired directly and indirectly from the text; it is modeled after the quirkiness of conversations and the association of ideas—the opposite of the sequential, linear way books are supposed to work.

I believe it is the diversions and distractions that inspire our thinking. I've tried to apply this to my book. It mirrors the way the mind works; it follows the natural, organic, wandering, informal model of a conversation, one of the most powerful models for surviving in the Digital Age.

2 THE BUSINESS OF UNDERSTANDING

When I came up with the concept and the name information architecture in 1975, I thought everybody would join in and call themselves information architects. But nobody did—until now. Suddenly, it's become an ubiquitous term. Of course, as is the case with any ubiquitous label, there are some information architects who legitimately meet the definition of the term, but there are lots who don't.

Effective information architects make the complex clear; they make the information understandable to other human beings. If they succeed in doing that, they're good information architects. If they fail, they're not. It's not unlike the case of a lot of people who practice law calling themselves lawyers; some of them are good lawyers and some are bad lawyers. There is a real variation of competence underneath the guise of a title.

The only thing we know is our own personal knowledge and lack of knowledge (our own personal understanding and lack of understanding). And since it's the only thing we really know, the key to making things understandable is to understand what it's like *not* to understand. What makes communication possible is my ability, sitting across from someone, to know what it is that person doesn't understand. If I don't sense a lack of knowledge or appreciate a person's capacity for knowledge, then I will have a hard time communicating.

> I roamed the countryside searching for answers to things I did not understand.
>
> – Leonardo da Vinci

When I was an architecture student and in my early 20s, I had an epiphany. My epiphany was not that I was an information architect, but that I wasn't very smart. I was, in a sense, an empty bucket—a bucket being filled up by others. All that I knew was what people were teaching me, with none of it coming viscerally from me. So I decided that I would put into that empty bucket only those things that I truly understood. How would I know if I truly understood something? I would know I understood if I could explain it to another human being. So my epiphany had nothing to do with architecture—only with my personal limitations, a collection of my own thoughts which had nothing to do with a career. In fact, it led to a very unsuccessful life (for quite a number of years).

> He was a self-made man who owed his lack of success to nobody.
>
> – Joseph Heller

Nobody cared about the fact that I was stupid or an empty bucket. Nobody cared at all. In fact, I was unpopular at meetings for admitting that I didn't understand what people were saying, because an admission of ignorance wasn't the behavior that was rewarded in our society. It wasn't—and still isn't—popular to ask questions rather than answer questions. Answering questions was rewarded; asking them wasn't. It also wasn't popular to try to understand the nature of failure. It was popular to try to replicate success.

I kept doing what I was doing, and success caught up to me when I was in my 50s. But I had a long run of not doing anything that was thought to be valuable to society—I'm talking about financial success, power, positioning in companies, positioning in society.

I'm a success when I do something that I myself can truly understand. That's step one. And if my understanding of things gets published in a book and people buy the book, and they like it and tell other people to buy it, then I guess I've done OK.

ODE TO IGNORANCE

To comprehend new information of any kind—be it financial reports, appliance manuals, or a new recipe—you must go through certain processes and meet certain conditions before understanding can take place. You must have some interest in receiving the information; you must uncover the structure or framework by which it is or should be organized; you must relate the information to ideas that you already understand; and you must test the information against those ideas and examine it from different vantage points in order to possess or know it.

But the most essential prerequisite to understanding is to be able to admit when you don't understand something. Being able to admit that you don't know is liberating. Giving yourself permission not to know everything will make you relax, which is the ideal frame of mind to receive new information. You must be comfortable to really listen, to really hear new information.

When you can admit to ignorance, you will realize that if ignorance isn't exactly bliss, it is an ideal state from which to learn. The fewer preconceptions you have about the material, and the more relaxed you feel about not knowing, the more you will increase your ability to understand and learn.

At the age of 26, I began teaching as an assistant professor of architecture at the University of North Carolina in Raleigh. I realized immediately that there was a binary choice: I could teach about what I already knew, or I could teach about what I would like to learn. I was more motivated by what I didn't know and was comfortable with admitting my ignorance, so I chose the latter. As a teacher, I directed my subjects of inquiry to that which I wanted to know and ran my mind parallel to the mind of a student, rather than acting as a director of traffic.

My expertise has always been my ignorance, my admission and acceptance of not knowing. My work comes from questions, not from answers.

When you can admit that you don't know, you are more likely to ask the questions that will enable you to learn. When you don't have to filter your inquisitiveness through a smoke screen of intellectual posturing, you can genuinely receive or listen to new information. If you are always trying to disguise your ignorance of a subject, you will be distracted from understanding it.

By giving yourself permission not to know, you can overcome the fear that your ignorance will be discovered. The inquisitiveness essential to learning thrives on transcending this fear. Yet this essential prerequisite to learning is a radical concept. As there are

> We are, I know not how, double in ourselves, so that what we believe, we disbelieve, and cannot rid ourselves of what we condemn.
>
> – Montaigne

> Failure is unimportant. It takes courage to make a fool of yourself.
>
> – Charlie Chaplin

few rewards and many punishments for admitting ignorance on a personal or professional level in our culture, we go to great lengths to mask a lack of understanding.

And the energy expended diminishes our ability to learn. The classic progression of conversations—especially those in the workplace—illustrates how destructive this process is.

Let's say two people are talking about a project they are both working on, and Person A introduces new material. This will most likely set off a warning bell in Person B, who will start to worry: "Should I have known this? How did he find this out? What's wrong with me? How can I pretend that I knew this too?" While Person B is berating himself with these questions, he is likely to miss the chance to make the new material his own, to ask the questions born of a genuine desire to learn.

The same people who would delight in confessing to sexual indiscretions or income tax evasion blanch at the idea of saying, "I don't know." Instead, we practice the "Uh-huh, ah, yes" defense. One of the things we all learn in school is how to respond with a look of thoughtful intelligence to even the most incomprehensible information. I probably could elicit this look from most Americans if I suddenly started speaking Swahili. The focus on bravado and competition in our society has helped breed into us the idea that it is impolitic, or at least impolite, to say, "I don't understand."

Most of us have been taught since childhood, at least implicitly, never to admit ignorance. We've all heard the parental admonition: "If you keep your mouth shut, the world can only suspect that you are a fool. If you open it, they will know for sure."

This plays on an almost universal insecurity that we are somehow lesser human beings if we don't understand something. We live in fear of our ignorance being discovered and spend our lives trying to put one over on the world. If we instead could delight in our ignorance, use it as an inspiration to learn instead of an embarrassment to conceal, there would be no information anxiety.

The refusal to admit to ignorance hampers us every day in our personal relationships and professional development. Collectively, it bears primary responsibility for the anxiety and frustration of

> A minute's success pays the failure of years.
>
> – Robert Browning

> I'm not a speed reader. I'm a speed understander.
>
> – Isaac Asimov

staying informed. The issues relating to ignorance and understanding are so highly charged and subjective that—human nature being what it is—we are all easily distracted from the intangible toward more imminently solvable concerns. It simply is easier, for example, to conceive of building a new corporate headquarters than creating a new corporate philosophy.

AN OVERVIEW OF UNDERSTANDING by Nathan Shedroff

Understanding should be thought of as a continuum from data to wisdom. The distinctions between the steps along this continuum are not terribly discrete but they do exist on some levels. Therefore, the distinctions between data and information, for example, seem like shades of gray; and on the other side of the continuum towards wisdom, not only are the differences difficult to understand,

but the concepts themselves are hard to define (such as what knowledge and wisdom are). This is mostly due to the fact that at this end of the spectrum, understanding gets increasingly personal until it is so intimate that it cannot truly be shared with others. Instead, only the process that leads to it can be shared.

Data and information, although words used interchangeably in our language and our culture, are not the same. Not only does information have more value, it takes more work to create and communicate. For all the talk of this being the Information Age, it would be more accurate to call it, instead, the Age of Data— though this is still not the case.

AN OVERVIEW OF UNDERSTANDING by Nathan Shedroff

"One of the best ways of communicating knowledge is through stories, because good stories are richly textured with details, allowing the narrative to convey a stable ground on which to build the experience."

Data

Data is not the new driving force of our age. It is true that we have never before had so much data in our lives and this tends to obscure the fact that it is nothing new. We have reached a new relationship with it, surely, but it doesn't define our time.

An example of data passing as information would be the trivia we call news. Whether it is the obvious (like CNN's "Factoids" that serve to ease audiences in and out of commercial breaks) or the subtle (just about anything included in a celebrity biopic), data has nothing to teach us. As Richard says, "if it does not inform, it can't be information."

A more precise way to identify data from information is to look at its context. Without context, information cannot exist, and the context in question must relate not only to the data's environment (where it came from, why it's being communicated, how it's arranged, etc.), but also from the context and intent of the person interpreting it.

Information

Information comes from the form data takes as we arrange and present it in different ways. One of the most confusing points for many people is that the presentation and organization of data are entirely different. The organization of data itself changes the meaning of it, or at least its interpretation. As much as we would like to think that information is objective, it isn't. Most people already suspect that "statistics can be made to lie," because without changing any of the data (no fudging of the figures, for example), they can still be moved around in different patterns to conceal or reveal what the informer intends. This is because the organization creates, or at least, shapes meaning.

The presentation of the very same organization of data can vary drastically, from verbal (or textual) to visual, to auditory, or to something else entirely. The presentation also creates meaning (or highlights it), but it always is based on the organization already determined, which can be ultimately more powerful since it operates on a conceptual level instead of a sensory one.

Imagine what we could accomplish if we spent the same time, energy, and money to use the information skills we already know as we do on the tools and technologies otherwise labeled as Information Technology. In fact, the culture of IT, including most of the people who call themselves MIS (Managers of Information Systems) or CIO (Chief Information Officer), is precisely the problem. By renaming an industry (and the people and techniques within it), we've succeeded in subverting the question of information altogether since we've now given all of the prominence to data exclusively. This makes it harder than ever to see the information in our work lives.

Knowledge

The knowledge industry fares a bit better, on average, because the focus, at least, is more on the people than the IT industry, but the problem still remains. The bulk of those working as "Knowledge Officers" are still too concerned with the mechanisms of the solutions rather than the meanings, understandings, or personal issues of how people learn from each other and share what they know. Technology forms a near-disastrous distraction from real information and knowledge issues.

What most differentiates knowledge from information is the complexity of the experience used to communicate it. By necessity, knowledge can only be gained by experiencing the same set of data in different ways and, therefore, seeing it from different perspectives. This is also why education is so notoriously difficult: because one cannot count on one person's knowledge to transfer to another. We all must build it from scratch ourselves through experience—and not, ultimately, through books. Only through multiple experiences and questioning can we see the patterns that mark knowledge's trail. It is these patterns of information that define knowledge and allow us to not only understand the subjects better, but understand those patterns so that we can use them in different contexts with different subjects. This is what education should be about, but too often it is only focused on information—and worse, data—simply because those are the only forms that are easy to measure.

The field of experience design is emerging to help define what great experiences are (so that knowledge can be built from them) and to discover processes for creating these experiences for others. It is, in some ways, a new field (never having been recognized as a professional endeavor before), but in reality it is as old as humankind. We have always been creating experiences for each other, with a growing complexity as our own tools, expectations, knowledge, and sophistication grow.

One of the more difficult aspects of knowledge for many people is that it is much more casual than information, and the experiences that create it are more personal. Without the opportunity, willingness, or openness to interact on a personal level, much of the

power of these experiences are not made available to us. People need to move past their fears of things (including information, certain experiences, and dealing with people personally) in order to learn on this level.

One of the best ways of communicating knowledge is through stories, because good stories are richly textured with details, allowing the narrative to convey a stable ground on which to build the experience, and often allowing multiple interpretations. Telling stories face-to-face can also allow the story to change with the reactions, interests, and experiences of the audience, making it even more personal. Conversation (the interactive analogy to storytelling) comes very easily to some people, and these tend to be the people who gain knowledge the quickest. In contrast, those who find conversation difficult or would see the act of telling a story to be a terrifying exposure of themselves gain knowledge with great difficulty. It is only when we find an internal confidence and start telling stories for ourselves that we can best begin to understand the stories others tell us.

Wisdom

Lastly, wisdom is an ultimate level of understanding in which we understand enough patterns and meta-patterns that we can use them for ourselves in novel ways and situations in which we didn't learn them. Wisdom is as personal as understanding gets—intimate, in fact—and it is a difficult level for

many people to reach. Like with knowledge, wisdom operates within us instead of outside us so the transmission or sharing of wisdom is next to impossible. What can only be shared is the experiences that form the building blocks for wisdom, but these need to be communicated with even more understanding of the personal contexts of our audience than with information or knowledge.

As with knowledge, our comfort with ourselves—our ability to confront ourselves on an intimate level—is crucial to building wisdom. We cannot trick ourselves into becoming wise, and we cannot allow someone else to do it. We must do the work ourselves (and hard work it is), and we must be willing to find out things about ourselves along the way that we did not expect. This takes the most courage but offers the greatest reward.

Recognizing and valuing wisdom in others is one way to start down this path, as it will help define the framework of wisdom in our own minds. Introducing the concept itself to people is a critical step, for without the concept of wisdom, we cannot see it nor can we motivate ourselves to achieve it. Also, we need to expose people to the processes of introspection, pattern-matching, contemplation, retrospection, and interpretation so that they will have the beginnings of the tools to create wisdom.

Nathan Shedroff
Experience Designer
(nathan@nathan.com)

AESTHETIC SEDUCTIONS

Seduction is not an adjective most people would associate with a computer interface or media, but whether they realize it or not, most people have been either seduced or have been the target of seduction by almost all forms of media. Successful seduction, however, is a careful art that is not easily mastered nor invoked. For example, I believe that it's important to view the interface as an opportunity to seduce people—not for nefarious reasons, but to enhance their experiences and lives. Seduction, in fact, has always been a part of design, whether graphic, industrial, environmental, or electronic. For many, seduction immediately connotes sex appeal or sexual enticement. In fact, the sexual aspect is not the essence of its meaning as much as enticement and appeal.

While numerous fields are involved with the storage and transmission of information, virtually none is devoted to translating it into understandable forms for the general public. As the only means we have of comprehending information are through words, numbers, and pictures, the two professions that primarily determine how we receive it are writing and graphic design. Yet the orientation and training in both fields are more preoccupied with stylistic and aesthetic concerns.

Despite the critical role that graphic designers play in the delivery of information, most of the curriculum in design schools is concerned with teaching students how to make things look good. This is later reinforced by the profession, which bestows awards primarily for appearance rather than for understandability or accuracy. There aren't any Oscars, Emmys, or Tonys for making graphics comprehensible. The departments of graphic design that offer valid courses on information architecture and information design are practically nonexistent. Recently, some lip service has been given, but the efforts and results have been shallow. The various books that have been produced on graphic diagrams have been devoted almost exclusively to the aesthetic of the beautiful diagram, the beautiful map and chart—not their performance, nor their system, and not the analysis and criticism of their performance. If you remember this, perhaps you won't feel so inadequate the next time a chart or graph doesn't make sense to you even though you have an urge to hang it on your wall.

I do believe there is the need for new words. I do believe there is the need for new actions relative to understanding. I do believe leadership for these words and actions comes from several communities:

- Thoughtful graphic designers
- Creative information architects
- Writers and journalists

The individuals who cross the boundaries of these three groups have the potential to become good information architects.

JUST THE FACTS, PLEASE

Writers also serve the golden calf of style and are easily seduced into sounding literary rather than writing clearly. **Iris Murdoch** once said that to be a good writer, you have to kill your babies. Cross out something you might think approaches brilliance because it doesn't belong or doesn't move your point along.

Writers are usually held somewhat in check by considerations of accuracy. Even writers of fiction strive to convey accurately their own inner vision of the world. However, serving the god of accuracy doesn't always translate into understanding. Facts can do just as much to cloud meaning as to clarify it. I believe there is a god of understanding out there, and the god of understanding is not served by just the facts. Facts in themselves make no sense without a frame of reference. They can be understood only when they relate to an idea.

Ideas precede our understanding of facts, although the overabundance of facts tends to obscure this. A fact can be comprehended only within the context of an idea. And ideas are irrevocably subjective, which makes facts just as subjective. This is why if you serve the exact same meal to 15 people and ask them to describe what they ate, no two descriptions would be alike. Some descriptions will emphasize taste, others smell or texture. There is a tendency to forget that facts are subjective, especially within the news industry, which worships objectivity with the zeal of Shiite Muslims. Try sending 15 reporters out to cover the same fire and see what happens. Based on their own understanding of the world and the influences under which they operate, each

"Designer," likewise, has acquired a new generic meaning that has nothing to do with solving problems, communicating, or exploring ways to fit human needs within the constructs of the physical world. Fraught with negative associations, "designer" now connotes some kind of petty, overwrought exercise in extravagance.

– Akiko Busch,
"Designer Vocabulary,"
Interiors (April 2000)

reporter will recognize certain details and miss others. They will report on the event through the context of their own understanding, which will determine what they choose to emphasize or omit. The pitfalls and seductions of writing and graphic design apply to anyone trying to understand or communicate information.

Accuracy, in itself, is not the means to making things understandable. Once you realize that absolute accuracy is impossible, you can be more relaxed and comfortable with your own choices as to the level of detail and to the point of view. The key to understanding is to accept that any account of an event is bound to be subjective, no matter how committed the recounter is to being accurate and objective. Once you accept that all information comes to you filtered through the point of view or bias of someone else, somehow it will be less threatening, and you can begin to understand it in perspective and to personalize it, which is what enables possession (the stickiness of the information).

PERSONAL TABLE OF CONTENTS

A table of contents is the road map to the organization of any book, project, or Web site. It mirrors the author's thinking and the organizational point of view and emphasis. This is what gives you a sense of the whole. This is what shows you the structure. Trying to wade through information without a sense of its structure is like going to the Library of Congress and aimlessly combing the shelves for a particular book. Once you have a sense of how the whole is organized, you will reduce the frustration of searching for a needle in a haystack. Even if the needle is all that you need, you should know how the hay is organized.

The following page spreads reproduce a great little book created and designed by the information architect **Nigel Holmes**. Here it's reproduced at 80 percent of its actual size. Few of you will read it without coming to a clearer understanding of things you thought you already knew. I think Nigel's book speaks for itself as a good example of information architecture in its simplicity and its success at making a complex topic clear.

Don't be too certain of learning the past from the lips of the present. Beware of the most honest broker. Remember that what you are told is really threefold: shaped by the teller, reshaped by the listener, concealed from both by the dead man of the tale.

– Vladimir Nabokof

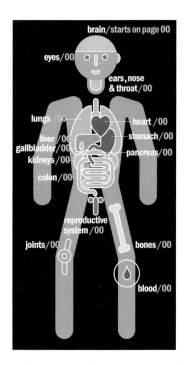

In my upcoming TOP books, *Diagnostic Tests for Men* & *Diagnostic Tests for Women*, I use a diagram of the human body as an index to medical tests.

GUIDE TO THE INTERNET by Nigel Holmes

NIGEL HOLMES

The smallest ever

GUIDE TO THE INTERNET
(for busy people)

The Internet
is a bunch of networks linked together.

A network
is a bunch of computers linked togther.

A user
is someone who accesses data
from these computers.

The smallest ever guide to the Internet
(for busy people)

COMPUTERS, PHONES & MODEMS

6 ☞ **9**
TRANSMISSION SPEEDS

10 ☞ **15**
WE ALL SPEAK THE SAME LANGUAGE

16 ☞ **19**
INSIDE THE WEB

20 ☞ **23**
INTERNET & INTRANET

24 ☞ **25**
COMMERCIAL TRANSACTIONS

26
COPYRIGHT PROTECTION

27
JUST A FEW BUZZWORDS

COMPUTERS, PHONES & MODEMS

Computers are **digital** machines. They produce a stream of pulses, on or off.

"on" "off"
pulse pulse

I00I0II0

The ones and zeros are
binary dig**it**s called **bits**.

To send or receive messages, computers are usually hooked up to phones. But unlike computers, phones are **analog** machines—they work by using sound waves.

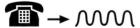

2

For messages to be transmitted from computer to computer over phone lines, the computer's digital language must be converted to the phone's analog language.

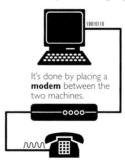

I00I0II0

It's done by placing a
modem between the
two machines.

The translation is called modulation (the word **modem** comes from **mo**dulation and **dem**odulation). At the other end of a message's journey, the process is reversed.

3

GUIDE TO THE INTERNET by Nigel Holmes

A modem's speed—the **baud rate**—is measured by the number of times a second it converts **100101** to .

9.6 & 14.4 baud rates are hardly used anymore; most people connect to the web with 28.8, 33.6 or 56k modems.

Baud rate is often confused with **bits per second (bps)** which is a measure of transmission speed—the number of bits that pass a specific point per second.

The computer uses eight bits to create a single character or letter. Those eight bits = one **byte**.

Right: 1,000 characters, about 166 words. Since each character, or letter, is one byte, this block of text is one **kilo**byte (1K*). A floppy disc holds one **mega**byte (1MB). A mega-byte is a million characters, or about 166,600 words—roughly 530 pages of text.

This block of text is 1,000 characters long. That includes every letter of every word, and all the spaces and punctuation marks between the words. When calculating the length of a block of type, it's common practice to say that, on average, words and their attendant spaces and punctuation are six characters long (in the English language). So that is why a kilobyte—1,000 characters—is calculated to be equal to roughly 166 words. (Remember; it takes one byte to create just one character). This block of text is 1,000 characters long. That includes every letter of every word, and all the spaces and punctuation marks between the words. When calculating the length of a block of type it's common practice to say that, on average, words and their attendant spaces and punctuation are six characters long (in the English language). So that is why a kilobyte—1,000 characters—is calculated to be equal to roughly 166 words. (Remember, it takes one byte to create just one character). So choose your words carefully. You are eating up valuab space with each keystroke!

4

*kilobyte=a thousand bytes / megabyte=a million bytes / gigabyte=a billion bytes
Purists correct my simplification here. A kilobyte is actually 1,024 bytes, because computers use base-2 numbers, instead of the familiar base-10 system. Hey, this is the kind of stuff I'm trying to shield you from!

The time it takes to transmit messages depends firstly on the speed of the modem, and secondly on the size of the message.

+

=

either

or

But bandwidth makes a difference to transmission time too…

5

TRANSMISSION SPEEDS

Internet messages travel down **pipelines.** The bigger the pipeline (more **bandwidth**), the faster a message travels.

Here's **how long** it takes to transmit the contents of a **floppy disc** (one MB, or a million characters of text) using different pipelines:

Using a 28.8 phone modem: **7 minutes**

an ISDN* line (64,000-128,000 bps): **3 minutes**

DSL (1–1.5 million bps): **8 seconds**

a T-1 line (1.5 million bps): **5.2 seconds**

a cable "modem" (3–10 million bps): **1 second**

*Integrated Services Digital Network (uses standard phone lines)

6

At the moment, phone companies and TV cable companies are racing to upgrade their services to match increased demand for speed (and for audio and video, which require a lot more bytes).

▸ **Phone companies** are developing **DSL** (Digital Subscriber Line) modems. If you live more than three miles from a local switching station however, you won't be able to get this service.

The service is called **ADSL** (Asymmetrical DSL) when the speed you send (upload) data to someone is slower than the speed that you receive (download) it.

▸ **Cable companies** are converting the one-way analog cables that bring you TV into high-speed two-way digital pipelines. While cable "modems" are available in parts of the US now, it will be some years before everyone can get the service.

And when we all can, the speed will depend on how many of us are logged on—at peak times cable service may be no faster than a 56k modem.

7

In the US, the backbones of the Internet itself (not individual connections to it) are built with fiber optic OC-3 lines that carry 155 million bits per second. Companies such as MCI Worldcom are now upgrading to lines that can handle 2.4 gigabits (2.4 billion bits) per second.

Businesses use T-1 lines and T-3 lines (45 million bps) to connect to these backbones, or build custom lines for routes they regularly use to cut down waiting time.

8

Next-generation Internet

The Abilene Project (also known as Internet2, or simply I2) is a cooperative effort of approximately 150 universities and companies including Cisco and IBM. They are designing a broadband network that will carry text, voice, video, and graphics fast enough to enable users to have real-time conferences. The new network will also ease the rapid increase in general net traffic.

This collaboration is a return to the origin of the Internet. In 1969, the Defense Department, in partnership with universities and other research communities, constructed the computer network ARPANET to share military and science data. In 1986, the National Science Foundation (NSF) started its own network. NSFNet took over ARPANET's functions, and in 1988 the whole system was referred to as the Internet. This is the same year that Tim Berners-Lee wrote the code for HTTP and HTML (☞ page 13), and created the World Wide Web.

9

WE ALL SPEAK THE SAME LANGUAGE

A common **protocol**, or language, is used on the Internet so that people with different types of computers all over the world can correspond with each other.

Internet protocol is called **TCP/IP**, which stands for **T**ransmission **C**ontrol **P**rotocol / **I**nternet **P**rotocol.

The function of the **TCP** part of this mouthful is to break down internet messages into small **packets** of data.

The function of the **IP** part of TCP/IP is to attach an address to the packets so that the internet knows where to send them.

10

Each packet contains a mere 1,500 bytes of data (about 250 words).

 Why so little data in each packet? Here's the reason:

There is **interference** on phones (it's the crackle you often hear on the line). If a computer message were sent as one continuous stream of binary digits and it encountered interference during transmission, the whole message would be destroyed and would have to be resent from the start.

 But with small packets, only the interrupted ones must be resent.

Sending and resending packets between many parties, in both directions simultaneously is called **packet-switching.**

FYI, **circuit-switching** is a conversation between just two people, on one phone line.

11

GUIDE TO THE INTERNET **by Nigel Holmes**

Within the machinery of the Internet, **IP addresses** are all numerical. The use of numbers rather than letters is less complicated for machines.

e-mail addresses substitute real names and words for numbers so we humans can remember them.

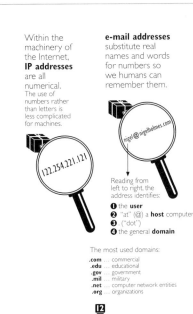

Reading from left to right, the address identifies:

❶ the **user**
❷ "at" (@) a **host** computer
❸ ("dot")
❹ the general **domain**

The most used domains:

.com .... commercial
.edu .... educational
.gov .... government
.mil .... military
.net .... computer network entities
.org .... organizations

12

URL stands for Uniform Resource Locator. It is another way of saying "internet address."

A URL (address) for a site on the Wide Web looks like this:

hypertext **t**ransport **p**rotocol: the computer language used by the web

world **w**ide **w**eb   World

the internet domain

the name of the file

all the "dots," punctuation and slashes are needed. Following the double slashes (across to the single slash) is the name of the machine on the Internet that you will access

the name of the web site. This one has the phone numbers of all **ISP**s (Internet Service Providers) in the world

everything following a single slash is a specific file on the site. Everything to the right of this slash is case sensitive. So type carefully!

denotes the file type. **H**ypertext **m**arkup **l**anguage is a format that enables the file to be read by a web browser

13

Routers, acting like traffic cops, control the vast numbers of packets criss-crossing cyberspace. They make sure that messages get to their destination by the fastest route.

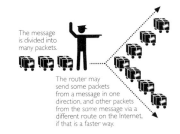

The message is divided into many packets.

The router may send some packets from a message in one direction, and other packets from the *same* message via a different route on the Internet, if that is a faster way.

It's as though you mailed a postcard to India from the US, but the Post Office cut your card in half, then routed the two halves in different directions around the world. They also make sure that both halves arrive in India at the same time and in the right order.

14

The common language of the Internet, TCP/IP is used only for traffic *between* computers. It is not the native language of any of the computers themselves.

So, at the end of the message's electronic journey, it must be translated back into the language of the receiving computer.

This translation is done by a **gateway**—software residing on the Internet provider's computer.

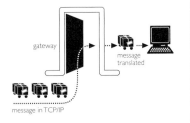

gateway

message translated

message in TCP/IP

15

INSIDE THE WEB

To find your way around the most popular part of the Internet, the world wide web, your computer needs something like a pair of reading glasses. This is called a **browser.**

Browsers such as Netscape or Microsoft Explorer help you to move to different sites on the web, and between pages within a site, by pointing and clicking on **links** within the text or on an image.

This linkage is made possible by **hypertext.**

16

In the text of a file, **hypertext** links are highlighted in various ways (as blue words, for example). These are keywords that have the address of a new page embedded invisibly under them. When you click on a highlight, you are linked directly to the new page.

Hypertext links may take you to other text, to pictures and graphics, to animations, to film clips, or to audio clips.

17

 Why is it sometimes so slow? These factors can affect the time it takes to retrieve data from the web (old joke—the World Wide Wait):

The **speed** of your modem

The type of **phone line** between you and the host computer/Internet **S**ervice **P**rovider. Also, **congestion** at your ISP

Interference on the line, which means that packets have to be resent

Routers, which are slower than the cables that join them

The popularity of the site you are visiting, meaning that you must wait until the **congestion** clears

Complex graphics at the site

The Internet is only as fast as the slowest link between you and the data you request.
—Stephen Manes, New York Times

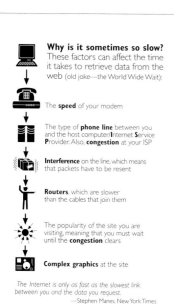

18

Too much design

Users will quickly go elsewhere on the net if it takes them too long to **download** (see) a page.

Web designers should take into account that many people are not using the latest, fastest equipment to download pages. They should design pages that are graphically **simple** and appropriate to the restrictions of the medium. There are estimated to be 320 million pages on the Internet. You may use one of the top **portals** (such as Yahoo, or Excite) to find information, and you'll thank the designers whose work gets onto your screen the fastest.

19

GUIDE TO THE INTERNET by Nigel Holmes

INTERNET & INTRANET While **the Internet** is many linked **networks...**

Within the networks there are **hosts.** A host is a computer that provides internet services to other computers on the network.

How many users are there? According to the US Dept. of Commerce, 80 million Americans and approximately 200 million people worldwide are connected to the Net. You'll find this and lots of other interesting numbers at www.internetindicators.com.

20

...**an intranet** is a private network within an organization—an internet inside a company.

All employees are linked together, streamlining communication. Here are some uses for intranets:

Employee training; benefits info | Company phone directory | Marketing materials | Libraries; research data | Technical databases; software library

21

Security for intranets is achieved with a **firewall** which prevents "outsiders" from gaining access to the intranet. "Insiders," however, may cross through the firewall to retrieve data from the net proper.

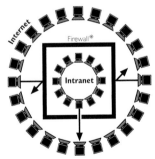

If an intranet is well-engineered, users will be unaware of whether they are inside or outside the firewall.

*The firewall works by disabling part of the packet-switching activity of the net.

22

A **Virtual Private Network (VPN)** is an arrangement between companies to open their firewalls to each other, allowing access to their respective intranets for a specific time—for example, on a joint project.

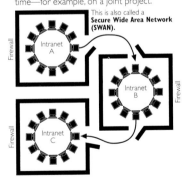

This is also called a **Secure Wide Area Network (SWAN).**

LAN = Local Area Network
(any internal network of computers in one company)
WAN = Wide Area Network
(the connection between different LANs)

23

COMMERCIAL TRANSACTIONS

It is estimated that worldwide Internet commerce could reach $3.2 trillion by 2003. That's 5% of total global sales. Security is a pressing concern for both buyers and sellers. Credit card companies and banks are jointly developing **Electronic Data Interchange (EDI)** technologies. Here's one way that financial transactions are made secure:

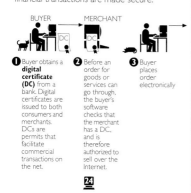

BUYER   **MERCHANT**

❶ Buyer obtains a **digital certificate (DC)** from a bank. Digital certificates are issued to both consumers and merchants. DCs are permits that facilitate commercial transactions on the net.

❷ Before an order for goods or services can go through, the buyer's software checks that the merchant has a DC, and is therefore authorized to sell over the Internet.

❸ Buyer places order electronically

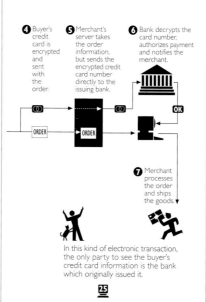

❹ Buyer's credit card is encrypted and sent with the order.

❺ Merchant's server takes the order information, but sends the encrypted credit card number directly to the issuing bank.

❻ Bank decrypts the card number, authorizes payment and notifies the merchant.

ORDER → **ORDER** **OK**

❼ Merchant processes the order and ships the goods.

In this kind of electronic transaction, the only party to see the buyer's credit card information is the bank which originally issued it.

24

25

COPYRIGHT PROTECTION

When the Internet was originally set up, there was no question of "ownership" of the information. Today, the web is as much a commercial medium as it is a place to exchange free information. Sites that charge users to download images, for example, naturally want to protect their property from pirates.

One way to safeguard unauthorized use of images is with a **digital watermark.** This technology encodes ownership information into the pixels of photographs. The brightness of certain pixels are changed enough to be electronically detected, but not enough to be seen.

A digital **worm** can then be sent to burrow through the Internet in search of stolen images that have this changed pattern of pixels.
The rest is up to the lawyers.

But, you know, **don t steal stuff.** Besides, lawyers have enough business.

26

JUST A FEW BUZZWORDS

Cookies are the coding left on your computer by websites you have visited.

Java is a programming language that can run on most computers. An **applet** (a small Java program sent to your computer over the Internet) can contain simple animation or complex math functions.

Mouse potato Someone who spends too much time at the computer.

MP3 is a format that compresses sound into files small enough for

internet transmission with minimal loss of quality.

Optical computers are the next generation. They process information by sending pulses of light along optical fibers rather than bursts of electricity along metal wires.

V-commerce is e-commerce that is speech-activated.

VoiceXML is a computer language that substitutes the human voice for a mouse, and the spoken word for a click. *BUY!*

Vortal = vertical + portal. A vertical portal is one that targets a *specific* group of users. [Yahoo (<➤ p. 19) caters to *all* users, and is thus a horizontal portal.]

XML (Extensible Markup Language) is a language like HTML (<➤ p.13) that uses **tags** (a code) to tell the computer what to display. Unlike HTML it also tells the computer what the information is. For example, in HTML, $9.99 is merely text, but in XML it can be 'tagged' as a price. This allows it to be searchable by information type.

27

L ocation
A lphabet
T ime
C ategory
H ierarchy

LATCH

The ways of organizing information are finite. It can only be organized by location, alphabet, time, category, or hierarchy. These modes are applicable to almost any endeavor—from your personal file cabinets to multinational corporations. They are the framework upon which annual reports, books, conversations, exhibitions, directories, conventions, and even warehouses are arranged.

While information may be infinite, the ways of structuring it are not. And once you have a place in which the information can be plugged, it becomes that much more useful. Your choice will be determined by the story you want to tell. Each way will permit a different understanding of the information—within each are many variations. However, recognizing that the main choices are limited makes the process less intimidating.

If you were preparing a report on the automobile industry, you could organize cars by place of manufacture (location), year (time), model (category), or *Consumer Reports* ratings (hierarchy). Within each, you might list them alphabetically. Your choice would depend on what you wanted to study or convey about the industry. If you wanted to describe the different types of cars, your primary organization would probably be by category. Then, you might want to organize by hierarchy, from the least expensive to the most. If you wanted to examine car dealerships, you would probably organize first by location, and then by the number or continuum of cars sold.

After the categories are established, the information about the cars is easily retrievable. Each way of organizing permits a different understanding; each lends itself to different kinds of information; and each has certain reassuring limitations that will help make the choices of how the information is presented easier.

Location. Location is the natural form to choose when you are trying to examine and compare information that comes from diverse sources or locales. If you were examining an industry, for example, you might want to know how it is distributed around the world. Doctors use the different locations in the body as groupings to study medicine. (In China, doctors use mannequins in their offices so that patients can point to the particular location of their pain or problem.)

Alphabet. This method lends itself to organizing extraordinarily large bodies of information, such as words in a dictionary or names in a telephone directory. As most of us have already memorized the twenty-six letters of the alphabet, the organization of information by alphabet works when the audience or readership encompasses a broad spectrum of society that might not understand classification by another form such as category or location.

Time. Time works best as an organizing principle for events that happen over fixed durations, such as conventions. Time has also been used creatively to organize a place, such as in the Day in the Life book series. It works with exhibitions, museums, and histories, be they of countries or companies. The designer **Charles Eames** created an exhibit on Thomas Jefferson and Benjamin Franklin that was done as a timeline, where the viewers could see who was doing what, when. Time is an easily understandable framework from which changes can be observed and comparisons made.

Category. Category pertains to the organization of goods. Retail stores are usually organized in this way by different types of merchandise, e.g. kitchenware in one department, clothing in another. Category can mean different models, different types, or even different questions to be answered, such as in a brochure that is divided into questions about a company. This mode lends itself well to organizing items of similar importance. Category is well reinforced by color as opposed to numbers, which have inherent value.

Hierarchy. This mode organizes items by magnitude from small to large, least expensive to most expensive, by order of importance, etc. It is the mode to use when you want to assign value or weight to the information, or when you want to use it to study something like an industry or company. Which department had the highest rate of absenteeism? Which had the least? What is the smallest company engaged in a certain business? What is the largest? Unlike category, magnitude can be illustrated with numbers or units.

If you understand, things are just as they are; if you do not understand, things are just as they are.

– Zen proverb

That is what learning is. You suddenly understand something you've understood all your life, but in a new way.

– Doris Lessing

> The most incomprehensible thing about the world is that it is comprehensible.
>
> – Albert Einstein

We already employ these modes almost subconsciously in many ways. Most of us organize our financial records first by time, then by category when we figure our taxes. We organize our CD and DVD collections, libraries, and even our laundry according to certain principles whether or not we are aware of them. But it is only the conscious awareness of these methods that will reduce the frustration of searching through information—especially new information. Uncovering the organizing principles is like having the ultimate hat rack. It is as essential when working with already existing bodies of information as it is in developing your own information programs. The time spent in comprehending someone else's method of organization will reduce the search time spent looking for individual components. When you arrange information, the structure you create will save you the frustration of juggling unconnected parts. Many people get into trouble when they mix the different methods of organization, trying to describe something simultaneously in terms of size, geography, and category without a clear understanding that these are all valid but separate means of structuring information. Understanding the structure and organization of information permits you to extract value and significance from it.

VANTAGE POINTS

> We come. We go. And in between we try to understand.
>
> – Rod Steiger

Once you have a sense of organization, however casual, you can relax with that knowledge and begin to examine the information from different vantage points, which will enable you to understand the relationship between bodies of information. Ask yourself: How can I look at this information? Can I move back from it? Can it be made to look smaller? Can I see it in context? Can I get closer to it so it is not recognizable based on my previous image of the subject? Can I look at the detail?

Whatever problems you have in life—personal relationships, putting together a business deal, designing a house—can be illuminated by asking these questions. How can I pull myself out of the situation? How do I see it by changing scale? How can I look at the problem from different vantage points? How do I divide it into smaller pieces? How can I arrange and rearrange these pieces to shed new light on the problem?

Each vantage point, each mode of organization will create a new structure. And each new structure will enable you to see a different meaning, acting as a new method of classification from which the whole can be grasped and understood.

CLASSIFYING LASSIE: THE DOG STORY

I could contact Avanta, an Italian company that makes stuffed animals, and ask them to make me a set of 296 life-sized dogs representing a male and a female of each of the 148 breeds recognized by the American Kennel Club. (My book *Dog Access*, produced in 1984, the source of the following illustrations, showed all the approved breeds at that time, arranged by size.)

To make dogs understandable to people, I could put this extraordinary bevy of stuffed animals on a gymnasium floor and organize and reorganize them. I could put flags on them denoting their country of origin and tie ribbons around their necks, colored according to which of the six different major groups in which they belonged: sporting dogs, hounds, work dogs, terriers, toys, and nonsporting dogs.

Then I could arrange them from the smallest to the largest, from the shortest to the tallest, from the lightest to the heaviest, from the shortest-haired to the longest-haired, by their level of viciousness, popularity in the United States, population, price, and the number of championships they have won.

Illustrations by William McCaffrey

CLASSIFYING LASSIE: THE DOG STORY

Every time the dogs are arranged in a different way, you can start seeing new information about the relationships. You might see that the most popular dogs are the shorter-haired ones, or that the most expensive dogs are the small dogs, or that in certain breeds the females are bigger than the males. As you observe these different types of dogs, you'll discover patterns, and finding and recognizing patterns is what leads to understanding. Each way I arrange these dogs tells you something different about them; each mode of organization provides additional information. The creative organization of information creates new information. The dogs don't change, but the information about them does. And it takes no prior knowledge or understanding to comprehend.

You can do this with many things; it makes your mind work differently because it shows the importance of relaxing and thinking about the arrangement of information before you make it complex. It's a process of simplification, not complication. And you realize that by simplifying, by taking one point of view, one slice, you can make something absolutely clear. Whereas if you tried to say this dog is the most popular in Wisconsin, and is of medium height, and said all these things at once, you would never get the mental map in your head, nor would you retain the memory of the information. Each way that you organize information creates new information and new understanding.

I could organize these dogs **alphabetically**...

Afghan Hound   Chihuahua   Komondor   Labrador Retriever   Pomeranian   Poodle   St. Bernard   Standard Schnauzer   Wire-haired Fox Terrier

Or by **category** (country of origin, for example)...

Egypt   England   Germany   Hungary   Mexico   Newfoundland   Poland   Switzerland

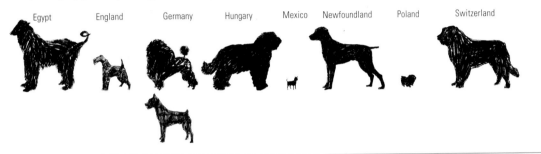

Or by **time** (for example, the year in which the breed was officially recognized by the American Kennel Club)...

1885   1887   1888   1898   1904   1917   1926   1937

Then again, I might arrange them in a **hierarchy** by weight in pounds...

4   11   18   19   40   60   70   90   175

Real learning about the dogs comes from comparing organizations. For example, you can see that the Afghan hound is taller than both the Labrador Retriever and the Komondor, but is outweighed by both.

THE SPACE BETWEEN THINGS

Part of the concept of looking at things from different vantage points is the idea of opposites. I see things in terms of opposites. I rather worship the space between things, the silence between good friends, the time between the notes of music, the break time during a conference, the space between buildings, negative space. I love the space on my desk better than the objects themselves. It makes me see clearer. It is the yin/yang of things. The opposites of things are just so much more fascinating than the things themselves. It's the way I approach everything. I look for a solution that has a valid oppositeness. Not a different way of looking at things, but an opposite way.

At dinner parties, I always look at the table with the place settings as the focal points; then I blink a couple of times and look at them as the backdrop for the table, which becomes the foreground. I try to look at cities the same way. In Venice, I look at the buildings as the space between the canals. Artists do these kinds of figure/field exercises all the time; we are all familiar with the drawing of the vase that becomes the profiles of two people facing each other. To see the opposite is illuminating.

Barry Diller, when he was the chairman and CEO of Twentieth Century Fox, asked a junior executive why a certain assignment wasn't finished. The young man said, "It's taking so long because I'm trying to do it the right way." Diller replied, "Did you ever consider doing it the wrong way?"

Opposites embrace the unexpected—what you look at every day but never really see or what you expect will never happen but does. With the advent of computers came the prediction of the paperless office, but just the opposite has proven to be the case: We developed desktop computer publishing capabilities. The VCR was predicted to supplant the movie theater, just as television was supposed to take the place of radio. More recent concerns have focused on DVDs, the MP3 music format, and Napster file-exchange software. The people who profit most from these new developments are those who can look at opposites. Only by looking at radical alternatives can you discover new possibilities and solutions—whether it's in architecture, writing, book publishing, graphic design, business, surgery, or science. It's a way of testing what has already been done, a way of finding solutions via the Hegelian formula of thesis versus antithesis yields synthesis.

Volvo designed its production process from an opposite. Instead of using the traditional industrial automobile assembly-line process, which calls for one person to perform one task, Volvos are built by small groups of people who each perform different tasks on the same car.

Numerous scientists were researching the possibility of developing a vaccine for polio, believing that it must be developed from a live virus. The Salk vaccine was developed from a dead virus.

Opposites inspire most scientific discoveries and business developments. Looking at opposites is a way of testing an idea to see if it works. It is a way of seeing, listening, and testing.

We recognize all things by the existence of their opposite—day as distinguished from night, peace from war, failure from success.

This should be the approach to interpreting information. You should ask yourself, "How can I look at this from different or opposite vantage points?" and "How would reorganizing the information change its meaning?" Instead of being bound by the accepted way of organization, what would happen if you mix everything up?

A learned blockhead is a greater blockhead than an ignorant one.

– Benjamin Franklin

If a little knowledge is dangerous, where is the man who has so much as to be out of danger?

– T.H. Huxley

THE SMART YELLOW PAGES® AND BEYOND

These were the questions I asked myself when I was asked to redesign the Yellow Pages in California.

The Yellow Pages are an ubiquitous reference that we accept without a thought. They are the path to the commercial environment, to our culture. Yet they are often confusing to use.

Companies are listed under one set of subheadings. If you don't happen to categorize information in the same way the telephone company does, they can be pretty inscrutable. For example, pencils are listed under the heading of Pens & Pencils—Retail, which is fine, but I would have never found them.

If you have an automobile and look up the word, you will find that fewer than ten percent of the total listings that have to do with automobiles begin with Auto.

So I asked myself, how could you look at the books from a different vantage point? How could you offer alternative ways of searching for information that would increase the chances that users could find it?

First, I decided that if the 2,300-plus headings could be grouped under larger categories, users would have a more manageable way to start their search. Also, they would be more likely to see categories that they might have never thought to look for. Home improvement, for example, would embrace the headings Carpentry, Building Supplies, Contractors, Hardware Stores. I realized it was logistically possible to assign the specific headings into general groups, such as Health-Care Services, Automobiles, Entertainment, etc.

I developed Subject Search Pages for each of the general groups. All of the specific headings were listed here followed by the page numbers of where they appear in the book.

With these books, you can skim a few pages and see things you might not think pertain to your car or home. You can use the Subject Search Pages like open stacks at a library, where in browsing through the shelves you might come across books you didn't at all anticipate finding. This approach permits you to follow your own thought process instead of the phone company's because it offers you alternative searching mechanisms.

Seek not to understand that you may believe, but believe that you may understand.

– Saint Augustine

Enabling the user to look at the information from different vantage points also suggested other ways to present or organize. Entries could be organized by their hours of operation or their location. For instance, I would like to know all the automobile places or car rentals, pharmacies, or restaurants that are open twenty-four hours a day in my neighborhood. You can access things by interest, then access them by task, and then by time in much the same way.

Each way of organizing the book provides new information. The listings stay the same, but the means of searching for them have been varied and expanded.

The product and service listings already exist; what I am doing is offering a variety of ways to access the same information, without barriers.

This is the complete 🔖 library for Guadalajara

MEXICAN YELLOW PAGES PROJECT

4 GUADALAJARA/OVERVIEW   MAPS 5

Businesses use these location numbers in their listings and advertisements

Los Belenes

Huentitán Bajo

Zapopan

San Juan de Ocotán

1   **2**   **3**   **4**

Huentitán Alto

See next page for **central area** in detail

Ciudad Granja

5   **6**   **7**   **8**

Centro

El Colli

9   **10**   **11**   **12**

Tlaquepaque

Santa Cruz de las Huertas

13   **14**   **15**   **16**

Santa Ana Tepetitlán

Nueva España

El Cerro del Cuatro

Las Juntas

San Pedrito

Santa María Tequepexpan

San Sebastianito

San Martín de las Flores

Mexican Yellow Pages Project

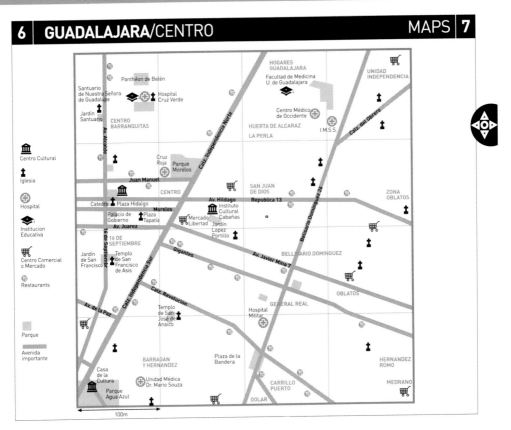

Recently, I have been consulting on a new Yellow Pages project planned for Mexico. We're producing a library of four separate Yellow Pages books: Home & Clothing, Transportation & Travel, Computers, Learning & Finance, and Health, Legal, & Government.

I welcomed this project, as it meant I could reintroduce some of my original concepts intended for the Pacific Bell Smart Yellow Pages, which were not implemented. And, best of all, I could introduce new features that I have come up with over the past 13 years to improve on my original concepts.

I'm fascinated with the word "source" and "find it" and the power that a company or product would gain were it to be thought of as THE SOURCE, the bible, the place to go to, the place to trust. When you combine this with our find-it society, a product in paper and electronic format that facilitates these notions is important.

I still like the phone. Perhaps that's too blasé of a statement. I love the phone. It is still my personal connection to the world (being a bad typist), my way of finding things, ideas, and exchanging information in real time.

This new set of books, which will also have an electronic iteration, will allow you to find out where something is, when businesses are open, the multiple ways of getting in touch with companies, and most importantly, the connections between products and services needed to complete a task—that is, everything having to do with your car, everything having to do with your house.

Shown here are some preliminary designs for this new library of Yellow Pages.

IN THE BEGINNING IS THE END

Before any solutions to any undertaking can be developed, a movement must begin to discover its beginning. Understanding the vein of the problem is the course to solving it. The best way to accomplish any endeavor is to determine its essential purpose, its most basic mission. What is the endeavor supposed to accomplish? What is the reason for embarking upon it? This is where the solution lies.

Originality is in the origins.

Let's say your community is thinking about building a hospital. On the surface, the purpose of a new hospital is to provide better medical services. But the purpose of medical services is really to improve health care, which in turn is to improve health. And the most essential purpose of all is to improve the quality of life in the community. Maybe the best way to do this is not to build a hospital; maybe the community needs only emergency medical services and more programs that emphasize preventive medicine.

There are two parts to solving any problem: What you want to accomplish, and how you want to do it. Even the most creative people attack issues by leaping over what they want to do and going on to how they will do it. There are many how's but only one what. What drives the how's? You must always ask the question "What is?" before you ask the question "How to?"

Here is a story about what is and how to. I'm in a desert. I'm dying of thirst. I see a trickle of water. It is not a mirage. I want that liquid in my mouth. Getting the water into my mouth is the what. How am I going to get it? First, I make a container out of my hands and scoop up the water.

I think, Ah! I can design a cup. So I make a cup, and it works, but it is too large for me to hold. So I make a smaller cup and put a handle on it, and I realize I have designed a spoon. I spoon that water to my mouth. I see some reeds growing. It occurs to me that I could put that reed in the water, draw the air out, and suck up the water. I have designed a straw. I get the water to my lips. These things all have to do with how to. Design is about how to. But first you have to understand the what. Only one what, but many how's. Each how has its moment in the sun.

Life is the first gift, love the second, and understanding the third.

– Marge Piercy

People want to buy lights before they understand lighting, which is what they really need. People go on diets before they understand nutrition, which would enable them to evaluate the relationship between their health and their food intake.

If you neglect to ask, "what is the purpose of the project?" your decisions of how to accomplish it become arbitrary and you will suffer nagging doubts. You will experience the anxiety of wondering would another solution have been more successful?

Many of us move too quickly into the how to before we fully understand what we want to do. Uncovering the essential purpose of any endeavor requires asking it what it wants to be and discovering how that relates to what you want or need it to be. In fact, I believe the design of your life evolves from asking these questions.

This practice can be employed on global issues, as well as on the mundane. It can mean asking questions about the national debt or on the design of your kitchen. Should your kitchen be a space for elaborate culinary undertakings or just an excuse for a microwave oven and an ice machine? Should your desk be just a surface or a place for storage?

I believe all information is out there and the trick is allowing it to talk to you.

We don't invent information; we allow it to reveal itself as it marches past. The parade must be encouraged, so that we can develop marvelous new organizational patterns that spark new understandings.

Ratio of Americans who say they trust TV news magazines to those who say they trust print news magazines: 2:1

Ratio of those who say they trust local TV news to those who say they trust C-Span: 2:1

Number of American children crushed to death by television sets since 1990: 28

Ratio of minutes that the three major networks spent on the Lewinsky story last fall to minutes they spent on Kosovo: 5:1

Number of words devoted to the Depression in Houghton Mifflin's fifth-grade history book, *Build Our Nation*: 332

Number devoted to the baseball career of Cal Ripken Jr.: 339

– Harper's Index
(January-April, 1999)

3 LAND MINES IN THE UNDERSTANDING FIELD

Since the advent of the Industrial Age, we have increased our use of a terrific word: *more*. It really worked for everything. When our roads became crowded, we built more roads. When our cities became unsafe, we hired more police officers, ordered more police cars, and built more prisons.

We built more schools for our children when we found they couldn't read. We solved our problems by producing endless products in greater numbers.

Now, however, the word that worked so well for a hundred years is creating the problems it once solved. More police officers don't necessarily mean less crime. More hospitals don't mean better health care. More schools don't mean a higher quality of education.

In fact, the opposite has become the case. In our desire to educate, we've penalized imagination and rewarded conformity. In our desire for revenues, we've encouraged deterioration by taxing owners for building improvements instead of penalizing them for letting buildings dilapidate. In our desire for mobility, we've scarred the landscape with highways that are always too narrow for the increase in traffic they generate. In our search for simplicity, we've created overly complex and expensive products that few can operate, let alone fix.

We have attempted to solve all problems with more solutions. We have asked ourselves only questions that produce more answers.

Less is more.

– Ludwig Mies van der Rohe

Somebody once said we never know what is enough until we know what's more than enough.

– Billie Holiday

There is an often-told story about **Gertrude Stein** that describes the moments before her death. People are huddled around her bed. Suddenly her face lights up. Her friends hover over her and say, "Gertrude, Gertrude, what is the answer?" Her eyes flutter and she says, "What is the question?" and dies.

People either don't know how to ask the right questions or they don't understand the value of asking them.

POLKA DOTS ON AN EDSEL

Social, economic, and cultural progress has historically been measured in terms of more or better or improved.

Any intelligent fool can make things bigger, more complex, and more violent. It takes a touch of genius— and a lot of courage—to move in the opposite direction.

– Ernst Fritz Schumacher

We attempt to solve problems with solutions that are only improved versions of what didn't work in the first place. We doggedly try to postpone that day of the grim reaper when we have to discount or throw away an idea. And a better version of what doesn't work is like putting polka dots on an Edsel.

We have a spackling-compound mindset that is geared toward products and product improvement. What we are missing is a language of solutions, a language that recognizes the concept of performance over product.

MORE, adj. The comparative degree of too much.

– Ambrose Bierce
The Devil's Dictionary

More answers don't describe the performance we need from a person or a product to solve the problem. The issue is learning, not schools; safety, not the number of police officers; mobility, not highways; communication, not signs. The issue is performance, not products.

Function is to Performance as a Model-T Ford is to a Ferrari. What's the difference between function and performance? A Model-T Ford is a car that functions as transportation; a Ferrari Testarossa is performance.

In architecture, the function of many buildings is that they keep occupants safe from the elements; far fewer perform. A building that performs is one where all spaces can be used efficiently, with neither too much space nor too little allotted for different activities; where the building systems are designed to accommodate the needs of the occupants; where the design is such that users feel comfortable in the interior environment. Performance is how well the building works. These concerns can be more important than construction costs. In the long run, an inefficient building will cost more.

Performance matters. What we need is a language that would allow us the power and ability to demand learning, safety, mobility, and communication. What we have is a vocabulary that encourages makeshift solutions that distract us from real problems.

We need the vocabulary that will enable us to understand the essential problems and to ask the questions that will produce answers that perform.

The emphasis on function produces sophisticated information technology without clear manuals that would enable people to operate it. The emphasis on function produces information anxiety.

> You can tell whether a man is clever by his answers. You can tell whether a man is wise by his questions.
>
> – Naguib, Mahfouz

> All promise outruns performance.
>
> – Ralph Waldo Emerson

TRAPS, DISEASES, AND MALAISES

The language of information transmission is laden with traps that lead us away from the concerns of performance and toward anxiety, confusion, and misunderstandings. By merely being wary of them, you can relax and learn. Keep them in mind as you dive into new information, when you peruse a newspaper, listen to the news, embark on a new endeavor, or take a new toaster out of a box. Understanding the pitfalls of communicating information will give you a defense against being intimidated or overwhelmed by it.

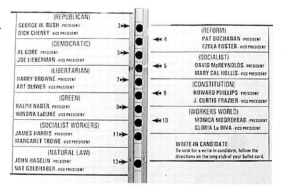

Just as this book was going to press, the controversy over the Palm Beach County ballot in the U.S. Presidential election became intense. See Susan King Roth's article: http://informationdesign.org/pubs/roth1998.html.

The following are misnomers, myths, and diseases that litter the information field, and unless you are aware of them, they will sabotage understanding. They afflict our ability to see the things we have always seen but have never really seen. They obscure our path to learning, and just by recognizing them, we can disarm their potential to mislead us.

- **The disease of familiarity**. Familiarity breeds confusion. Those suffering from the disease of familiarity are the experts in the world who, so bogged down by their own knowledge, regularly miss the key points as they try to explain what they know. You ask them the time, and they will tell you how to build a clock. We have all had teachers who are extraordinarily bright, yet we cannot understand what they are saying. They fail to provide the doorknob or the threshold into each thought so you can grapple with the learning connections along the journey.

- **Looking good is being good.** The disease of looking good is confusing aesthetics with performance. A piece of information performs when it successfully communicates an idea, not when it is delivered in a pleasing manner. Information without communication is no information at all. It is an extremely common, insidious malady among graphic designers and architects to confuse looking good with being good. The cure obviously is to ask how something performs.

- **The "uh-huh" syndrome.** This occurs when our fear of looking stupid outweighs our desire to understand. The manifestations are involuntary head nodding and repeating "uh-huh, uh-huh," pretending to a knowledge that we do not have. Rather than admit we don't understand the principle of quantum mechanics, we nod our heads as if we were intimately familiar with the subject, desperately trying to give the impression that we understand terms or allusions that are in reality incomprehensible to us. This only prevents us from learning and exacerbates our suspicion that everyone else knows more than we do.

- **Unhealthy comparisons.** Comparing unknowns or intangibles is uninformative; so is comparing things that have nothing in common. People warn of the dangers of comparing apples to oranges, when this is a perfectly reasonable comparison. Apples and oranges share many common characteristics: both are globular fruits that grow on trees. An unhealthy comparison would be to compare the cost of a loaf of bread or a movie 50 years ago to the cost today. The dollar had a completely different value then. The informative value of this comparison is very little. Whereas healthy comparison is one of the most powerful information tools—for example, comparing the cost of a loaf of bread relative to a movie 50 years ago and today.

- **If it's accurate, it's informative.** One doesn't necessarily follow the other. The cure is learning to get beyond the facts to meaning and to recognize the nature of the receiver. Accuracy

---

Form follows function.

— Louis Henri Sullivan,
Lippincott's Magazine
(March 1896)

Today, if you are not confused, you are just not thinking clearly.

— U. Peter

Despite the pain felt at the pump, gas prices are not really all that high by historical standards, according to the American Petroleum Institute. While retail gasoline averaged $1.57 a gallon last month (March 2000), the highest it has been since 1990, that still compares favorably with inflation-adjusted prices from 1920 ($2.53), 1930 ($2.03), 1940 ($2.23), 1950 ($1.88), 1960 ($1.78), 1970 ($1.56), 1980 ($2.51), and 1990 ($1.58).

"Crude Economics,"
New York Times Magazine,
(4/23/00)

or facts do not necessarily make things understandable. Quoting a price in pounds won't help someone who understands only dollars and cents. Barometric pressure is another example. I would say there is one person in a thousand who knows how barometric pressure is derived or what it means; yet weather commentators slavishly offer it up in every forecast.

- **Unnecessary exactitude.** Rounding off is not a sin. Not only is extreme accuracy not always informative, it is often not necessary. For pilots, knowing the exact altitude of the plane is important. But whether the plane is flying at 32,000 feet or 32,112 doesn't add to the experience of flying. In the business community, an accountant needs exact figures, but someone making a presentation on sales projections might just as well say that projected sales will be $90,000, rather than $91,653. Just because the technology exists to provide accuracy to the nth degree doesn't mean that we have to take advantage of it. Sometimes, extreme detail prohibits you from seeing the bigger picture. Even the federal government permits rounding dollar amounts on tax forms.

- **Rainbow worship or adjectivitis.** This is an epidemic belief that more color and more colorful language will in itself increase understanding. An area where this is particularly insidious is in sports reporting, which has adapted the dramatic language of war. Teams are annihilated, destroyed, massacred.

- **Chinese–dinner memory dysfunction.** This is characterized by total memory loss one hour after learning something. This has been caused by the educational system's emphasis on short-term memory. The cramming of unnecessary information about unnecessary subjects for unnecessary examinations to get unnecessary grades. The cure is very simple; the key to learning is remembering what you are interested in and that through interest comes understanding.

- **Overload amnesia.** This is a permutation of the Chinese-dinner memory dysfunction that occurs more specifically as a response to overloading yourself with data. When overtaxed, your memory will not only release the data that you were trying to retain, but may arbitrarily download other files as well. This is often experienced when trying to assimilate data over which you cannot

An example of excessive precision from one of my itineraries:

8:01 am: Depart on US Airways Flight 183, seat 3C.
Arrive in Philadelphia at 9:10 am.

A man may imagine things that are false, but he can only understand things that are true, for if the things be false, the apprehension of them is not understanding.

– Sir Isaac Newton

control the flow—for example, in a classroom, conference, or lecture. This is why after listening to a particularly ponderous speech, not only can you *not* remember a thing the speaker said, but you forget where you parked your car too.

■ **User-friendly intimidation.** "User friendly" has to be one of the most absurd terms in the language of technology. Like many other words in techno-talk, this usually means the opposite of itself. Any piece of hardware or software that has to be described as user-friendly probably is not. Often, the appearance of friendship with silly graphics is only a camouflage of incoherent instructions. Besides, why should a computer be friendly? We have the right to expect technology and equipment to perform for us, save us time, and make our lives easier. But if we expect friendship from it, we are bound to be disappointed.

■ **Some-assembly-required gambit.** I have no doubt that somewhere in the instructions for building a Saturn rocket are the words "Some assembly required." This is instant intimidation, a phrase lightly tossed off, designed to make the user feel that any boob could put this machine together during a network station break. I suspect it's sheer business chicanery, a trick so that the manufacturer can collect on a house call and a repair bill after you have failed miserably at the some-assembly-required test.

■ **The expert-opinion syndrome.** There is a tendency to believe that the more expert opinions we get—be they legal, medical, automotive, or otherwise—the more informed we will be. But we tend to forget that expert opinion is by no means synonymous with objective opinion. Unfortunately, most experts come with a professional bias that makes obtaining truly objective information almost impossible. Take the second-opinion movement in medicine that is even being promoted by health insurance programs, where patients are encouraged to consult more than one doctor before undergoing non-emergency surgery. Surgeons are trained to respond to problems by performing surgery, so it is likely that they will see surgery as the solution to a patient's problem.

- **Don't tell me how it ends.** The popularity of the suspense genre in books and movies has encouraged people to extrapolate this notion when conveying new information, for example, when a salesman unveils a new product. I think not knowing how something ends makes us apprehensive; it prohibits us from understanding how something was done while we frantically try to guess how it might end. People love **Shakespeare** because they know the endings; an opera is more pleasurable when you know the whole story before the curtain rises. The Brandenburg Concertos are like old friends because you know them. While suspense has its place, it does tend to induce anxiety, which is not an optimum state to receive new information. If you know the ending, you can relax and enjoy the manner in which something is being presented. I've seen more new ideas squelched in committee meetings when the person trying to sell them got bogged down in introductions. An audience will be more receptive to new information if they aren't kept in suspense, made anxious trying to guess where someone is going. Many people can't really listen to an idea until key questions about it have been answered in their minds.

- **Information imposters.** This is nonsense that masquerades as information because it is postured in the form of information. We automatically give a certain weight to data based on the form in which it is delivered to us. Because we don't take the time to question this, we assume that we have received some information. My favorite example of this is cookbook recipes that call for you to season to taste or cook until done. This doesn't tell you very much. Why bother? Information imposters are the fodder for administrativitis.

- **Administrativitis.** This is a disease manifest in schools, institutions, and in big business where the individuals think that they are running the system, but in actuality just the opposite is the case. It is characterized by a preoccupation with the details of operation—administrative issues, salaries, square footage of office space, and supplies—and a neglect of the purposes for operation. It has reached global proportions and is the fundamental curse of our society.

- **Edifitis.** This is a condition characterized by the belief that a better building or a more lavish office or a flashier annual report will solve all problems. Many a business has crumbled trying to improve its corporate headquarters instead of its corporation.

COMMUNICATION EQUALS REMEMBERING NOT KNOWING

The more one knows, the more one simplifies.

– Elbert Hubbard

Information feeds all communication in that the motivation behind all communication is to transfer information from one mind into another who will receive it as new information. Thus, perhaps, the most universal information trap is the one that inevitably occurs when attempting to communicate information. It is the trap of forgetting what it's like not to know. The minute we know something, we forget what it was like not to know it.

We can't remember what it was like not to read, to walk, or to know the names of objects. To some extent, we all fall victim to this when we explain something to another, because once we know something, we can't remember what it was like not to know it.

For many years, I had an idea in my mind of what the Pantheon in Rome looked like. Then, the instant I saw it, I forgot the picture of it that existed only in my imagination. It's as if there was a file in my mind under the heading Pantheon. Once I saw the real thing, the image ran over or erased the original. Once you see or understand something, you cannot conceive of what it was like not to have seen or understood it. You lose the ability to identify with those who don't know.

The villany you teach me I will execute, and it shall go hard but I will better the instruction.

– William Shakespeare

In the business community, millions of dollars and man–hours are lost in the training of new employees because the trainers can't remember what it was like not to know. If you could remember what it was like not to know, you could begin to communicate in terms that might be understood more readily by someone who doesn't know.

We may not be able to completely transcend this trap. By at least trying to put ourselves in the place of someone who knows nothing about what we are talking about, we can anticipate some of their questions and become better information transmitters. If we can simulate what it is like to be blind by covering our eyes, we can try to remember what it is like not to know when communicating new information to others.

LOOK OUT FOR THESE INSTRUCTORS

If you notice that your employees often cock their heads sideways and look at you with a glassy-eyed, loose-lipped stare, either they are suffering from narcolepsy, or they do not understand you. One way or the other, your directions are not getting through to them, and you are wasting your money paying people to carry out incomprehensible instructions.

Unfortunately, the very characteristics that tend to make successful executives—creativity, ambition, and mercurial thinking—also make for poor instruction-givers. They often lack the time or patience to explain themselves clearly. Thus, they misinterpret clients' needs, bewilder and aggravate employees, diminish creativity, hinder an employee's ability to do a job, and set themselves up for constant disappointment.

Bad instruction-givers squander talent and time as well as money. Their habits are perpetuated because they direct their staff in such a way as to confirm their preconceived notions. A boss who keeps peering over an employee's shoulder, fearing that he or she is incapable, is bound to make the person nervous and mistake-prone. This is a vicious cycle; the boss redoubles surveillance and makes the employee even more nervous.

Remember the frustration the last time you tried to figure out an equipment manual? Did you curse and throw the manual at a wall, complaining that "I can't understand a damn word of this thing?" This may be just what the people who have to follow your instructions feel like. The next time you accuse someone of "doing exactly what I told you not to do," entertain the possibility that what you wanted them to do wasn't exactly what you told them to do.

If you think that you are a masterful direction-giver and that your faithful followers always understand exactly what you want, then you might be in real trouble. Owing to the inherent shortcomings of communication, this just isn't possible. Our understanding of language is colored by our own experience and perceptions—aspects of humanity that have infinite variations. No two people will express ideas in the same way. Brilliant instruction-givers, people who can direct their staff to perform their tasks with exquisite precision, do exist. But even they can improve their techniques.

The most important fact about Spaceship Earth: An instruction book didn't come with it.

– R. Buckminster Fuller

A different language is a different vision of life.

– Federico Fellini

Once you are willing to admit there is room for improving your instruction technique, the next step is to understand just where your shortcomings are in the instruction department.

The following describes a variety of bad bosses who haven't learned how to give directions. They don't represent different people as much as different delivery styles. You may recognize yourself in more than one.

Illustrations by Ed Koren

Cover Your Ass. These bosses are not comfortable with their own position, so their primary motivation in giving you an assignment is to make sure that if anything goes wrong they will have someone other than themselves to blame it on. Finding excuses becomes a religious quest in itself. Their employees don't get to spend much time with assignments because they are occupied with trying to find a scapegoat in case things go wrong. The favorite words of Cover-Your-Ass bosses are focus group, test market, and mall-intercept study—the Holy Trinity. With religious fervor, they fight off the evil temptations of personal judgment and intuition—their own or anyone else's. Every night, the entire market-research industry says a prayer for these people.

I'm an Important Person, I Don't Have Time to Explain. These people are usually thinking about the next task before they have made the first one clear. They regard explanations as a waste of precious time, and they brag that they won't stoop to hand-holding their employees. Their time is very precious because Important Persons spend most of it trying to correct the mistakes made by their subordinates, usually with new directions that they never take time to deliver properly. Of course, to do the job right the first time would save twice as much time, but then the Important Persons wouldn't feel so important and so needed. The Important Person's favorite expression is "For heaven's sake, I don't have all day."

Crisis Managers are a contradiction in terms, for nothing is managed as much as it is attacked. They take their working style from kamikaze pilots. Their speech is peppered with cliches like "going for broke, staying on top of everything, the whole ball of wax, and shooting the wad." Foreplay to Crisis Managers is calling an emergency meeting. They thrive on exorbitant rush charges, overnight delivery services, last-minute changes of plans, and hearing someone else say, "The sky is falling." Their phones

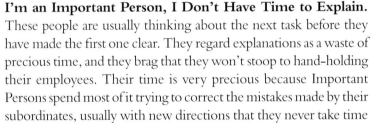

never get put down as much as slammed down, and they sound like they are on the commodities trading floor even when they are sitting in their offices. They appear to be in imminent danger of suffering from massive coronaries, nervous breakdowns, and apoplectic fits. Don't let this fool you though. They can live long and happy lives in this state. The ones who collapse are the people who have to follow their directions.

Mr./Ms. Taskus Interruptus. With flawless timing, these bosses assign a task and, just when their employee has become immersed in it, they interrupt the person with a new request. Thus, their employees are deprived of a sense of accomplishment because they never get to finish a job. Sometimes, this behavior is caused because people fear that their employees might donate the company to charity if they had a free moment. More likely, it results from arrested development on the part of the instruction-giver. When an infant's pacifier falls out of its mouth, getting it back becomes the most important quest in the world. An infant doesn't understand that the house might be on fire; mother might be rescuing brother from the washing machine; or she could be in the middle of an important phone conversation. As they mature, most children are forced to accept the idea of limited time and resources; they learn to adapt to this phenomenon by setting priorities. This escapes many executives. Whatever comes to their minds is what needs to be done *now*. Employees soon learn that the new request is always more important than what they were doing. Task Number 1 gets put aside for Task Number 2. While doing Task Number 2, they are fair game for further interruptions. Sometimes, tasks undergo generations of interruptions. It becomes increasingly difficult to remember all the tasks that were put down temporarily. Employees are likely to get confused and make mistakes. "Let's see, where was I? Was I supposed to review the Barber case or case the barber?" You might think working under such a person would be intolerable, but, fortunately, Mr. and Ms. Taskus Interruptus tend to retain other more appealing traits of childhood as well. They are often very creative, optimistic, playful, and just plain fun to be around, but underlings can grow resentful if they are expected to act in a more mature manner than their bosses.

Over-the-Shoulder Supervisor. These people fear that they are the only ones capable of doing anything and that the only way you are going to be able to carry out their orders is if they supervise you at every step of the way. Of course, this kind of approach tends to make subordinates nervous, and, in a state of heightened anxiety, they are likely to commit just the kind of errors the bosses were sure they would make in the first place. The bosses give elaborate step-by-step directions that are so detailed that they tell you not only who to call, but how to use the phone. Then, five minutes after giving the instruction, they poke their heads into your office and say, "You're staying on top of this now, aren't you, Miss Jones?" Their employees get so caught up in the intricacies that the goal gets lost in the shuffle.

Why Don't You Let Me Do That for You. No one could possibly do the job as well as these people. These are the obsessive-compulsive versions of the Over-the-Shoulder supervisors who, while they may watch you like a hawk, will not take tasks away from you. The problem is that Let Me Do That's have such a fixed idea of the solution that no one can do the job in the exact way that they would. Their employees are also prevented from going beyond their bosses' directions or from coming up with better ways to do things. These bosses have been told by everyone—and usually are aware of it themselves—that they should learn to delegate authority, but when they try to assign tasks, they invariably wind up repossessing them. These people live at the office and are surrounded by a staff of people who take very long lunch hours, keep in close touch with their friends, and surf the Internet at their desks to pass the time.

If You Love Me, You'll Do This, or Management-by-Guilt. This type may be a workaholic who has no life outside the company and assumes that no one else does either. They play the role of parent with varying degrees of good nature. If an employee has to tell her MBG boss that third quarter sale figures will not be available until after the fourth quarter, what does she fear most? Getting yelled at? Getting fired? Being embarrassed in front of her co-workers? No. She fears that baleful, bassett-hound look. "Oh, Ms. Foididdle. This makes me very sad," says Mr. Management-by-Guilt, as he shakes his head slowly. "I'm so disappointed. I just don't know what to do with you. You're like a daughter to me." MBGs are fond of familial references, and they tend to attract susceptible underlings who imagine that their boss is really their father or mother. The employees of these people are usually so burdened by guilt that they barely have the strength to work. But eventually they realize that their bosses will not come over when the babysitter cancels, make canapes for cocktail parties, or remind them of their anniversary. When this happens, employees tend to get very bitter.

Free Associators. These people throw out vague requests that sometimes seem contradictory or confusing. They speak in stream of consciousness, read New Age literature, think in hyperbole, and vacation in exotic places. They are always animated, expostulating on harmony in the office and the creative spirit. An assignment given by a Free Associator might sound like this: "I want you to show the connection between art and science. Where is that point where they merge? The question is in the answer. The answer is in the question. Education is all about connections." The employee suspects that this might be an assignment to design a poster for a museum exhibit, but is never quite sure. These people can be positively evangelical; they are great at eliciting enthusiasm and make great bosses as long as they don't turn out to have some specific goal in mind despite the vagueness of their requests. As long as they are as flexible as their instructions, these kinds of instructors can be quite inspiring for they permit the takers to use their own imagination in completing assignments. One of the most dangerous types is an outward Free Associator in the body of an Over-the-Shoulder Supervisor.

The Cro-Magnon Manager. The communication skills of these people never developed beyond the crib. Consequently, they hide behind an attitude that communication, as well as quiche, is for sissies. Their directions are barked out in one-syllable grunts, and they have the patience of hand grenades. It is a peculiar phenomenon that such types tend to surround themselves with people who live for language and devote themselves to reforming their Cro-Magnon bosses. A typical exchange with such a person goes as follows:

"Sir, what did you think of the letter of agreement I drafted with Blank Page Printing Company?" says the loquacious lackey.

The Cro-Magnon Manager, rifling through the mountains of memos on his desk, responds without looking up. "Huh?"

"The letter of agreement, sir, did you get a chance to read it?"

"Huh? Oh, yah," he says, as he glances at the document and seems to notice something disagreeable. "Argh."

"Is there a problem?"

Finally, resorting to an approximation of English, he responds, "Wrong. It's wrong."

"What is the problem, sir?"

"It's just not right."

"Could you be more specific?" the lackey asks, ever optimistic.

"I said it's wrong," says the manager, as he goes back to rearranging the piles of paper on his desk.

At this point the employee gives up and shuffles back to his or her desk to try another version with no idea of what was wrong with the first one.

Do As I Mean, Not As I Say. These bosses may have a clear picture of what needs to be done, but the idea gets garbled when they try to explain it. Their instructions are muddled in contradictory phraseology, unclear descriptions, and errors in meaning. Do As I Meaners say West Coast when they mean East Coast, say Fred when they mean Ethyl, and call General Motors Major Motors and expect you to know exactly what they are talking about. These bosses prevent their staffs from getting clarification on any directions by accompanying them with remarks such as:

"You know what I'm talking about, don't you?"

"You can see the writing on the wall, can't you?"

"I don't have to spell it out for you, do I?"

Underlings are understandably reluctant to admit that they don't, they can't, and you do, because the implication to these questions is that you would have to be an idiot not to understand. So employees spend most of their energy trying to pretend that they do. It may be of some consolation that Do As I Meaners are as frustrated as their employees.

Henry/Henrietta Higgins. This couple thinks their employees were created in their own image. All they have to do is think of an idea and their underlings will understand it. The employees automatically know what they know, so there is never any need to put an instruction in context. This couple believes that all of their knowledge and information gets transferred to their employees by cerebral osmosis. They mistake their employees for mind-readers. The Higginses' behavior manifests itself in two diametrically opposed personalities—a supreme egotist who views underlings as merely extensions of his or her own persona, and a pathologically fearful sort who is terrified of insulting anyone else's intelligence by unnecessary explanations. Either way, this couple appears to have blind faith in their employees, and blind is what the employees working for them feel like. When they tell you to call Smith, you are supposed to know that they mean Fred Smith, who is president of Smith & Smith in Smithville. Even if you can piece this together, you still need to know that Smith is vacationing in Brazil at the time, but don't expect this helpful information from a Higgins. An identifying characteristic is that they usually pound their fists on the table, wailing, "Why can't my employees think more like I do?"

The Carrot-on-the-Stick Wavers. The wiliest form of instruction-givers, their instructions appear to be complete, but they have directed their employees to a goal that is only a step along a much longer road. Just when their employees think they have realized the goal, they are discouraged to discover the road is still ahead. Satisfaction is still around the corner. These bosses probably had fathers who used to tell them, "Now that you've finished cleaning the garage, you can mow the lawn." Working for a Carrot-Waver will remind you of that detested camp counselor who kept telling you the top of the mountain was only a few yards up when, even at the age of six, you knew she was lying through her teeth.

Ping-Pongers. Ping-Pongers seem to operate on a different level of consciousness than the rest of the people in the world. While many people define things in terms of their opposite—that is, ("Don't do anything cheap or small time" means "I want ritzy"), these people spout out mutual exclusives. In describing his design concept to his staff, a Ping-Ponger in the architecture field might say, "I want something grandiose, but intimate; playful, but serious; large, but small." You bounce back and forth between these opposites desperately waiting for the ball to land in one court or the other, but it never does. Trying to interpret their bosses' instructions requires defying all of Western thought—a feat for which few junior designers are prepared. Ping-Pongers work well with Zen Buddhists, people from California, and anyone else who has ever seen a rock grow.

INSTRUCTION-TAKERS GUARANTEED TO GET IT WRONG

As an instruction-giver, you feel accused unjustly. The above types just don't apply to you. You always speak in a language that is understood by the taker; you clearly outline what is expected of your employees; you never give an assignment without giving the reason for it; and you are the epitome of patience. Yet, there are communication problems in your office, and your employees still have trouble following your directions. Is it possible that while you are a divinely perfect instruction-giver, they are hopelessly human and flawed in the instruction-following department?

Yes. It is possible that you are surrounded by poor instruction-takers. After all, you can't be blamed for everything.

Incompetent instruction-takers are just as costly as instruction-givers in terms of dollars spent and time wasted. They can also be more dangerous. The CEO of an airline can be a lousy instruction-giver. An airline pilot who can't follow the instructions of an air-traffic controller doesn't have that luxury. Those operating the equipment can do a lot more physical damage than those who buy it.

Do you recognize yourself in any of the following instruction-takers?

Just Give Me the Details. These people are always trying to second-guess you. You have just started to explain what you want them to do and they are running out of your office muttering, "Yeah, yeah, I know what you are talking about. I'll get right on it." They are in such a hurry to carry out your directions that they don't have time to listen to the request. But you don't find out that they don't know what you are talking about until they return with the evidence of the finished project. When you point out that they have done the wrong thing, they get even more flustered and harried trying to correct it. You may be tempted to yell at these people, but this will only get you more mistakes. Just-the-Details types are likely to be afraid of you, figuring that the less time they spend with you, the less chance they will incriminate themselves. One approach might be to handcuff them to a chair in your office while you fully explain what an understanding, patient person you are.

The Pacifist. This inscrutable form of poor instruction-taker is the most difficult to spot. These persons will patiently listen to all of your directions, nodding at all the right moments. Pacifists have mastered a look of intelligent attention; you are just sure they are hanging onto your every word—until you see the results of their efforts. You wonder: Did you explain it to them correctly? Did your message get through? You never know with Pacifists. They will never argue with you, so you have no idea whether they just don't understand you or choose not to pay attention to you. These are the types that one day start shooting at people from building tops, and their neighbors claim in the ensuing news accounts, "I don't understand it. He was such a nice man."

Toadying Sycophants. In less polite circles, these instruction-takers are referred to by a term that rhymes with Pass Misser. They hover over you; they are the first to run for your coffee, to volunteer for any assignment, to fight any fire. You might ask, isn't this the best kind of instruction-taker? It is if you expect only wanton flattery, for they will look you in the eye and insist that your most preposterous ideas make perfect sense. If you are president of a company that manufactures dental prostheses and suggest that the company introduce a new line of false teeth made of balsa wood, your toady will be on the phone with the local lumber yard.

The Terminally Obtuse. These people are easy to recognize because their mouths hang open, their shoulders droop, and they can maintain one facial expression for extended periods of time. Their favorite word is "Huh?" They move so slowly that they could walk through a room of duck down without ruffling a feather. At first, you may be tempted to suspect that they are a few pickles short of a barrel. This is not necessarily the case. The

appearance of extraordinary denseness isn't always an indicator of low intelligence. The Terminally Obtuse may be trying to get out of doing something they don't want to do. If you suspect that someone is feigning stupidity, look for signs of inconsistency, such as responding to high-potential-for-reward instructions with a keen mind and low-potentials with a dim wit. For example, if the obtuse person always remembers to bring coffee to the ringmaster but forgets to clean out the lion cage, you have a strategist on your hands.

I'm Just All Thumbs. This is a more appealing variation of the Terminally Obtuse. Where the former plays the moron, the latter aims for helplessness, which, when cultivated, can be quite fetching. Strategically, it is a superior tactic, for the Terminally Obtuse person will succeed only in avoiding a task; Mr. and Ms. Thumbs will get you to do it for them. They are masters in the Art of the Ditz, whether trying to park a car or to put together a barbecue grill. "I can't seem to get it. I'm such an idiot at this kind of stuff," they say while batting their eyelashes. Make no mistake. While they appear to be engaging in self-pity, they are really bragging about their inabilities. They aren't apologizing; they are advertising all of the things they can't do and machines they can't operate. This is part of their technique for getting someone else to do the job they don't feel like doing.

Wild Goose-Chasers. Always on the run (usually in the wrong direction), they have boundless energy, and no idea how to harness it. You can find them searching for left-handed monkey wrenches or unsalted herring. They are easily distracted. You could ask them for the price of beef, and they might embark on a study of hoof-and-mouth disease and go on to colleges that offer animal husbandry programs. They are so earnest and intent on making you happy, it's hard to criticize them. They work well under Over-the-Shoulder Supervisors who can keep them on track.

Style Meisters. These people are obsessed with the appearance of their work. It is always neat and organized—with footnotes and margins in perfect order and replete with graphs, tables, and charts. They adore flashy graphics and four-color printing. They wear unstructured clothing and read only that which is printed on chrome-coated paper. Their desks are always immaculate; their taste is exquisite; and they can be counted on to know the most chic restaurants and bars in any given town. The only thing they cannot seem to do is fulfill the substance of your assignments. Their obsession with style is at the expense of content, and their work is long on glitz and short on ideas. But Style Meisters tend to flock together, so they usually wind up working in places where their shortcomings are never noticed.

Don't Boss Me Around. These belligerent types perceive every instruction as an order and will never fail to let you know that they have no intention of following it. They are experts in labor law and know the number of the local Labor Relations Board, which they regularly threaten to call should you be tempted to violate any of the rules. Strangely enough, though, these people invariably follow directions quite well and, if you can stand their attitude, make competent employees. They are often quite intelligent and concomitantly unpopular. Just don't ask them to buy a present for your spouse. They work best in environments that don't involve much interaction with others—like in ice-fishing or patrolling borders, perhaps.

Too Smart for Instructions. This is a variation of the DBMAs above. The DBMAs are just pushy; these people are arrogant—the kind who will empty a tank of gasoline driving around hopelessly lost rather than ask directions. They see themselves as being above the need for instructions. Their egos are always on the line. Their favorite expressions are "I know that" and "You hardly need to tell me." On the positive side, they usually make a lot of mistakes so you have a good chance of getting the last laugh.

The Paper Warrior. This one believes that all problems can be solved with more information. If you ask him or her to get you the figure for gross sales this month, you will get a plastic binder stuffed with charts and graphs. You will get gross sales for every year since the company was founded. You will get gross sales of all your competitors. And the only one who spends more time than this person is the one who has to wade through all the unnecessary data to find the information that was requested.

The Overkiller. This is a more expensive version of the Paper Warrior who believes that all problems can be solved with more: more technology, more money, more manpower. Instead of imagination, the overkiller uses heavy artillery. Like the Pentagon, this person is expensive. Beware of the person who starts sentences

with "If we only had...." You cannot afford him. This type originated with the Carthaginians, who after killing their enemies would pour salt on them. Overkillers just don't know when to stop; the equation "enough is enough" computes as more in their minds.

Guaranteed to Miss the Forest for the Trees. This common type gets so caught up in the details of the instruction that they miss the intent altogether. They thrive on the convoluted and the complex, the abstruse and the arcane. The direct line between any two points is the last place you will find them. If you asked them to count a herd of cows, they would add up the legs and divide by four. Ask a Forest-for-the-Trees type what's for lunch, and you're liable to get the chemical composition of a bologna sandwich. These employees can often be found searching for overcoats that they happen to be wearing and looking for papers that are under their noses. However, they try so hard it is painful to watch them at work and few bosses are steel-willed enough to reprimand them.

Sure, Oh Shit. These poor souls try to please everyone. No matter what you want them to do, they will promise to do it and then wonder how in the world they are going to manage it. They understand the word "No," but they will never use it. They will work harder and longer trying to do the impossible. Unlike toadies, who will butter up their bosses to improve their own position, SOSers selflessly want to make their bosses happy. If you asked for a report yesterday, they would try to deliver it as requested. But they are often catastrophe-prone. Their cars break down en route to important meetings; they spill mustard on presentation drawings; and their buildings collapse on the day before the real-estate closing is scheduled. Somehow the adulation they seek is denied. The SOS personality was probably made to feel inadequate by parents incapable of praise and is determined to win it from a boss or other parental figure.

MANAGEMENT STYLE VERSUS WORK STYLE

Sometimes, communication problems aren't so much the result of individual personality types as the result of poor combinations of personalities. Just as bosses have different techniques for directing, workers have different styles of carrying out directions.

Each will function best in a different environment, either alone or in groups, in an orderly or chaotic room, on a fixed deadline or at one's own pace. Certain types of instruction-takers can function perfectly well with certain instruction-givers, whereas others might bring work to a standstill.

Pairing someone who manages by guilt with a Sure, Oh Shit personality would benefit only the company psychologist. An Over-the-Shoulder Supervisor is liable to meet his or her demise at the hands of Mr. Don't Boss Me Around. But pair a Free Associator with someone who thinks he or she is too smart for instructions, and you could have a productive team, especially if that someone really is smart. And the union of Here Let Me Do This for You and I'm Just All Thumbs is a marriage made in heaven.

If you can determine what types of personalities you embody in the instruction department, you can correct some of your own shortcomings and look for compatible partners who will work with the flaws you can't correct.

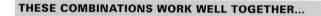

THESE COMBINATIONS WORK WELL TOGETHER...

Just Give Me the Details

and

I'm an Important Person, I Don't Have Time to Explain

THESE COMBINATIONS WORK WELL TOGETHER...

I'm Just All Thumbs

and

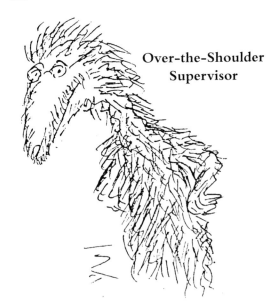

Why Don't You Let Me Do That For You

Toadying Sychophant

and

Over-the-Shoulder Supervisor

THESE COMBINATIONS SPELL TROUBLE

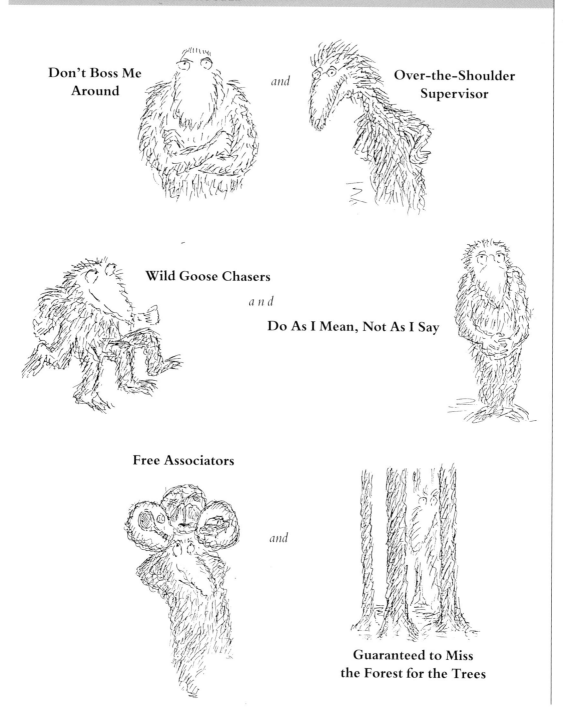

Don't Boss Me
Around

and

Over-the-Shoulder
Supervisor

Wild Goose Chasers

and

Do As I Mean, Not As I Say

Free Associators

and

Guaranteed to Miss
the Forest for the Trees

Carl Jung devised a classification system for supervisors based on whether one is extroverted or introverted and how one perceives and makes judgments. His system can be applied to determine a work style as well. He believed that people perceive either by sensing directly through our five senses, or by intuition, indirectly comprehending ideas through the unconscious. People judge by thinking (by a logical system motivated by objectivity and impartiality), or by feeling (a subjective and personal system). Based on different combinations of these characteristics, he outlined eight types:

- **Extroverted Thinking Type.** "But the facts are." This type is analytical, decisive, a good organizer, and a disciplinarian, but lacking in perception and concern for others.

- **Introverted Thinking Type.** "I'll have to give it some further thought." These people organize facts and ideas, but not people and situations; are independent, persevering, and good at problem solving. However, they tend to be stubborn, reclusive, and lacking in communication skills.

- **Extroverted Intuitive Type.** "I have a hunch." These enthusiastic innovators possess imagination, confidence, and an ability to stimulate others. Their biggest problem is an aversion to routine and details.

- **Introverted Intuitive Type.** "Silence, genius at work." These intense types are inspired by the problems no one else wants to tackle. They are creative, driven, determined, and need little companionship. They tend to be single-minded and blind to the conditions and counterforces that might affect their solutions and sometimes have the reputation of impractical geniuses.

- **Extroverted Sensing Type.** "The right tool for the right job." These adaptable realists are driven by facts. They notice, absorb, and remember more of the world around them than others. Their natural sense of economy, keen perceptions, and tolerance make them generators of integral solutions to problems, instead of imposing rigid or external ideas. On the down side, their dependence on observations sometimes precludes vision.

- **Introverted Sensing Type.** "The real meaning is not what it seems." Dependable and observant, these types rely on facts, but see them differently. They are adept at getting to the heart of the matter; they are persevering, and they are patient with details and routines. They make good administrators, but have trouble empathizing with divergent ideas, and they are rather impersonal and passive socially.

- **Extroverted Feeling Type.** "The more the merrier." These hale fellows are sensitive to the emotional atmosphere, friendly, tactful, and sympathetic. They get along well with people, but don't do well on their own and are impatient with slow or complex procedures.

- **Introverted Feeling Type.** "Still waters run deep." These types are also sensitive, but they care more deeply about fewer things than their extroverted counterparts. They don't need to impress or persuade others and are tolerant of others as long as their own convictions aren't threatened. Adversely, they can be overly sensitive and frequently suffer a sense of inadequacy.

Which of the above types do you resemble? Perhaps just ask four people who have to follow your instructions to read this chapter and circle the personalities that most resemble you.

If you are unhappy with your type, you could always hire a coach to readjust your personality or your communication style. Business coaches use role-playing, videotaping, and behavior adjustments to correct personality problems.

"Indeed, private coaching is on the upswing, and for good reason.... For high-level people, lack of skill is not usually what gets in their way," said **Bernard M. Kessler**, a divisional president at Beam-Pines Inc., a New York-based consulting firm. "Their styles are just inappropriate for team playing."

The next step is to recognize some of the larger forces at work that defy some of our best attempts to communicate instructions in the office.

Tell me and I forget,

Teach me and I remember,

Involve me and I learn.

– Benjamin Franklin

DRAWING THE LINE

Red Sox legend **Ted Williams** was the last person to hit .400 and probably the greatest hitter of all time. He disliked the press vehemently. In one rare interview, a reporter brought up the subject of Williams's vision, which was 20/10. Yes, he said, his eyes were better than normal, and he had a lot of walks because he really understood exactly where the strike zone was. The reporter said that Williams could get more hits if he swung at some balls just slightly out of the strike zone. Yes, Williams replied, he could get more hits; however, he never swung at pitches outside of the strike zone. Well, the reporter asked, why if you could get more hits, don't you try to do that? Williams said, "Because then there is no place to draw the line." And that was the interview. (Another way of looking at this: even at the height of his career, Ted Williams didn't even get on base 60 percent of the time.)

That story has stayed with me since I first read it when I was twelve, and it became a talisman for me in my uncompromising and rebellious days. In many ways, I carry it with me today—trying to understand where the strike zone is, and the seduction of things right outside the strike zone, and how that seduction always reduces the clarity of your ideas.

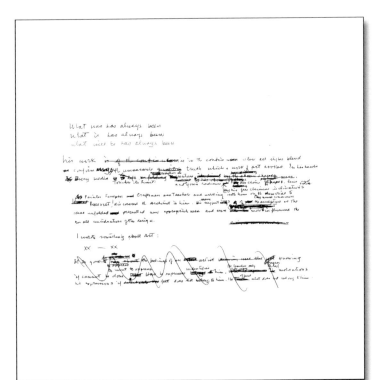

I compiled a book on the architect **Louis Kahn** called *What Will Be Has Always Been*. The cover was a page from one of his notebooks—a messy scrawl with words inserted and scratched out. The publishers of the book, Rizzoli International, didn't like the cover. They wanted a photograph or something pretty on the cover. They wanted all the things that would make the book more salable, but less clear. The book is about its cover, about somebody's words, the difficulty he had with the clarification of ideas, the working over and over of an idea, trying to find his way through the mistakes, and the failures to the clarity. The book isn't about Kahn's buildings; it is about his ideas of the man-made world and of learning. How do you express an idea? How do you avoid being seduced and allow that feeling to flow into a finished product that has clarity? How do you make a connection between the idea and the image?

Ideas that aren't attached to images are forgotten. If you are trying to understand the DNA molecule, you could memorize all the formulas or you could read the story of **Francis Crick** and how he unlocked its secrets. The image of the man and his work would help you remember the formulas.

Learning is like Velcro. An unfiltered fact is not a complete fastener. Only one side of learning is made up of facts; the other consists of stories—that is, ideas and images.

WHAT YOU TAKE FOR GRANTED YOU CANNOT IMPROVE

When we take something for granted, we give up the possibility of changing or improving it. This applies to monumental issues like marriages, jobs, law, religious doctrine, and to more pedestrian concerns, such as a recipe or a room color.

People take it for granted that if they go outside when it is raining, they will get wet. But why couldn't cities be built with arcades—like Bologna?

The information traps outlined in this chapter exist because people take them for granted—looking good is being good; if it's accurate, it's information; an expert opinion is an objective opinion. We accept that tax forms should be confusing, legal documents should be written in legalese, and that we should spend hours every day trying to decipher charts and graphs.

All of these conceptions cloud our understanding of information because we accept them as givens. If we questioned them, we would see them with different eyes. In this way, we wouldn't be such easy victims of preconceptions, and we might begin to see the new paths around them to understanding.

> What is now proved was once only imagined.
>
> – William Blake

4 AN AGE OF CONNECTIONS: INTEGRATED MESSAGES

What do escalators, bananas, bathroom stalls, and chair backs at movie theatres have in common? They are all new media for marketing. Advertising messages have become so pervasive that the world surface area *without* them is disappearing faster than the rain forest in South America.

Ads are everywhere, but most of them aren't connected in a meaningful way. I've seen stickers for Coke on bananas, and bridal gowns on bathroom door walls. The media conflicts with the message. Bananas are a healthy sources of potassium; Coke is sugar-laden and vitamin-sapping, and would you really want to associate weddings with bathroom stalls?

Are you speaking to your customers in ways that embed positive messages in their minds? Are you showing them the connections among your products? Does your market have a sense of who you are, what you stand for, the qualities or characteristics of your product?

Companies are learning new ways to communicate and to converse with their employees, existing customers, contacts, and potential business prospects. With more vehicles for communication, it's become more important to unify your messages—to pull together and look at all aspects of interaction with customers, not just ads and sales brochures. Are you communicating in a unified voice so a message in one medium augments a message sent through other channels?

Customers around the globe are becoming increasingly more savvy, informed, demanding, cynical, price conscious, and empowered, with a relentless appetite for quality, service, customization, convenience, and speed. There's only one way to reach their hearts, minds, and wallets: through *communication*, which is the process that people engage in to share understanding and meaning. Communicating with individual customers across all contact points requires painstaking *integration*, which is commonly defined as the process of achieving a unity of effort in various organizational subsystems. Ergo, *integrated communications* is the stuff that profitable relationships are built on in the Customer Century.

– Anders Gronstedt
"The Customer Century: Lessons from World-Class Companies" in *Integrated Marketing and Communications*

It's all about consistent messaging, and the key is not to have technology for technology's sake, but to create something that consistently delivers information to your audience. Design in the Digital Age will increasingly require integration of words, pictures, sound, and touch—exploring all ways to communicate.

Consider, for instance, this year's Super Bowl advertising. According to **Mavis Scanlon** in an article "Only a Couple of Super Bowl Ads Stuck with Viewers. The Lesson?" in *Internet World* (4/15/00), out of 55 advertisers, 18 were dot-coms. The bigger news: Viewers couldn't remember them after the game. More than 400 participants in an *Adweek*-sponsored survey couldn't name one of the dot-com brands they saw advertised. The ones who did remember a dot-com recalled E*TRADE, mostly because of its dancing chimp ad, which combined humor with a clear, resonating message.

So, what is E*TRADE's real secret? It's more than dancing chimps. A multi-tiered, brand-building approach is the key, Scanlon says. Its marketing campaign includes seasonal television, radio, and print ads. Its consistent and clear messaging across all media have helped the dot-com boost its brand awareness to more than 90 percent, up from 28 percent in the fall of 1998. Just because the Super Bowl offers a huge audience for distribution of a brand, E*TRADE didn't make the mistake of moving away from the one it had already established.

Amazon is another company that has built a colossal brand in only a few years based on a consistent message about streamlining the purchase of goods. Customers know if they purchase a product from Amazon.com, the process will be pared down to the essentials. Ten years ago, if you'd heard the word Amazon, you'd think of a river and crocodiles and the tropics. Now what does Amazon conjure? The answer you'll hear is books, CDs, and shrinking market capitalization.

MAKING YOUR OWN CONNECTIONS FIRST

One way we have of understanding the world is comparing unfamiliar ideas or concepts to familiar ones. For example, if you've never made concrete before, the whole concept can be rather intimidating. However, if you've ever made homemade

> Ogilvy preaches the gospel of 360 Degree Branding™ to ensure that wherever the customer has contact with the brand—be it in a telephone call, or in a reception area, or choosing something off the shelf—the experience is a positive one.
>
> – Mike Walsh, CEO of Ogilvy Europe

clay, you can simply transfer the experience to the creation of concrete.

With the Internet, we've got an entirely new set of concepts that have no prior experiences. We don't even know what the right questions are that apply. National Public Radio commentator **David Weinberger** explained on an *All Things Considered* broadcast (4/2/00) how the Internet has made our frames of reference disappear because we have nothing with which to compare today's information revolution.

He explains that the Internet has specialized in "framejacking" our normal frame of reference. For example, we treat email almost as a conversation—short, sweet, and to the point, or long, rambling, and informal. However, the lawyers treat it as a letter, which we used to spend much time drafting, writing, editing and rewriting. Written, paper-based letters and email are similar in that we write them, address them, and send them, but we have an entirely different set of expectations from them.

Weinberger points out that the the Internet makes "things that used to be clear now seem hopelessly complex." With the Internet, we've got to develop entirely new analogies because the old ones don't apply to this new frame of reference. As Weinberger puts it, "The familiar has become completely unfamiliar."

In order to cross this barrier, you must become familiar with the unfamiliar. Participate in the chance for dialogue that the Internet provides. Develop protocols that you're comfortable with and stick to them. Something is only hopelessly complex until you familiarize yourself with it. Then realize that your peers, customers, and prospects may not know what you know.

> The more associations we make when learning material, the easier it is to remember the material.
>
> – Peter Russell, *The Brain Book*

REMEMBERING WHAT IT'S LIKE NOT TO KNOW

Those designing the messages for people who are trying to make those leaps have to do the almost impossible: Remember what it's like not to know? Try explaining to someone how to walk or how to tie your shoes. Once you know how to do something and understand how something works, it's almost impossible to put yourself in the place of the person who doesn't know.

When you are presenting information to your audiences, remember that although you're exceptionally familiar with the topic, they may not have any idea what you are talking about. In every presentation, begin with something familiar. Give your audience at least one fact they already know and tie that into the new material you are presenting. Give them something slightly familiar so they have a starting point, an initial connection to the new world that you're bringing to them.

When you are designing information for your target audience, remember they may have no access to the knowledge you take for granted. And their not having this knowledge could confuse them to the point where they give up and move on to information much less confusing, perhaps information your competitor is willing to provide in a much simpler fashion.

Companies are finding creative ways to think like customers and to remember what it's like not to know. Take Whirlpool, for example. The home appliance titan is using a hands-on method of teaching its new employees to understand the products and gain invaluable insight into how their products are used from the customer viewpoint. New hires spend two months living in a Whirlpool house near Lake Michigan. They use the appliances every day. As they learn the nuances of each machine, they'll become better salespeople. They'll be able to communicate not only what they learned about the products, but also what they learned about what it means to be a consumer of those products.

You have to hone your ability to understand what it's like not to understand, which will allow you to communicate more clearly with your audiences, no matter who they are. Remembering that will allow you to tailor your message toward understanding, no matter the medium.

The most common frustration I have is trying to use the "Help" section on a specific family of software products that I'm sure many of you use every single day. Have you ever wondered how to set up a spreadsheet so that a certain column will print on every single page? Do you know what they call that process? I don't either. Which is why every single time I want to accomplish this task, I spend about the same amount of time searching the help

> Be patient toward all that is unsolved in your heart. Try to love the questions, themselves. Do not now seek the answers, which cannot be given because you would not be able to live them. And the point is to live everything. Live the questions now. Perhaps you will then gradually, without noticing it, live along some distant day into the answers.
>
> – Rainer Maria Rilke, *Letters to a Young Poet*

> An education isn't how much you have committed to memory, or even how much you know. It's being able to differentiate between what you do know and what you don't.
>
> – Anatole France

menu for what I think this topic should be called as I did creating the spreadsheet.

Occasionally, I'll get lucky and accidentally happen upon what that topic is called. In the same way, don't require that your readers learn exactly how you think before they can learn how to use your products. They may give up and go to a different vendor.

Fernando Flores, former Chilean finance minister under Allende, has become an expert at teaching companies to communicate. He's broken down the theories of what you don't know based on comfort levels.

Your communication hinges upon building that trust. In addition to extolling the benefits of your products and services, you must provide an atmosphere where consumers can trust your products, where your employees can trust the information you give them about the organization, and where your shareholders know you are taking good care of their money.

When you are communicating with others, let them see that you don't understand everything either. If you talk to them with the attitude that you know everything, you will stifle their natural curiosity about your product or ideas because you will intimidate them into silence. Facilitate learning as you teach by being open to the interaction between you and your audience. With a truly open question-and-answer experience, everyone benefits because all parties are learning from each other.

CREATING INTEREST

Learning can be seen as the acquisition of information, but before it can take place, your customers must have interest; interest permeates all endeavors and precedes learning. In order to acquire and remember new knowledge, it must stimulate curiosity in some way.

Interest defies all rules of memorization. Most researchers agree that people can retain only about seven bits in their short-term memory, such as the digits in a ZIP code or telephone number. Yet, most people who saw the movie *Mary Poppins* and liked it could remember the word "supercalifragilisticexpialidocious." Children who couldn't for the life of them remember the capital of Idaho could not only remember, but also could probably spell this word.

The World According to Flores exists in three realms. The first is the smallest—and the most self-limiting: What You Know You Know. It is a self-contained world, in which people are unwilling to risk their identity in order to take on new challenges. A richer realm is What You Don't Know—the realm of uncertainty, which manifests itself as anxiety or boredom. Most things in life belong to this realm: What you don't know about your future, your health, your family. People are always trying to merge this second area into the realm of What You Know You Know—in order to avoid uncertainty, anxiety, and boredom. But it is the third realm of Flores' taxonomy to which people should aspire: What You Don't Know You Don't Know. To live in this realm is to notice opportunities that have the power to reinvent your company, opportunities that we're normally too blind to see. In this third realm, you see without bias: You're not weighted down with information. The language of this realm is the language of truth, which requires trust.

– Harriet Rubin, *Fast Company* (January 1999)

Learning can be defined as the process of remembering what you are interested in. And both go hand in hand—warm hand in warm hand—with communication. The most effective communicators are those who understand the role interest plays in the successful delivery of messages, whether one is trying to explain astrophysics or sell a car.

INTEREST REQUIREMENTS

In his book, *Freedom to Learn,* **Carl Rogers** states that the only learning that significantly influences behavior is "self-discovered, self-appropriated" learning. Only when subject matter is perceived as being relevant to a person's own purposes will a significant amount of learning take place.

When designing a building, an architect considers observers' interest. As **Eugene Raskin** explains in *Architecturally Speaking*, the sequence of interest points in a structure—what comes first, what comes next, how long it takes a person to experience each hallway, each entrance—determines the extent to which the structure will intrigue the eye. Like interest in learning, interest in a building "…needs to be revived and renewed by constantly increasing doses of stimulant. While these doses…may be alternated for effect with transitional periods of relative dullness, the overall plan must be one of rising interest."

Information anxiety results from constant overstimulation; we are not given the time or opportunity to make transitions from one "room" or idea to the next. No one functions well perpetually gasping for breath. Learning (and interest) requires "way-stations" where your customers can stop and think about the ideas you are presenting before moving on to what you want them to know next.

Don't let them get lost on the road to interest. The importance of piquing and maintaining interest crosses all media or expression. Any written or spoken presentation should be developed to incite interest along the way. The path should be flexible enough to allow the reader or listener to see the connections between the topic at hand and other topics. If you are presenting a proposal for a marketing study on a new analgesic, you are not bound to only the drug itself. You can tie it to other analgesics, the development

Anyone who stops learning is old, whether at twenty or eighty. Anyone who keeps learning stays young. The greatest thing in life is to keep your mind young.

– Henry Ford

The more you learn, the more you can learn; the more you have to associate new learning with.

– Roger Merrill, *Connections*

of painkillers, or the history of medicine. Understanding the connections between one interest and another encourages people to chart their own paths.

You can follow any interest on a path through all knowledge. Interest connections form the singular path to learning. It doesn't matter what path you choose or where you begin the journey. A person can be interested in horses, or automobiles, or color, or grass, or the concept of time, and, without forcing the issue whatsoever, can make connections to other bodies of information.

Someone who's interested in cars could move into a fascination with the Porsche and the German language, or the physics of motion, or the growth of cities and the pattern of movement and defense, or the chemistry of fuels. Various cars are made by various countries that have different languages and histories. Studying Italian automotive design, you gain entry into the study of roads, the Appian Way, the plan of Rome, and the history of transportation itself.

Make interest connections. The idea that you can follow or pursue one interest into a variety of other interests makes your choices less threatening. You can jump into a subject at any level, and not only can you follow the subject to greater levels of complexity, but you can follow it to other subjects.

If a computer company wanted to develop an exhibit that would make computers less intimidating to the public, it could start at a basic level with the idea of opposites, which could move into "on" and "off," then into binary numbers, the workings of a circuit panel, and into computers themselves. Everyone can identify with the idea of opposites. The simplicity and universal appeal isn't threatened with self-limitations or exclusivity. It becomes a path to new interests and to higher levels of complexity.

I have always been passionate about architecture, and it was as an architect that I started my professional career, but I discovered that about everything interested me, and I couldn't channel the practice of architecture to recognize my curiosity. I needed quicker gratification; I needed to be able to follow my interests. As an architect, you can't do anything until someone asks you to do it.

You may take a horse to the water, but you cannot make him drink; and so you may take a child to the schoolroom, but you cannot make him learn the new things you wish to impart, except by soliciting him in the first instance by something which natively makes him react.

And the maximum of attention may then be said to be found whenever we have a systematic harmony or unification between the novel and the old. It is an odd circumstance that neither the old nor the new, by itself, is interesting; the absolutely old is insipid; the absolutely new makes no appeal at all. The old in the new is what claims the attention—the old with a slightly new turn. No one wants to hear a lecture on a subject completely disconnected with his previous knowledge, but we all like lectures on subjects of which we know a little already, just as, in the fashions, every year must bring its slight modification of last year's suit, but an abrupt jump from the fashion of one decade into another would be distasteful to the eye.

– William James
Talks to Teachers

You can't get up in the morning and say, "I've got this great idea for a factory. I think I'll design one today." You always depend on the client. The same goes for business.

Unity of concept is important to any creative endeavor. An architect must form a clear concept of a project in human and social terms before beginning. Then shapes, scale, color, harmony, ornament, rhythm, dominance, subordination, and other devices are used to enhance the basic concept. All of your messages, whether via the Web or the mail, need to maintain consistency, as well.

My work has to do with solving the thoughts with which I have discomfort. My own understanding or lack of it is enough. Committee meetings and market research are not part of this process. I don't believe in using such a method to determine what subjects or cities to tackle. Having confidence in your own understanding, acceptance of your ignorance, and determination to pursue your interests are the weapons against anxiety.

SAVVY COMPANIES DRIVE CONNECTION OPPORTUNITIES

Most Americans drive cars. Most Americans use salt. What makes a Honda different from a Saturn? Why can't most Americans name their brand of salt?

If you build it, they will come. Articles and books abound extolling the financial prudence of courting the customer with post-purchase service, and manufacturers are heeding the lessons. Paying attention to what customers need after paying for the product makes particular sense with commercial consumers, who not only invest money in the initial equipment, but also must store, maintain, and update the documentation for it at phenomenal cost.

Savvy companies cruise for connection opportunities, opportunities to build relationships with their customers; they don't take the customer relationship for granted. Hondas are known for reliability. Saturns are known for their owner loyalty. During the 1950s, made in Japan meant made to be cheap and fall apart. However, during the 1960s, as Americans ignored **W. Edwards Deming**, the Japanese embraced his concepts of quality and began to turn around their products. By the 1980s, it was the Japanese cars Americans considered to be of quality and the U.S. cars that Americans associated with cheap and falling apart. When Saturn began, it had to be a "different kind of car company." It had a lot of obstacles to overcome to become an American brand considered "of quality."

How did Saturn do it? Saturn doesn't build cars—it creates relationships. Saturn makes selling a car an event. Each "retail outlet," as Saturn dealers consider their showrooms, makes a big deal out of every purchase. They celebrate a Saturn's exit for its new home by taking photos of the car with its new owners and doing a little cheer in celebration. Each owner is also personally invited to visit the factory in Spring Hill, Tennessee. More than 45,000 people have used their vacation days to visit the factory. Saturn owners can find each other via the Web. They have service groups—of both Saturn employees and owners—that build children's playgrounds. Saturn doesn't sell cars—it builds communities.

As Saturn honors its relationships with its customers, it also honors its relationships with its employees. When General Motors began Saturn, it went to the union to explain what its goals were with Saturn and why it did not want the Saturn employees to unionize. GM made its case so well that the UAW allowed the experiment called Saturn to begin. That experiment has turned into one of the most successful brand and product launches for the automakers in years. Saturn isn't the only organization creating special moments with its customers. What would McDonald's be without its Happy Meal? Have a Coke and a smile!

Bring business relationships from traditional media to the Web. Creating a connection is more than just placing advertisements. It's leading your customers from their first phone call to your image brochure to a face-to-face meeting to your Web site and coming out on the other side with a consistent perception of you—what you do, and how you do it. Most people now register for my **TED** conference on our Web site.

When did we start becoming truly connected? When did we begin to experience mass culture? Although you can trace the development of mass communications and shared experiences back to the trade routes and the Silk Road, modern mass communication began with the telegraph. **Mr. Morse** gave us the capability to tell our cousin in St. Paul that we'd love to come up from St. Louis to see her. Mr. Bell allowed us to pick up the phone and arrange a date. You could even say the party line was the first Internet connection. Mr. A could hear what Mr. B was saying to Mr. C. The Internet is a giant party line; we can discover what is going on with our neighbors across the street and across the world. Think of how the growth of USENET groups has created entire global villages around obscure topics from medieval role playing to ballroom dancing.

The obscure can quickly become the infamous. The Love Bug from the Philippines disturbed an extraordinary number of email systems across the United States. The Internet has brought back the chain letter to the extreme. Microsoft will give you $100,000 if you pass this to 30 friends; the Gap will give you a $25 gift certificate if you send this email to 15 of your friends, and so on, and so on.

Where do you stop? How do you get noticed among all of this noise? It is time to create value for your customers, not just talk about creating value. At the heart of every transaction is customer interaction. How do you bring people to your Web site? Your museum? Your store? What tools do you use to reach your audiences? You sell over the Web; you sell over TV. Just don't sell empty promises.

Connect to your customers the way they want. Remember when everyone was home watching ABC, CBS, NBC, FOX, or PBS? Now, if you were to randomly call 10 friends, you would get 10 different answers of what television or radio stations they were tuned in to.

The proper use of data can be a powerful tool for making sure that the right people are getting the right message. Before the modern era, you could send out thousands upon thousands of letters, postcards, and faxes just to make a single sale. Now you can break down your customer base and determine that 4,000 of your customers prefer phone calls from your sales reps, 6,000 will respond to your email, and 9,000 of your customers like getting your direct-mail pieces.

Data mining helps you find the right niche. Using sophisticated computer modeling, now available in any good database system, you can find your customers and design your communications materials to fit them accordingly. As with any database information, remember that data is nothing without the knowledge to use it wisely. What does knowing that 95 percent of your customers are right-handed matter if you are selling socks? Having access to an extraordinary amount of data can be a curse as well as a blessing. At the heart of everything is making sure all of your media of communication convey the messages you want to communicate.

Your goal as an information provider is to keep all stakeholders informed. The same concepts you are telling your managers and employees, your internal customers, also need to be communicated to your external customers. If you are an organization where customer service is what you live and die by, be sure that your IT people understand this just as much as your frontline customer service representatives. Everyone in your organization needs to be providing the same messages, walking the same walk, talking the same talk. Every single employee is a spokesperson for your organization.

In *The Customer Century,* **Anders Gronstedt** expounds upon the importance of integrated communication. All messages across all parties need to be consistent. Gronstedt cites the following selling points:

- Integrated communications build customer relationships, which are the only sustainable source of competitive advantage in today's commoditized marketplace. Loyal customers are less costly to maintain, less price-focused, and more inclined to give references to others.

- Integrated communications forge relationships with other stakeholders as well, which reduces the cost of litigation, regulation, and boycotts, making money by attracting investment capital, skilled employees, and positive media coverage.

- Integrated communications are more *effective* because they give companies greater control of the messages and contact points that will ultimately be integrated in the customers' and stakeholders' minds, enabling companies to better manage and cultivate relationships with them.

- Integrated communications are more *efficient,* saving time and money by leveraging efforts and reducing duplication and waste.

- Integrated communications strengthen employee relationships, by valuing and acting on their ideas, sharing their resources, and giving them the information they need to do their jobs.

CHANNEL CONFLICT

There's a downside to too much integration. The Web has expanded the world of integrated marketing. Catalogues have turned into stores. J. Crew came out as a catalogue. We have stores that now have catalogues. We have catalogues that started as stores that now are Web sites. Land's End started as a catalogue and leapt to the Web. J. Peterman went into bankruptcy when it went from catalogues to stores. Sotheby's went from an auction house to designing its own auction site, scuttled it, and bought into a relationship with Amazon.com. In Internet time, what would be considered a strange relationship between someone who started as a bookseller now hooked up with two major auction houses is simply part of the integration of goods and services brought on by the Internet Age.

eMarketer determined that 81 million Americans sent 2.1 billion personal and business messages per day, with advertisers sending an additional 7.3 billion. That's almost 10 billion per day. To contrast, the U.S. Postal Service delivers about 107 billion pieces of first class mail in a year. That means there were over 30 emails for every piece of first-class mail.

The Web is a powerful tool for any business. Building and keeping relationships with your customers is critical, but you must be careful how your Web relationships affect your other corporate relationships. The Internet has made it easier to play both wholesaler and retailer, to sell B2B to the masses, and conflicts are likely to arise when one end of the chain feels like it's being squeezed out by the other.

Channel conflict, also known as disintermediation, is an issue you need to consider when you consider direct-to-consumer e-commerce sales. Taking advantage of the Internet to increase sales without harming long-term vendor relationships is a difficult proposition. Some companies, such as Microsoft and Dell Computer, have managed to pull it off.

One way to balance channel conflict is to provide value-added information to your consumers, while reminding them that you are the wholesaler, not the retailer. At www.LizClaiborne.com, the site highlights the different aspects of its fashion line and provides general fashion advice and education: If you don't understand a fashion term, you can look it up. Moreover, if this isn't enough, the featured items on the site change with the seasons so Liz's customers always have an excuse to come back. The site also provides a store locator, allowing its retailers to benefit from the site.

Travel is an industry where channel conflict has always been an issue, even before the Internet became a factor in our lives. Once a plane takes off with an empty seat or a ship leaves port with an empty cabin that revenue is gone. The Internet gives travel companies an extra tool to dump those perishable resources. With airlines, customers have always had the choice about using travel agents or calling the airlines directly. Cruise lines, once entirely in the travel-agency domain, are beginning to use the Internet for customers to book cruises, and they also are using it as a database collection tool so they can send out mass emails to promote "specials."

Channel conflict is an issue you need to consider when you add content and e-commerce to your Web site. Determine what messages you want to send to your customers, your retailers, your wholesalers, your distributors, and your staff before you decide the best Internet strategy for your organization.

DESIGN IN THE DIGITAL AGE

In the Digital Age, you need to focus on the connections among all of your design elements: medium, words, pictures, and sound. You'll have to look at each message and explore all the ways to communicate it. Then, in your quest to stay connected, don't forget to be clear, too.

It is ideas that precede our understanding of facts, although the overabundance of facts tends to obscure this. A fact can be comprehended only within the context of an idea. Ideas are irrevocably subjective, which makes facts just as subjective.

Where words meet pictures meet sound creates understanding. Are you a value-based organization? A service-based organization? A quality-based organization? Are you all three? We test communication by conveying a message and having the recipient understand it, be interested in it, and remember it. Any other measure is unimportant and invalid.

A new study shows that mommy rats have better memories than childless rats.

I chew my toast and stare at this news article.

I wonder, what am I supposed to do with this information?

My dad always said that for the alchemy of the mind to turn information into understanding, mere hints are best. Exhaustive information clogs the mind, which needs roominess to do its work.

"If you would control the minds of men," he said, "either deny them information or set them afloat in information—the end is the same."

— Adair Lara,
San Francisco Chronicle
(1/25/00)

Always design a thing by considering it in its next larger context—a chair in a room, a room in a house, a house in an environment, an environment in a city plan.

— Eliel Saarinen

QUALITY CHECK FOR YOUR INFORMATION CONNECTION

The quality of information is judged not only by its accuracy and clarity, but also by how it acts upon your customers.

- Is it useful and relevant?

- Does it have meaning or is it merely facts?

- Is it feedback to the customer's question?

- Does it have the power to change or expand the customer's knowledge?

Most successful designers will be ones who can make their products more understandable through design, but these designers will also realize that it is the medium that has to influence the design.

Consider what you look for when you go into a grocery store. You wander up and down the aisles, seeking out familiar brands. Your customers look at the Web in a similar way. If a customer needs information about Brand X, she'll simply go to the Brand X Web site to seek out information.

When you are designing for the Web, make sure that your customers can see logic in your chaos. Although Net surfing is structured like conversation—talking about pizza leads to anchovies to fishing to the beaches of the New England—you need to remember there is some logic in the chaos.

You could design a Web site like I design my **TED** conferences. The most important part is the pacing: Where and when will there be entertainment, when will it be serious? When do you have a dark room, a bright room? When do you create a break for your participant? What is the first thing you see when you come back from a break? What calms them down? How do you start the day? What would I like to see in an afternoon? What kind of experiences do you want to give them when they arrive? When they leave? **TED**'s middle name is Entertainment—remember that on your Web site. Don't just inform, expecting your customers to find their own ways through your Web site; entertain them too.

> Eventually, if you can't find what you're looking for, you'll leave. This is as true on a Web site as it is at Sears. You'll leave when you're convinced they haven't got it, or when you're just too frustrated to keep looking.
>
> – Steve Krug, *Don't Make Me Think! The Common Sense Approach to Web Usability*

You also need to address these three factors when designing your Web site:

- Ease of navigation

- Quality of information

- Time savings

Your site needs to be easy to navigate; it should have a logical flow from piece to piece. Although people traditionally jump around on the Web, remember that people read in a Z pattern.

As more and more people get plugged into the Internet, television viewing has been plummeting. People are choosing to be plugged in and interactive instead of couched-and-potato-chipped. Give them a reason to come to your site; give them quality content, quality products, quality services. Your site must provide quality that they cannot get elsewhere. Perhaps you are a motorcycle dealership. You don't need to spend the money printing brochures about the history of the motorcycle for distribution in your showroom. Instead, make it a value-added benefit to keep people at your site.

Even though people are watching less television and spending more time on the Internet, you should worry about time savings because your customers want it smarter, faster, cheaper, *and* right now. As an online retailer, create instant pathways allowing your customers to view their accounts, make transactions, or get information quicker and easier. If you're an online bank, provide a single button on your site that allows regular customers to log in directly.

If you're a magazine, give the headlines across the top with links to each of the relevant stories. Make your sites, your brochures, and your promotions simple for your audiences to navigate, and they'll leave feeling refreshed rather than frustrated. Make sure your Web sites inspire both terror in the competition and confidence from your customers. You have to have programs that intelligently go out a couple of steps, that stretch people. Just don't promise them anything you cannot deliver.

I tuned in to 99 Lives when someone at a BrainReserve TrendProbe said, "Today I don't even have time to realize how busy I am."

I predict that by 2010, 90% of all consumer goods will be home-delivered.

Time is the new money: people would rather spend money than time.

80% of Americans are looking for ways to simplify their lives.

78% want to reduce stress.

Home meal replacement is now a $100 billion business.

– Faith Popcorn, *99 LIVES Observations*

CONNECTING YOUR MESSAGES

My Understanding USA project is an example of a book and a Web site (www.understandingusa.com) that complement each other with their different contributions to my objective of helping us understand our country at this important time.

You can't hang a book on a wall and call it an exhibition. The medium has to influence the design. However, you can look at a book and the Web and see how they are related in the Age of Connection. The relationship between the Web and a book is more similar. Both are one-to-one conversations through words. These words make a connection, allowing the transfer of ideas.

Ensure that your ideas are consistent across all media, and you'll stay connected to all of your audiences.

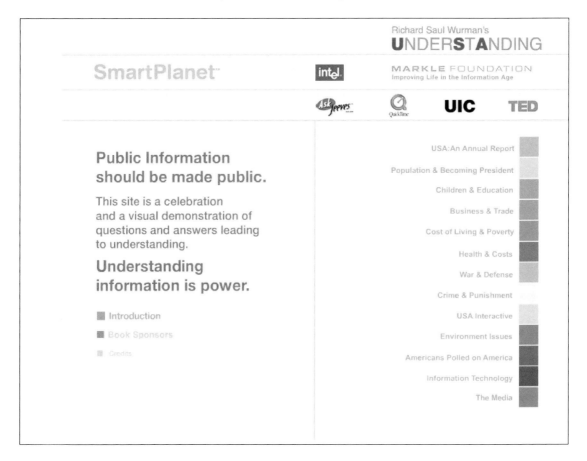

5 THE STRUCTURE OF CONVERSATION

This page is like a conversation. The quotes in the margins are like a "let-me-put-this-another-way" feature of conversations. You hear a voice when you read it. Like a conversation, the page explores asides and anecdotes and trails off to distractions. It has diversions; it stops and starts. It makes leaps, and one thought doesn't always link to another in a linear fashion.

The structure of conversation is organic, constantly changing, and people are continually exploring new ways to communicate with one another because conversation is not governed by any established set of rules. A conversation goes from story to joke to incident to fact to story to issue—all in a natural, organic way.

Yet, if you diagrammed a conversation, it is amazingly complex. Conversation is more complex than any writing, yet it is often more likely to lead to understanding. The whole apprenticeship system of education, sadly nearing extinction today, is based on the beauty of conversation, of the wise and experienced imparting of wisdom to the young through the medium of an extended conversation that unfolds in the workplace.

There are boundless applications for it and thus great value in finding out how a conversation works. I'd like to uncover the structure of a good conversation that could be used to develop maps and charts. How could they be designed so they would talk to the user, allow the user to say, "Wait, what I want to know here is this."

> Conversation is an art in which man has all mankind for competitors.
>
> – Ralph Waldo Emerson

> A single conversation across the table with a wise man is worth a month's study of books.
>
> – Chinese proverb

> The power of conversation goes well beyond its ability to affect consumers, business, and products. Market conversations can make—and unmake and remake—entire industries. We're seeing it happen now. In fact, the Internet is itself an example of an industry built by pure conversation.
>
> – Christopher Locke, Rick Levine, Doc Searls, and David Weinberger, *The Cluetrain Manifesto*

> Hedonomics means extracting the last drop of fun out of every buying experience. Today, culture, demography and technology are all fostering hedonomics. With their major life purchases behind them, baby boomers are returning to their hedonistic roots. Young people are "multi-tasking," entertainment-surfing the Net, listening to CDs and watching TV, all at the same time. Feeling they have less free time than ever, adults are seeking fun in more concentrated doses. As a result, the personal savings rate is near an all-time low, while spending on entertainment and recreation is at an all-time high.
>
> – Michael Wolf, author *The Entertainment Economy* "at Random" interview

I think we don't use it as a model because it is so obvious and so natural that we don't see its perfection of form. It doesn't seem pure or elegant, as it is always adjusting; it is changing its emphasis, its level of detail. It is not consistent, it is not the way you are taught to write, but it is exactly the way you think. I'm able to have a conversation, break into a joke, and come back. You couldn't write like that because it wouldn't flow properly. Yet, in a conversation, the digressions are permissible; nothing has more flow than a good conversation.

Unlike writing, conversations are not bound by principles of logic, transition, and clarity. The spontaneity of conversations prevents them from being edited to a sterile purity. Lapses, non sequiturs, and quirky associations are accepted in the best conversations.

Not only is the conversation unbound by traditional principle and logic, it is ever changing. There are more opportunities to communicate with consumers today: cable television, radio, network television, local television, magazines, newspapers, Web sites, email, satellites, cellular phones, fax, direct mail, chat rooms, newsgroups, and message boards. The world seems to be in a nonstop state of conversing.

There is a new marketplace being created by the changing structure of conversation. There is no such thing as a traditional consumer, mostly because the Internet has given people the power to choose how and what kind of information they wish to take in. We have 16-year-olds who are running successful online businesses. There are dot-com billionaires and self-proclaimed e-divas who have started online businesses—anything from industry news sites to online communities to upper-crust gossip sites.

Why? Because you can be as fantastic as you want to be online, and you have ultimate control. The Internet is unimpeded. It's this capability for control and demand for targeted information that is changing the structure of conversation within your market.

MAPPING CONVERSATION

If you think back to the days of imperialism, the days of colonies, magistrates, and wealthy kingships, you see a key to success. Those who owned a map of the world had ultimate power. They possessed the ability to create commerce, build riches, conduct business, and monopolize.

Today, most information isn't presented in the detailed form of a map to direct and guide us to new lands where we can find wealth (or a wealth of information). Rather, it's fired at us like buckshot, with the hope that some might hit a target.

In response, a group of people is emerging that feels a life force—an undeniable drive—to make life understandable. They feel compelled to create a new world map with this barrage of data. They are the information architects.

Today's information architects must get through to a population that makes choices every day about what to view and what not to view. People are bombarded from all sides by television, print, and online ads. We have newspapers, magazines, journals, newsletters, e-zines, and online news sites where we can tailor our daily dose of news to fit personal interests.

It seems that media and advertising design has largely been based on Baby Boomer sensibilities, with little attention being paid to the viewing habits of younger generations. According to **Cliff Zukin**, Professor of Political Science and Public Policy at Rutgers University, the Generation X television audience is very visually oriented, able to quickly scan text and graphics for meaning. They are likely to be "perpetual surfers," meaning they turn on the television and start dialing around, stopping here or there as something catches their interest for a moment and then moving on to something else. Gen-Xers are multi-taskers, and do other things while they watch. They demand interactivity with the media.

Markets, your clients, and prospects are not only seeking conversation, they're searching for intelligent conversation. They're wading through scores of options to find someone who can provide quick, helpful information on their subject of interest. They're looking for a community of intelligent, like-minded people in which to exchange information.

It seems to me we're living in a time of "extreme capitalism," where the marketplace rules as never before. We're living in a time when almost everything (news, politics, advertising, the computer revolution) is a form of entertainment. And we're obviously living in a time when the culture generally, thanks to technology and the aging of the baby boomers and the end of the Cold War and feminism and a hundred other reasons, is in a state of thrilling, terrifying flux and newness.

– Kurt Andersen, author,
Turn of the Century
"at Random" interview

CONVERSATION AS A TRANSACTION

Exchanging information is a form of transaction. To transact is to carry out business or affairs. Conversations are transactions; they are exchanges of words and ideas between groups of people or individuals.

Too many companies are trying to separate these transactions into different areas. They treat each transaction separately with different divisions for bricks and clicks. I believe the most successful will be the ones that look at the commonalities among all transactions.

That's why a lot of old companies have made better use of new technology than some of the start-ups that are looking at the Internet as a separate world rather than an extension of the conversation. I heard General Electric is selling about 45 percent of its refrigerators over the Web. Sotheby's is another example. The old-line company attracted millions of new potential art buyers by using its site to sell more affordable artwork.

As the Web changes the face of how business operates, businesses are going from brick and mortar to click and mortar. Still, all the dot-coms are probably not going to do as well as a group as these brick-and-mortar companies that are now going on the Web. Having the years of experience as a storefront has given the newest Web entrants a head start on the solely dot-com organizations. Brick-and–mortar companies are accustomed to dealing with customers on a day-to-day basis, talking with them, and discovering their wants and needs. They can go into the design of their Web sites with the perspective of knowing how their customers already shop in real-time, and then apply it in Web-time.

The challenges and issues between the world of bricks and clicks are more similar than different. Just ask dot-coms that have seen customers fleeing in droves from poor service and broken promises.

Both online and brick-and-mortar transactions involve human interaction, yet they are treated as different worlds. I think we should pull them together rather than make them separate fields. When you look at all business in the form of a transaction, how is that reflected in the way products are designed and presented to the world?

TRANSACTIONS

Conversations

Stores

Shopping centers

Catalogs

Phone calls

Direct mail

Billboards

Museums

Schools

Television

Entertainment

Web sites

The above are all forums for the exchange of information, where the possibility for a transaction could occur—be it a sale of goods or an exchange of information. What applies to a good conversation can be applied to almost any transaction.

CONVERSATION WITH AN INANIMATE OBJECT

You can have a conversation with a machine. Industrial designers can create products that talk to users. The Hewlett Packard OfficeJet R series is a great example of how a company thinks not just about technology, but about how people are going to use it. You don't need to read the manual to know how to operate this multifunction machine. You know how to operate it just by looking at the buttons. They correspond to your experience with copying machines. The instrument panel has buttons with sensible names like "Paper Type," "Number of Copies," a blue button for "Color" copies, and a button that says "Black" for black-and-white copies. It is like having a technician right there talking to you. "See, here are the fax buttons. They are separate from the copy buttons." You don't need a manual to figure out which is which. There are small guides printed on the document tray for the printer and the fax options that show you which way to position paper or envelopes. The savings on misaddressed envelopes alone is worth the price of the machine.

Someone has thought about what people need to know when they want to send a fax, make a copy, or print an envelope.

Hewlett Packard recognizes that its customers don't want to read a manual just to print an envelope, and that dazzling features aren't worth much if you don't get the instructions that will tell you how to take advantage of them.

Ever buy a Volkswagen? You feel comfortable, almost like someone is right there helping you use the car. Lexus and Jaguar are known for certain things, but each component seems like it was designed by someone different, so learning to use each system requires figuring out a new set of buttons and icons—like trying to speak five languages at the same party. With a Volkswagen, the dials, door locks, glove box, and seats were made using the same logic: making the vehicle a cohesive package with a distinct personality.

Conversation doesn't have to be two-way. You can have conversations with cars or with computers. I'm waiting for someone to design a computer that nods when it understands you. You can have a conversation with a lecturer. I think that the best lectures are conversations with the audience—even if the audience never gets to talk.

> The next time you're feeling bereft of intelligent conversation on your favorite topic, fire up the computer and go search for some kindred spirits in cyberspace.
>
> – Greg Knollenburg, "Finding Intelligent Conversation Online," (www.writerswrite.com)

LET'S MAKE A DEAL—BARTERING AS CONVERSATION

Let's say you own a small public relations firm and one of your contacts happens to own an accounting business. Your accounting friend could use a little PR, and you could use the services of an accountant, but neither one of you has any extra money in your budgets for these services. What do you do? You give your friend some free PR in return for a few free financial evaluation sessions.

What was there before currency? People offered their goods and services in exchange for another's goods and services. Bartering is an age-old tradition. It's much more personal than the exchange of currency. Throughout time, money has become more abstract, an evolution that has taken the system further from its roots.

In the Colonial era—the 17th and 18th centuries—money was so scarce that colonists relied primarily on the bartering of beaver pelts, corn, musket balls, nails, tobacco, and deer skins (where the term "buck" was coined). During the Great Depression, money was again scarce. People responded by forming barter groups such as The Unemployed Citizens League of Denver and the National Development Association.

Then, in the 1980s, bartering became popular again when the United States experienced a long recession. In fact, $10 billion in corporate deals were bartered in 1980 alone. Magazines and books hailed bartering as the new way to do business, and hundreds of barter clubs were created across the nation. More companies learned about and began implementing bartering processes in their own industries. Why? Because bartering allowed companies to pay for many expenses without spending cash—most often advertising and promotion, or employee benefits.

Today we're more abstract than ever. The bartering process has moved to the Internet. Sites like BigVine.com, Ubarter.com, Trade-USA.net, and Barter-n-Trade.com offer companies and individuals the opportunity to trade goods and services online.

Who is trading, and what are they trading? Lawyers, accountants, moms, kids, restaurant owners, auto supply stores, big-name hotel chains, and construction companies are among the bartering crowd. They're there to trade within categories including advertising and

> Sixty percent of all companies in America have set up a barter division within their own company to help them move merchandise more effectively.
>
> – M.J. McConnell, president of Business Exchange

> Salary. This word originates in the Latin word, "sal," from which we derive the words "salt" and "salary." Salt was used to pay the wages of Roman soldiers; today, we might say that an employee is "not worth his salt."

promotion, art and collectibles, auto, boat and motorcycle, business and office, computer products and services, construction and renovation, financial services, real estate, and more.

Goods and services are paid for in "trade dollars" instead of actual money. The seller of a product or service sets a price—typically close to the price it would be worth in real currency—or lists a price as "negotiable." You can actually earn a surplus of trade dollars through an exchange. Bartering does have its advantages, but unfortunately, it's not completely free. Most online services charge a commission for brokering the deal, anywhere from five to eight percent. And don't expect to avoid income taxes. All exchanges are recorded, and any trade dollars you earn are reported to the IRS on Form 1099B. (Unfortunately, the IRS won't accept barter for tax payment.)

But one principle is a given: Bartering is a conversation between two parties. Go to Barter-n-Trade.com, and you'll see a list of conversations waiting to happen. One man offers his cabinet-making services for land in Maine. Another hopeful wants to trade cigars for a used multicopier/fax/printer. You can be as general or specific as you like on the site. It can be as easy as posting, "1969 Mercedes Benz." Wonder what they want for that?

NEWSPAPERS AS A CONVERSATION

The form of interaction that occurs in traditional publishing is very different from the discussions that take place in face-to-face settings or online communication. It's still conversation though. People look to newspapers to perform a variety of functions. According to the American Society of Newspaper Editors (ASNE), 80 percent of Americans see the role of the news media as crucial in a free society.

Americans expect journalists to have a deep understanding of what is important to people in the community, to explain difficult topics in depth, and to help the community focus on important issues. They look to newspapers as a means to give all people in the community a voice, providing access to different perspectives. They see the newspaper as a careful watchdog that spurs people to talk about issues and confront problems.

A barter of services says I value what you do so much that I will trade my most precious asset for it: my time. It becomes part of the language between friends.

– Adair Lara, *San Francisco Chronicle*
(10/19/00)

The function of the press in society is to inform, but its role in society is to make money.

– A. J. Liebling

Nationally, more than 56 million newspapers are sold daily, with an average of 2.2 readers per copy. And on Sunday, more than 60 million newspapers are sold, with an average of 2.3 readers per copy.

– Newspaper Association of America
(NAA)

And readers do talk to each other about articles they read, issues at hand, and the general state of things. They form tight-knit communities and feel close to the reporters who deliver the news and spur them to think. They also communicate with the newspaper itself through email, letters, phone calls, and general opinions.

EVERYTHING TAKES PLACE SOMEPLACE

About ten years ago the late **Jim Batten** of Knight-Ridder, asked me to examine the future of information architecture in the newspaper. I initially focused on the front page. The phrase "everything takes place someplace" kept on rebounding in my head. I used it as the organizing principle of news and daily events.

Each day there would be a slightly changing group of maps navigating you through the news from the world to local with all the main headlines that appear throughout the newspaper on the left and right margins. I still believe it is a good idea and it could also work as the organizing principle for the nightly news on television, or on the Web.

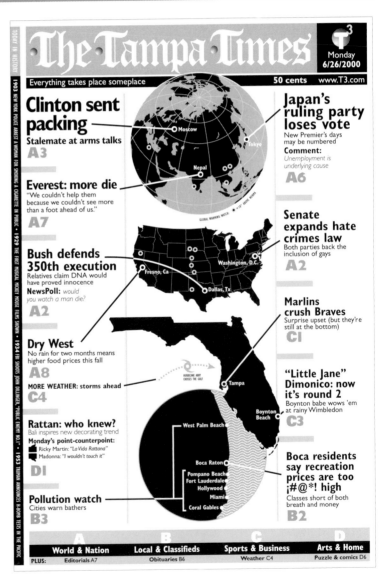

What does all of this mean? It means that the newspaper is an important part of this society's communication process. It means it's not dying like some said it would when the Internet came of age. In fact, it's quite the opposite. According to the Competitive Media Index, newspapers saw impressive growth in 1998. Readership remained steady, while spending on advertising finished the year up 6.3 percent over 1997. Newspapers were a $54 billion industry in 1998.

THE EVOLUTION OF THE CLASSIFIED AD

Rebecca Gardyn, in her May, 2000 *American Demographics* article, "The Future of Fine Print," states, "Classified ads are conversations. A majority of Americans remain intensely loyal to their local papers. A whopping 71% of residents in non-metro areas read their community newspapers regularly and 86% of those say they use ads in their community newspaper to find bargains locally, according to the National Newspaper Association. Says Edward McKersie, president of Pro Search, Inc., a recruitment firm in Portland, Maine, 'Ninety percent of people looking for a job, even in today's global marketplace, are not looking to relocate. The transaction is a local one. So, in that sense, newspapers have a strong advantage over the monster.com's of the world.'"

Does anyone want to buy my restored 1963 Ford Falcon? Here's the story on it.

No newspaper has done a major change in classified ads because it is the biggest revenue generator for that medium, and the print world isn't about to let go of valuable revenue streams with-

"No newspaper has done a major change in classified ads because it is the biggest revenue generator for that medium, and the print world isn't about to let go of valuable revenue streams without a good fight."

out a good fight. Revenue from print classifieds totaled $18.6 billion in 1999, a 4.3 percent increase over 1998, according to the NAA (Newspaper Association of America).

Yes, many newspapers have put classifieds online to offer greater search capabilities and opportunity for images. About two-thirds of the country's 1,500 daily newspapers now have electronic versions, and more than 500 of them post their classifieds online. In another decade, even small-town papers will migrate to online classifieds. The online classifieds extend the capabilities of conversation. They allow the seller to draw a picture, to point to the product, to say, "Will the people selling laptops please raise your hands."

COMPLEXITY DOESN'T NECESSARILY MEAN CONFUSION

AOL has triumphed because it fundamentally understands the customer. No, it doesn't always get it right. Nobody has ever always gotten it right. AOL has made huge mistakes, but it has never wavered from keeping it simple for the customer. The customer has responded, because while many of us parade a hip complexity, below the surface the vast majority of us crave a simple life.

Gerry McGovern,
"Unsexy and Unstoppable"
ClickZ Web site
(1/26/00)

How can we recreate the real-time experience of communication on a printed page, on the Web, on TV? How much of this page can you read? How much of this will you understand? When will you be drawn to an illustration? What happens when I draw an arrow?

When you are driving down Highway I-95, you want to know whether you are headed to Boston or Baltimore. You don't want to see a list of 8,000 cities and their distances when you're driving 75 miles per hour. You don't want to drive out of your driveway and see a sign for 20 cities. You just want to get downtown. The choices are fewer at any one moment. When you go across the bridge to Jamestown, R.I., you don't need information about San Francisco. That's just more than you want to know.

We are able to do an extraordinary job of processing information. Nothing is preventing us from doing an extraordinarily better job except the disease of familiarity and the communicators' and designers' sense of humanity. We all want information that takes us just past what we want to do. We want conversations that answer our desires and needs at the moment. We want books that way. So we are in an ever-expanding world of understanding.

We don't want a Web page to look like the cockpit of an airplane with hundreds of dials, buttons, and lists. We want to be taken on the journey that a conversation takes. When you have a conversation, you don't see signs with 500 topics, off-ramps, on-ramps, parking garages, or views of the horizon.

Drive down a highway in Tuscany, and you can choose to visit the tower or a restaurant that serves truffles, but you don't see all options in front of you at all times. This is exactly what today's conversationalists need—concise information that takes them just past where they want to go. Show them how to get there and then give them a teaser. What's their next stop after they find what they're looking for?

HOW TO MAKE INFORMATION LESS THREATENING

A few years ago, I was trying to make a list of the generic books in our society. One is the cookbook. I took all our cookbooks at home and started looking at them. As I looked, I realized that many cookbooks brag about how many recipes they contain: 400 recipes that can be made in under an hour, 100 recipes for healthy eating, and so on. But, when you really look at the choices, there aren't that many. We don't eat many things. We don't have many choices—and they are limited, not infinite. The choices for a (nonvegetarian) main course are beef, chicken, fish, pork, and lamb. It struck me that cookbooks could really be clarified and reduced to empower the cook.

At the top of the pyramid would be the five main-course choices. At the next level would be the different means of cooking (broil, bake, grill, fry), then the different sauces to complement each meat. By giving readers simple choices with subcategories, it empowers them to do more with the information, and you wouldn't have to repeat the same information over and over.

Under the category of poultry, I'd put basic instructions for stewing, frying, grilling, roasting, and baking poultry. Then there would be many sauces. This way you wouldn't have to repeat the basic cooking instructions. **Martha Stewart** was interested in the cookbook, but we couldn't agree on whose name would be on the cover. She wouldn't do it if my name was on the cover, and I wouldn't do it if my name wasn't.

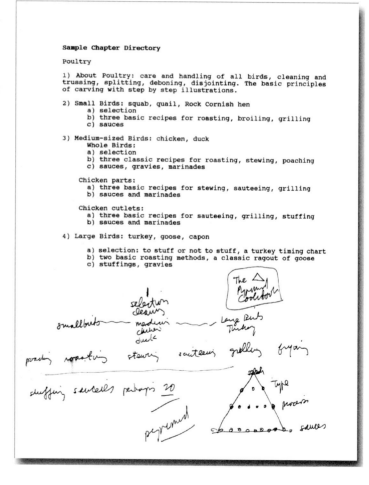

Sample Chapter Directory

Poultry

1) About Poultry: care and handling of all birds, cleaning and trussing, splitting, deboning, disjointing. The basic principles of carving with step by step illustrations.

2) Small Birds: squab, quail, Rock Cornish hen
   a) selection
   b) three basic recipes for roasting, broiling, grilling
   c) sauces

3) Medium-sized Birds: chicken, duck
   Whole Birds:
   a) selection
   b) three classic recipes for roasting, stewing, poaching
   c) sauces, gravies, marinades

   Chicken parts:
   a) three basic recipes for stewing, sauteeing, grilling
   b) sauces and marinades

   Chicken cutlets:
   a) three basic recipes for sauteeing, grilling, stuffing
   b) sauces and marinades

4) Large Birds: turkey, goose, capon

   a) selection: to stuff or not to stuff, a turkey timing chart
   b) two basic roasting methods, a classic ragout of goose
   c) stuffings, gravies

We're living in an era of explosive abundance. The challenge is to manage our freedom and to strike a balance in the face of endless opportunity. I've realized that I must find the discipline to say "no" more often.

It sounds easy, but it's not. Just when I've convinced myself that what I have is more than plenty, the phone rings, and someone offers me something that I can't resist. But then I ask an important question: How thin can I spread myself before I'm no longer "there"?

– John Perry Barlow, co founder of the Electronic Frontier Foundation

Most commercial Web sites have finally realized that the best way to serve their audience is to get out of the way and let them accomplish what they came to do. Still, there is a vestige of designers who continue to demand that *users* conform to *their* whims.

– Jeffrey Veen, *The Art & Science of Web Design*

Can you empower your audience to use the information you give them? It's all about making the best use of interactive mediums. If you make cars, and a customer calls to find out why he is having problems with his transmission, let him talk to a mechanic, not the company spokesperson. While the spokesperson may be the best candidate to speak to the media, the mechanic will be the best person to help your customer figure out his transmission problem. Too often, companies forget about having real, honest conversations with their market, spoiling the image they're trying so hard to promote and protect. The key: Get rid of the corporate speak and get down to the real conversation.

Design also can make information less threatening. If the design is simple, functional, and yields a lot of information, users will be satisfied and propelled to continue their interest. **Wendell Z. Roberts** addresses this challenge in his article "Designer Websites" (*Critique* magazine, Spring 2000). He uses the local chapter sites of the American Institute for Graphic Design (AIGA) as an example. They are flashy, provocative, and even "oh-so-cool," he says. But they actually achieve the opposite effect in their usability. "In essence, they play into the stereotype that designers have a fascination with empty decoration," he comments.

"As interface designs, home pages can't tolerate random, nonfunctional visuals," Roberts says. "Purely decorative elements should be segregated from functional graphics because users have high expectations and little patience. They believe that any round object or word/graphic combo is a link. If they click and go nowhere, you lose them."

In an interview posted on the EIU (Economist Intelligence Unit) e-business forum, (5/23/000; www.ebusinessforum.com) Ogilvy CEO **Mike Walsh** talks about the importance of usability in branding your business online. He stresses that the online environment makes it crucial to get things like the speed of the site, navigation, responsiveness, and value right the first time around. Walsh uses Boo.com as an example of an online company that lost prospects because of usability issues. "Boo.com had a very good brand image but was let down by the oversophistication of the site and failed to deliver to consumers for that reason," Walsh says.

The lesson: It goes back to the basic rule of technology—don't have technology for technology's sake. Make sure your Web site and collateral materials are clean and easy to navigate. You can have a splashy site or a trendy image brochure, but if the design is difficult, you'll only lose clients and prospects in confusion.

THE ARCHITECTURE OF INSTRUCTIONS

When we communicate, we usually have some idea we are trying to share, but don't always know if that corresponds with the picture we have planted in someone else's mind. When we give instructions, we test our ability to communicate information and gauge how much we really know about a process or place, by how well our instructions are followed. When people ask me what I do, sometimes I tell them that I give good instructions.

There are only three means of description available to us: words, pictures, and numbers. The palette is limited. Generally, the best instructions rely on all three, but in any instance one should predominate, while the other two are used to serve and extend. The key to giving good instructions lies in the ability to choose the appropriate means.

If I were going to describe my office, I could tell you in words, but it would take forever. I could tell you in numbers, but you would be left without a sense of the texture of the environment— you would have statistics without context. Clearly, the most appropriate way to describe my office would be in pictures, with a few dimensions and words of explanation.

If I were going to describe a person, a picture would never convey the complexities of personality. Only words might possibly do this, with a picture to enhance the description.

If I were going to describe a company, I would probably rely on numbers—that is, gross sales, profitability, or market share because these would be the easiest to compare to help you understand a company in terms relative to others of its kind.

In the Information Age, you don't teach philosophy as they did after feudalism. You perform it. If Aristotle were alive today he'd have a talk show.

– Timothy Leary

The choices are not always so clear. Often, the situation requires asking yourself: How can I most faithfully describe the thing, which means would be the most economical in terms of time and money, and which means would enable my audience to relate my description to something they might already understand? Despite all the high tech options we have for communicating in general, and in particular for communicating instructions, the conversation is still perhaps the most effective means available. Emails bounce, cell phone calls get cut off, and understanding exactly what people mean can be very difficult when they are not talking back and forth, face to face.

6 TALK IS DEEP

The industrial design critic **Ralph Caplan** was talking to a woman who was trying to explain something to him. "I know what I want to say, but I just can't put it into words," she told him. Puzzled, Caplan asked her, "Can you tell me what form it is in now?"

There is still only one method for transmitting thought, for communicating information in a manner that somewhat captures the spirit of the mind: the medium of conversation. Conversation can be a mirror of the mind, a petri dish for ideas. It enables us to communicate our thoughts in a manner that closely models the way they occur in our minds.

Without words, we would be severely handicapped in both shaping our thoughts and communicating them to others. While not the only tool, words elevate communication and lend an unparalleled degree of sophistication to expression.

The implicit and explicit goal of all conversation is understanding. Whether conversations occur between lovers, friends, relatives, or business associates, they have as their express goal to get one's point across, to make a connection between one's thoughts and another person—that is, the outside world; conversations are an understanding machine, an imminently satisfying forum for the exchange of information.

> The best of life is conversation, and the greatest success is confidence, or perfect understanding between sincere people.
>
> – Ralph Waldo Emerson

> Education begins a gentleman. Conversation completes him.
>
> – Thomas Fuller

A conversation forms a two-way communication link. There is a measure of symmetry between the parties as messages pass to and fro. There is a continual stimulus-response, cyclical action; remarks evoke other remarks, and the behavior of the two individuals becomes concerted, cooperative, and directed toward some goal.

Time and time again, studies have shown that the best communication occurs face to face. We just can't deny that. People still fly halfway across the world to meet clients for the first time. In many organizations, 40 to 60 percent of the workday is spent in meetings. Managers need to be talking to their employees, real-time, one-on-one, telling them what is going on in their organization.

> **Natural human conversation is the true language of commerce.**
>
> – Christopher Locke, Rick Levine, Doc Searls, and David Weinberger, *The Cluetrain Manifesto*

Your clients and prospects are talking about your business and, in fact, they're molding it. They're telling each other the truth in very human voices. The Internet is transforming your market and your employees as we speak. You must find a way to enter the conversation, even encourage it by giving your market the information it desires, packaged the way the market needs and wants it.

To be a success in today's competitive, connected market, you can't afford to reside on the fringe of this conversation. You must be an instigator and a leader in your industry, and you must always be listening to the conversation at large.

> **A powerful global conversation has begun. Through the Internet, people are discovering and inventing new ways to share relevant knowledge with blinding speed. As a direct result, markets are getting smarter—and getting smarter than most companies.**
>
> **These markets operate like conversations. Their members communicate in language that is natural, open, honest, direct, funny and often shocking. Whether explaining or complaining, joking or serious, the human voice is unmistakably genuine. It can't be faked.**
>
> – *The Cluetrain Manifesto*

John McCain is a politician who understands the allure of conversation. He isn't blow-dried and over-hyped by spinmeisters. He is just a guy talking. Sometimes he says the wrong thing, too. Authenticity reduces anxiety. Imperfections can inspire trust and compassion.

"The truth is the human voice [and it] remains the most powerful and persuasive tool in the sales and service arsenal," says **Stan Vestal** in "Turning Browsers Into Buyers" in TMCnet.com (5/22/00). "By providing online shoppers with the opportunity to ask questions or seek assistance from agents in real time, e-commerce sites can make shoppers much more comfortable about their Web purchasing experience. Comfortable shoppers are more likely to complete their e-commerce transactions....In the parlance of e-tailing, browse-to-buy ratios improve, and so does revenue."

THE LOST ART OF CONVERSATION

Alas, too often the human voice is lost, and our communication skills come up short. As **Henry Miller** once said, "We do not talk—we bludgeon one another with facts and theories gleaned from cursory readings of newspapers, magazines, and digests."

Nowhere is this more apparent than in the business community. Studies have shown that poor communication is one of the main problems facing businesses today. Executives consistently rate communications among themselves as their main area of difficulty, according to **Robert Lefton**, president of Psychological Associates Inc. in St. Louis. High on the list of employees' complaints are lack of communication with management and difficulties getting along with co-workers. If companies can't communicate among themselves, how well can they be talking to clients and customers?

As **Malcolm Gladwell** writes in *The Tipping Point*, we use influence to convince our clients and prospects to believe in us. We use the art of persuasion and consistent messaging to build trust with employees and our market.

When we are trying to convey an idea or attitude or product tip, we're trying to change our audience in some small yet critical respect: We're trying to infect them, sweep them up in our epidemic, convert them from hostility to acceptance. That can be done through the influence of special kinds of people—people of extraordinary personal connection.

Conversation is a viable, appropriate model for the communications industry, but it is largely untapped. It is a simple-minded principle imbued with extraordinary complexities, nuances, and ephemeral magic.

This is a book about clarification. And the most basic conversation that we have takes into it an enormous complexity, comments about weather, dress, nuances of the visual (someone nodding, blinking eyes, promptings, or lip movement) that show they want clarification or want to interrupt. It's the best of what we do, the most complex thing we do. It has in it the possibility of great creative activity.

New ideas have the potential to flow from a conversation with a single human being. When we understand these dumb things, we can understand the more complex. My conversation is

> Conversation, the commerce of minds.
>
> – Cyril Tourneur

> The best kind of conversation is that which may be called thinking aloud.
>
> – William Hazlitt

> She had lost the art of conversation but not unfortunately the power of speech.
>
> – George Bernard Shaw

different depending on who is here. A conversation with two is different than a conversation with three or more. This is not a value judgment, but an exercise in sensitivity to how people communicate. When I do the **TED** conferences, I'm sensitive to when people are listening and not listening. I'm not only going into myself, I am watching that audience. I can see almost everyone in an audience of 500 people. What they want, what resonates with them, what does and doesn't interest them.

THE ART OF LISTENING

> It takes two to speak the truth—
> one to speak and another to hear.
>
> – Henry Thoreau

Good communication skills are among the most valuable assets you can bring to your job. This means not only being able to speak eloquently and express your thoughts clearly but also registering what others tell you. Since most people remember a mere 15 percent of what they hear, good listeners are at a premium.

Here are some tips on being a better listener:

- Having two ears and one tongue, we should listen twice as much as we speak.
- Don't try to formulate your reply when the other person is speaking.
- The person who starts a sentence should be the one to finish it.
- Don't let your fear of silence propel you to fill it with air. A moment of silence can be the most revealing part of a conversation.
- Remember that listening is not a passive endeavor, but an activity that requires great energy. Try to listen with the same intensity you use to talk.

Almost all cultures have proverbs that extol the benefits of listening. Here are a few:

Italian
From listening comes wisdom and from speaking repentance.

Native American
Listen or thy tongue will keep thee deaf.

Chinese
If you wish to know the mind of a man, listen to his words.

Jewish
No one is as deaf as the man who will not listen.

WHAT THE TECHNOLOGY INDUSTRY CAN LEARN FROM OPRAH

How well do you listen to your audience? What do you know about them? Picture yourself having a conversation with a "typical" client. How would you talk to him or her? What kinds of questions would he or she ask? What kind of answers would you give? What kinds of answers would satisfy your client?

How can we recreate the real-time experience of communication on a printed page, on the Web, or on TV? How much of this page can you read? When are you drawn to an illustration? What happens when I draw an arrow?

Think about how **Oprah Winfrey** develops a personal connection with each member of her audience and with her viewers. She isn't phony, and she doesn't hide behind her failures. She is very real and accessible to her audience.

Human beings crave interaction. **Joanna Smith Rakoff** illustrates this perfectly in her article on *The Atlantic Unbound* (5/24/00, www.theatlantic.com). Recalling "The Million Channel Universe," a Columbia School of Journalism conference on the future of broadband, Rakoff shares one defining moment. "**Steve Rosenbaum**, CEO and president of the TV production company Broadcast News Network (BNN), asked a room full of journalists a question: Would we rather have digital television or interactive television?" remembers Rakoff. "The show of hands was overwhelmingly in favor of the latter—the right answer according to Rosenbaum, who not only believes in rising "consumer demand for a less passive experience," but also has based his latest business venture, a streaming-media site called Camera Planet.com, on both this supposed demand and the ostensibly impending expansion of broadband."

You must keep this craving for interaction in mind when designing information or products for your customers. Make it as if you're having a casual, informative, and interactive meeting about your product or service. Tell your audience the basics, anticipate their questions, supply them with the answers, and give them extra tools to increase their own usability and empowerment. Most of all, make it fun, and make it real.

PUTTING VELCRO ON FACTS

Conversation can put "Velcro" on facts. Within them are a myriad of self-adjusting systems. As we speak with another person, we constantly readjust our language based on the cues we get from the listener. Do they looked baffled or excited, bored or angry? We need to build in ways for customers to look baffled and to get an explanation.

There is nothing else we do better when we do conversation well. There is no other communication device that provides such subtle and instantaneous feedback, nor permits such a range of evaluation and correctability.

When Oprah was little someone asked her what she wanted to do when she grew up. She said, "I want to lead people." The person asked, "Where?" Her answer: "To themselves."

Sweet discourse, the banquet of the mind.

– John Dryden

Words are strung together seemingly without hesitation in phenomenally complex sequences and thoughts. They, in turn, work with each other to form new meaning. By its existence this process allows for the development of new ideas. Ideas are created in conversation. **E.M. Forster** used to say that to "speak before you think is creation's motto." Although spoken language is learned, it becomes natural and seemingly it becomes instinctive. It is our pipeline to understanding. We have more skills to put thoughts together by language than we do visually.

WORD OF MOUTH

Why books are bought:
Planned:	54%
Impulse:	46%
As Gift:	17%
For Self:	83%

Book purchasers of adult titles:
Under 25:	5%
25-29:	6%
30-34:	9%
35-39:	10%
40-44:	14%
45-49:	13%
50-54:	12%
55-64:	15%
65+:	16%

What do you recommend?
(The top ways adults say they generally select the books they read):
Recommendation from someone they know: 27%
An author whose books they like: 27%
Browsing bookstore/library: 26%
Book reviews: 6%

– USA Snapshots, *USAToday*

One of the most dazzling features of the Internet is its ability to act as an ongoing global conversation with the world. Web conversation is so powerful that it is almost impossible to control, as many a company has found out when fraudulent rumors about its products became part of the global rumor mill. Remember flesh-eating bacteria on Costa Rican bananas, antiperspirants causing breast cancer, mutant chickens from KFC, the so-called Neiman Marcus cookie recipe, and Mountain Dew as a contraceptive, to name just a few.

If word-of-mouth advertising is the hardest to control when it's used against you, word-of-mouth referrals are still the number one way to gain new business. In fact, a recent study conducted by the Graphic Visualization & Usability Center at the Georgia Institute of Technology (GVU) found that most users find Web pages through friends and other pages (96 percent) along with magazines (64.3 percent) and Usenet (59 percent). If people find 96 percent of Web pages through their friends, that's how they'll find your Web pages or at least hear about your company.

Consider the Faberge Organic effect. During the 1970s, Faberge Organic shampoo had an advertisement extolling the product, with the spokeswoman explaining how she told two friends and they told two friends, and so on and so on. No matter how well you communicate with your customers, how well they communicate among themselves really determines the success of your message.

Remember how critical word of mouth can be. Remember to create and promote "the buzz." You buy a book when your best friend says that it is really a great book. You go to a movie because someone told you it's great. These people told you personally, so you believed them. Do you really believe a blurb on a book jacket?

Consider the book *Divine Secrets of the Ya-Ya Sisterhood*. **Rebecca Wells**' bestseller didn't get there all by itself. Her book is a classic example of the power of word-of-mouth. It's a testament to the true power of groups and individuals passing along persuasion to other groups and individuals.

Think about Honda. They didn't do much advertising. The word went around that the car didn't need repairs. It was a value for the money. It actually worked, unlike the American cars people had at the time. Now think about Jaguar—beautiful cars. But everyone knows how hard they are to repair and keep repaired. Who told them?

One of the great ironies of the Internet is that its macro-universality makes it so effective for reaching people at the micro-local level. It's everywhere, so it can be in your little burg, too. So, buzzsters need to look at how they can reach that local level. Where do you find the consumers who might buy your product?

> Precision of communication is important, more important than ever, in our era of hair-trigger balances, when a false, or mis-understood word may create as much disaster as a sudden thoughtless act.
>
> – James Thurber

> All conversation is exaggeration.
>
> – Richard Saul Wurman

THE ART OF PROMOTION

From **Terence Gower**, *a costume designer and creative producer at Eisnor Interactive, quoted in an article, "She Builds Online Brands on the Street" in* Fast Company *(December, 1999). Here are three tips for effective promotions:*

Engage all the senses.
Consumers have become good at filtering out the messages that bombard their eyes and ears. We always put samples in people's hands.

Keep to the concept.
As an artist, I'm always going back to the essence of a project. We did a program for Staples.com at Internet World. We began working from the theme of utility, convenience, and a do-it-yourself attitude, so we skipped the glitz of the typical booth and created a dusty supply closet.

Work the street appeal.
We define street as edgy and grounded. At the Internet World launch of another client, iCast, a create-your-own-movie site, EI sent people out wearing orange jumpsuits. They shot footage of Internet World, which was later shown on the iCast Web site.

Sometimes, bananas might be just the right medium for buzz-making. Say you're a pharmaceutical company selling a potassium-draining diuretic. A lot of the people who buy your medication are going to be cruising the produce department for bananas.

Look at line items when you want to introduce a product. Instead of an advertising budget, how about a buzz budget. EI, Eisnor Interactive, specializes in buzz. **Di-Ann Eisnor**'s agency was the first offline promotions agency for online ads. She helped miningco.com announce its change to about.com. She takes online brands and translates them to the offline world—through buzz. For a campaign on changing the name of miningco.com to about.com, she had posters and stickers, graffiti, and sandwich boards plastered with the message: "Hello is anybody out there?" There was no company name or identifier other than a URL. The site got more than 100,000 hits, and it also received comments by leading talk-show hosts.

DESIGNING FOR WORD OF MOUTH

From *NYC Access*, 1983.

If you're going to create buzz, you want your product to back it up. You can design for buzz in the product itself. Look at the Volkswagen bug. There has to be something behind its ability to maintain its popularity for the past 40 years. In addition, the new one is even better than you expected. It's more comfortable; it has better vision; it's easier to use; it has more room; it's quirky and different. The lesson of the Volkswagen is that it is a real-time, 3D product that has buzz designed into it. What Volkswagen has done is put its product where its mouth is.

Tim and **Nina Zagat** created the marvelous *Zagat Guides*, which are frozen word of mouth. They are one of the great successes in publishing partly because they've captured conversation. The short and pithy comments from readers are more important than advertising. It's a book that is a poll, like the Harris Poll. It's word of mouth in print. You hear a voice when you read the comments.

In the early 1980s, I did my first volume of *NY City Access* while staying at the Meridien Hotel, and I had hired a guy to help with restaurants who was the food editor for the *Daily News*.

He said you ought to see this thing that a couple of friends are producing. They were just copying it on a Xerox machine. Tim Zagat came and brought me one. He was practicing law at the time. I told him if you give me permission, I'll run this in the back of my *NYCAccess* and I did, along with a note to call Tim Zagat.

Soon after, Zagat's guides went from photocopies to printed books. What he's done since then has been to create one of the best managed, intelligently run operations going. He's done an amazing job. The focus has been extraordinary. Tim just sold a tiny part of his business for $20 million. He met his venture capitalists at the **TED** conferences, something else that works because it's like a conversation.

ATTRACTING ATTENTION IN THIS SEA OF INFORMATION

Creating buzz doesn't always require big bucks. A hospital in Overland Park, Kansas, wanted to increase awareness of its obstetrical unit, which was underutilized. The director of communications came up with a blindingly simple but brilliant idea. She had a tape of Brahm's Lullaby played over the hospital intercom every time a baby was born. It created a tremendous buzz. People were asking, "Why are they playing it?" Soon, you could just look at the smile on a nurse's face to know why it was playing. Soon, it was not only creating awareness, but joy in the patients and staff. For a few minutes several times a day, the entire hospital smiled. Human relations aren't big things; they are thousands of little things.

The important concept is how you connect with the customer, not how much money you spend. You need to make them feel good about your product or service, to make it personal.

Donna Hoffman and **Thomas Novak** note in their paper (www.ascusc.org/jcmc/vol1/issue3/hoffman.html), "Commercial Scenarios for the Web," that the Internet is creating a revolution away from the typical model of "one-to-many" marketing communications. Individuals are able to customize their information needs from companies. Hoffman and Novak believe that this will increase brand loyalty because the Web will build stronger interactive relationships between firm and customer.

In the early days, the Internet was little more than brochure-ware. Companies threw their catalogues on the Net. Then came the shopping cart, and the companies started promoting online shopping. This is far from enough, as many a company has found.

Click-happy **Kelly Mooney**, who Web shops for a living as the intelligence director of Resource Marketing in Columbus, Ohio, contrasts the real-world experience of shopping at Dean & Deluca with their Web site. "When I visit one of its stores, I salivate over its products: I want to eat every cheese wheel in sight. But when I go online, I wonder, 'Is this the same company?' The Dean & Deluca site is boring and uninspired. I feel like I'm buying parts for my car."

According to an article on Mooney in *net company* (Fall 1999), "There's a big difference between owning a lot of data about customers and owning the customer experience. One of the main responsibilities of an online retailer is to make its site easy, intuitive, and accessible—to get a customer to click because he's engaged, not because he's confused. In part, that means getting better at asking the customer about the types of information he wants to receive."

DANGERS OF CUSTOMIZATION

Moving to the one-to-one model is positive in that it makes it possible for a single company to have a personal conversation with many customers. Yet, there is a tendency to go overboard toward customizing when you try to give people only what you think they want.

Everybody is talking about customization: how to customize newspapers, the Web experience, marketing. What a worthless idea. Companies have invested millions in this idea. They are all missing the fact that people often buy what they didn't know they wanted, or are most interested in what they didn't know they were looking for. That's why print newspapers survive. You can learn about something that wasn't on your "topics of interest." That's the whole serendipitous appeal of newspapers. No matter what you put in, you should never be given exactly what you ask for because you never know the limitations that puts on you. If you get everything you want, you don't get much.

Sometimes, our lives need to be unedited. When I talk about navigation, I never talk about getting from Point A to B. I talk about side ramps, going off into the parking lot. The diversions are what dial up your ability to see patterns between things. Creativity is the observation of patterns, that if you are lucky, you are seeing for the first time.

My work with one thing is what allows me to do another. How can I do a cookbook, a medical book, an Olympic book, a money book, and a city guidebook? Each one helps me see the pattern in the other.

Sometimes, people make bad choices. The results are that you don't get to see patterns. You don't get to see connections. If I did a survey of people's interests, they would never list jugglers, etymologists, vibraphone players, or science advisors. But the jugglers, bug person, vibraphonist, and science advisor to the "X–Files" were what everyone remembered about last year's **TED** Conference.

Sometimes, I see that the pattern in one area doesn't apply to another. Being able to find this out about things is wonderful. One of the ads for the Discovery Channel is "we allow you to see the things that you didn't even know you were interested in." For example, the lost tribes of Israel. I would never buy a book on that subject, but I watched a fascinating program on the subject that looked at settlements of people in China, India, and Africa that have had no contact, yet so much of their culture is similar.

Would you ever turn that on? *No*. Yet, it made me think about history and treks across the world. I've been talking to **Yo Yo Ma**, and he's interested in the Silk Road and the musical connections. Nothing about what he does has anything to do with the lost tribes of Israel.

FILTERS OF YOUR CHOOSING

I like to find out about boxing. Most newspapers don't have a lot of information on the subject, so I might turn to the Web for information about boxing. What if I filled out a form and just listed "boxing?" Maybe I am interested in violent sports or two-person sports. Maybe I would be just as interested in Sumo wrestling or tennis or chess.

If the form gives you back what you asked for, you limit your opportunities. A truly intelligent search mechanism would go two or three levels beyond your original request. When I listed boxing, it would come back and say, "What other sports do you like? Do you like to watch the whole match or just the final 15 minutes?"

Most forms don't give you that kind of direction, the kind that might locate what you didn't know you wanted. The forms don't see the patterns in your searching habits, the filters of your choosing, your design. That's a problem with artificial intelligence filters.

THE FIRST CONVERSATION

A company is only as good as the people in it who deal with the public. Have you ever called to complain about poor customer service only to have a company executive excuse poor service by saying, "We hired a lot of new help and some of them aren't up to speed yet?" That rarely makes anyone feel better. Besides, it reflects poorly on the company in not making the effort to train the most important link to the customer: the frontline. That's why our impression of McDonald's is formed by the person at the counter, not the CEO.

How to give good phone. The phone often is the first line of contact customers and prospects have with your business. In the beginning of a conversation, I will often start with some disarming piece of humor or honesty to establish the rapport. At the end of a conversation, I'll say I'm short, fat, and have a beard. That self-deprecation allows callers, in turn, to be honest about themselves or about the next thing they are going to say.

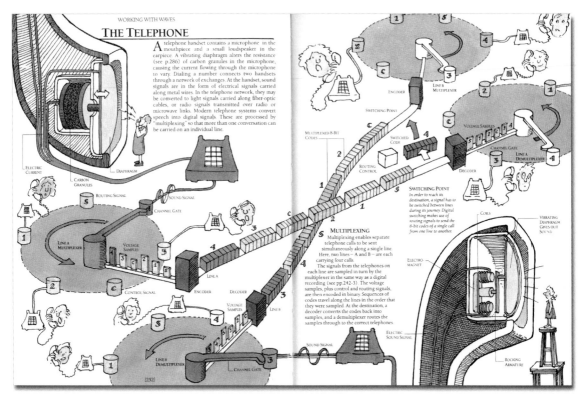

Illustration from
The Way Things Work,
by David Macaulay

A lot of my life is spent talking on the phone; no one taught me how to talk on the phone. The basic premise: Treat others as you would like to be treated. My gift is thinking about me in the other person's position. Talking on the phone in real time is a pervasive issue. I give good phone. I think about a phone call. I disarm people; I ask for things; it's not like a cold call.

I read somewhere that to run a business successfully, you should answer the phone in your office. I try to answer about one out of ten calls. Every week, I spend an hour answering the phone at my company.

There's no better way to learn how a company is or isn't running. I find out what kind of information people are seeking, where our books are out of stock, what kind of people our customers are, and what is or isn't getting done by the staff. I think all company presidents should spend a little time answering the phone. They might be surprised at what they can learn. At least they would exercise the ability to communicate with their clientele.

You should make public the name of your top executive, and customers should always be able to reach that person, even through an assistant. People want personal attention, they want to speak with a person, not get lost in voicemail hell. They don't want to speak to a bland, generic recording. They want to know that they matter, not just to the assistant but to the executive. Spend time talking to your clients and prospects; you'll be surprised by how much business you see from it.

Conversation via phone is an important part of the ongoing conversation you have with your market, and practicing proper phone etiquette is the first step in opening the lines of communication. I find that if someone's assistant answers the phone at a corporation and is terse or unfriendly, then I assume the person I'm trying to reach isn't friendly either. The word etiquette comes from the French word etiquette, meaning "ticket." More specifically, the court's rules and codes of conduct were written on tickets and passed on to lords and ladies to observe and obey.

Developing and using proper etiquette sets the stage for the rest of your relationship with clients, and it can make or break your success as a business owner. Are you on the right track to establishing open lines of communication? Since the phone is often your first contact with customers or prospects, it's an important part of your image and a great way to establish trust within your industry.

Then think about applying phone etiquette to email. Although email will never take the place of a phone call, it can mimic it in the ways that people appreciate and in the ways that people need. Email may seem like the perfect form of communication, but be aware of its limitations, and ask yourself if it's appropriate for the message you're trying to send. The common email pitfalls include missed signals, lack of context, permanence, and unfamiliarity.

It's hard to say something with a smile or happy tone in an email, and it's all too easy to misinterpret an offhand remark as a personal attack. Without the context of voice or face-to-face encounters, it's difficult to communicate more complex subjects via email, not to mention that emails can be deleted before they're even read, kept for years, or forwarded to unintended—or unimagined—recipients. Save hiring/firing issues for personal meetings, and matters of detail for a phone call.

AN UNDERSTANDING MODEL

There are so few things we do in our life where the absolute goal is to make things understandable. We have conversations all around us, yet we don't appreciate them as channels for the transmission of information, nor do we exploit their positive principles in other endeavors. No one seems to trust them. The favorite end to most business conversations is "Why don't you put that in writing?"

While the informality and amorphous structure of conversation will not (nor should it) replace the written word, it could be used much more as a model for the exchange of information in many areas.

Planning meetings. Agendas of meetings should be arranged so that they allow for everyone present to contribute. They should have built-in mechanisms for explaining new ideas and for adjusting the level based on the responses of those present. They should be flexible enough to permit diversions and changes in course. And ideas should be offered in such a way that they spark others to think and not as if they were handed down from Mount Sinai. I think there ought to be a five-minute new idea rule, where no one can say anything negative about a new idea for at least five minutes after it has been suggested. I think many wonderful, creative ideas get squashed this way, when they are too fragile and ill-defined to endure criticism, but may nonetheless be valuable seeds.

Employee training and education. Any program should involve new employees in their own training. They should be allowed to tailor their own programs, to learn at their own rate. They should be given the opportunity to ask questions, to stop and test their learning en route. Their training should be plotted like an extended conversation.

Social exchanges. Conversations play an increasingly insignificant role in our lives, contributing to feelings of alienation and isolation from society. Everyone has the opportunity to use conversation as a model for communication. While this seems absurdly simple, and most people would reply that they do this every day, what we are really doing most of the time is lecturing. Conversation, in its purest form means listening, responding to new stimulus, and exchanging ideas. It requires thought, attention, and patience.

Applying the structure of conversation could add meaning to multiple experiences. Conversations can tune themselves. We make adjustments, simplify, repeat, and move between various levels of complexity based on continuous feedback—a quarter-inch nod of a chin, the lowering or raising of eyes, strange guttural noises that say "uh-huh, uh-huh," blinks, shrugs, turns of the head, loss of eye contact, the making of eye contact. A symphony of signals occurs during even the briefest of conversations.

By mapping the complexity of conversation, we can use the oldest form of communication to make the newer modes of communication more understandable.

7 THERE IS ALWAYS A QUESTION

There is a Danish proverb that the one who is afraid of asking questions is ashamed of learning.

Questions can enlighten our world, expand our understanding of the universe, and help us assess what we know and what we don't know.

I've always found that asking the right question will take you a lot further than getting the right answer, yet the emphasis of most educational institutions is on finding answers. In school, we are rewarded for answering, not asking. Think how much more we could learn if it were the other way around. Educators should spend at least as much time on teaching us how to ask questions.

Certainly questions are more abundant than answers. A search at the Google.com site on the word "questions" turned up 2,160,000 entries. A search on "answers" turned up only 805,997.

Questions are the best checks of understanding messages or instructions. They test for clarity and tell us if we are on the right track as bearers of instruction or as the receivers. "The questions which one asks oneself begin, at least, to illuminate the world, and become one's key to the experience of others," according to **James Baldwin**

Isador Isaac Rabi, a Nobel-prize winning physicist, attributed his success to the way his mother used to greet him when he came home from school each day. "Did you ask any good questions today, Isaac?" she would say.

"How do you know so much about everything?" was asked of a very wise and intelligent man; and the answer was "By never being afraid or ashamed to ask questions as to anything of which I was ignorant."

– John Abbott

Why is the sky blue? Why is the grass green? Where is God? How do birds fly? Why are you laughing?

Children are masters at the spontaneous global questions for which there are no easy answers. Their appetite for acquiring information is far greater than their need to appear informed.

However, somewhere along the way of growing up, this inquisitiveness gets squashed by parents, by teachers, by a growing self-consciousness that prompts us to be wary of appearing uninformed. You can tell when kids are growing up because they start asking smaller, more proscribed questions.

We don't lose the curiosity, but we gain a fear of being unmasked as not knowing. Have you ever noticed in meetings the looks of undying gratitude directed toward the person who isn't afraid to raise her hand when the speaker says, "Does anyone have any questions about this material?"

> A good question is never answered. It is not a bolt to be tightened into place but a seed to be planted and to bear more seed toward the hope of greening the landscape of ideas.
>
> – John Ciardi

TEACHING WITH QUESTIONS

Socrates was the first teacher to use questions as a way to bring in-depth answers from his students. Unfortunately, his method has only continued its use in our law schools. Instead, in today's schools, you are rewarded for answering. But there is so much more to be learned by asking than answering. A real teacher isn't someone who asks the questions and lets you discover the answers. A real teacher is someone who helps you formulate your own questions. Embedded in most questions are the stirrings of the answer.

When the emphasis is placed on finding answers, we stop thinking about asking the innocent questions and start pretending that we know the answers.

Do these phrases sound familiar: "Stop asking questions," "Damn it, just do it," "Shoot first, ask questions later," "Wait till I'm finished, then if you still have questions"—that is, "if you're so dense you still don't understand...." These wholesale phrases, designed only to make the lives of parents and teachers easier, tend to repress the natural inquisitiveness associated with children—a repression that manifests itself in some peculiarly counterproductive behavior in adults.

> The greatest gift is not being afraid to question.
>
> – Ruby Dee

Adults learn to use questions to show off their own acumen rather than to acquire information from others.

Questions that are designed to elicit information or clarification of a problem are innocent questions that produce solutions. Questions that are designed to show off one's own erudition or prove someone else in error are destroyers of learning.

The "dummies" books published by IDG are a case in point of someone who asked innocent questions, like "What would make books on complicated subjects more approachable?"

At first, the concept was so radical that some book chains, like Waldenbooks, refused to carry the titles. Even IDG executives were opposed to the concept, which they thought was insulting and contrary to the company's image.

The publisher, **John Kilcullen**, prevailed because he asked the right questions. What intimidates people about technology? What might comfort them? He understood that customers new to the world of computers would be attracted to the "dummies" concept that would explain the foreign in understandable, even playful language. The concept resonated with consumers making the "dummies" books one of publishing's favorite success stories, with *Windows For Dummies, Gardening For Dummies, Antiques for Dummies*, and so on. There are more than 350 titles in the series and 50 million books in print.

The ability to ask questions borne out of original curiosity will serve one well in almost any circumstance—be it solving a problem, asking for directions, clarifying an assignment, or just having a conversation with a friend.

The person who asks the question usually learns more than the person who answers the question. If I ask you how old you are and you tell me 45, I have learned something. You knew you were 45 before I asked the question, you haven't learned anything.

In a good question is the answer and in the brilliant answer is the good question.

It is not only by the questions we have answered that progress may be measured, but also by those we are still asking.

– Freda Adler, *Sisters in Crime*

THE FIRST QUESTION: WHAT DO YOU DO?

The first question that most consumers are going to ask about your company is what do you do? This is one of the most profound questions that the business world will ever answer; yet, most do an abysmal job of answering it. You can open the pages of any technology magazine to see how poorly many companies answer this question.

Just watch some of the advertising on television. Quick: Is the commercial selling jeans, beer, or a car?

Companies need to rethink how they answer this most essential question: What does your organization really do? In much the same way adults try to sound informed and thus deprive themselves of an opportunity to learn, companies trying to sound hip and sophisticated deprive their potential customers of an opportunity to understand their businesses.

Here's a quick quiz. Tell me the difference between SYSCO and Cisco Systems. You've seen the SYSCO trucks on the highway, and you've heard Cisco Systems mentioned as a hot Internet stock. And that is all most of us know.

But SYSCO knows its site visitors may be confused, and it wants to clarify its position in the marketplace right off the bat. This paragraph appears at the very top of the Web site, before any of its site navigation.

> SYSCO is the largest marketer and distributor of foodservice prod-ucts in North America. Operating from 105 distribution facilities, the company provides products and services to nearly 325,000 res-taurants and other foodservice operations across the contiguous United States and portions of Alaska and Canada. (sysco.com, 5/00)

Additionally, the graphical image at the top left of the Web page is an 18-wheeler, reminding visitors that they've seen SYSCO in their daily environments. The image also tells site visitors that this organization deals with some sort of transportation issues.

Cisco, however, gives only a single clue to its *raison d'etre* on the first page of its Web site: "The Worldwide Leader in Networking for the Internet." Getting more information about the company and its line of work required traversing the site to get to this:

No question is so difficult to answer as that to which the answer is obvious.

– George Bernard Shaw

To spell out the obvious is often to call it in question.

– Eric Hoffer,
The Passionate State of Mind

Mission: Shape the future of the Internet by creating unprecedented value and opportunity for our customers, employees, investors, and ecosystem partners. (cisco.com, 5/00)

Eventually, you reach the explanation:

Cisco Systems is the worldwide leader in networking for the Internet. Cisco's networking solutions connect people, computing devices and computer networks, allowing people to access or transfer information without regard to differences in time, place or type of computer system.

This still leaves me baffled about what the company really does. When you see the word "solution," you know that you're not going to take away a clear visual impression.

DOES YOUR ORGANIZATION HAVE "SOLUTION SICKNESS?"

No one sells software or hardware these days; instead they provide "technology solutions." A technology solution could be anything. My toaster is a technology solution to the problem of untoasted bread.

Here are a few tag lines from the first few advertisements in the May 8, 2000, edition of the *Industry Standard:*

- Solutions for the surge economy (Intel)

- Pandesic: the e-business solution

- Rely on Active Software's eBusiness solutions to speed up your business

- Choose the solution that leaders like GE Capital, Nortel, Best Buy, Dell, Chemdex, and dozens more turned to (Calico)

Do you get any idea what any of these companies do from these ads?

TOP-SECRET MISSION STATEMENTS

The right mission statement can lead your employees to action, engage your customers, and point your company in a prosperous direction, but you've got to be able to find it first.

Quick, what's your company mission statement? No rifling through file cabinets or employee handbooks allowed. If you don't know, you aren't alone. With great fanfare, companies spend thousands of dollars and hundreds of hours producing turgid mission statements. Then, most mysteriously disappear.

An informal survey of 36 companies revealed that fewer than 14 percent had employees answering the phones who could identify the company mission statement. Less than 50 percent could produce someone who knew or could at least locate a mission statement. Many queried suspected that their companies *did* have one, but said they were lost or misplaced—missing in action you might say.

Here were some of their responses:

- "We're a *car* company. We don't have a mission statement."

- "We have a very lengthy mission statement, but it is not for external publication."

- "I thought I had it on my computer, but I can't find it now."

- "You might call our ad agency. Someone there might have a copy."

- "What's a mission statement?"

At best, mission statements can be mantras that glue companies together behind a common purpose. They can help you choose which way to go at crossroads, attract the right employees, and help convince investors to loan you money. (Some banks require a mission statement.)

"A mission statement should articulate the fundamental purpose of the company," says **Ted Davis**, president of Grace Consulting Services in Leavenworth, Kansas, and a towering general in the mission-statement army. "It should send a signal as to why it's worthwhile to be a part of the organization."

Davis, whose company offers strategic management advice and leadership development, estimates that more than 60 percent of companies have mission statements, but only a handful are usable. Other experts agree; most mission statements are sorely lacking.

"Most are either so lengthy or so lofty that no one understands them," says **Sally Winship, Ph.D.**, Dean of Continuing Education and Community Services at Johnson County Community College in Overland Park, Kansas. "It has to be meaningful to everyone in the company."

LeAnna Wilson, director of the Johnson County Community College Center for Business and Technology, has taught an organizational behavior class for 12 years. Every year, she asks her students to bring their company's mission statements. And, every year, she gets the same results. About 45 percent can't find one; 25 percent manage to locate one, but it's the first time they've seen it; and 30 percent know it by heart.

She's noticed something else that is just as predictable: The 30 percent who know the mission tend to come from the more prosperous companies. "The companies that move forward are the ones where the mission statement is shared," she says. "This gives employees a path to travel down."

Missions as road maps. Few do a more outstanding job of paving the path than Hallmark. The company mission, "to help consumers express themselves, celebrate, strengthen relationships, and enrich their lives," is part of the fabric of the company. It is reinforced by leaders, made the subject of presentations, published in employee communications, and held dear to the hearts of most Hallmarkers.

"Everyone might not get the words exactly right, but everyone here gets the spirit right," says **Ralph Christensen**, senior vice-president of human resources for Hallmark. "The mission statement has a lot of power to move people. People come and stay at Hallmark because they want to be part of that mission."

Management relies on the mission statement to evaluate new products and business opportunities and to make decisions based on how well they reinforce the mission. Christensen cited the recent entry of Hallmark into the floral business as an example of a product that clearly helps consumers celebrate and strengthen relationships.

"Our mission statement helps us stay focused," he says.

An ale and hearty mission. You don't have to be a corporate colossus to create a keepsake mission. Boulevard Brewing Co., a small brewery in Kansas City, Missouri, formalized one as part of its 10th anniversary celebration last year. **Jeff Krum**, chief financial officer, wrote the first draft, and then the rest of the management team discussed it at a planning meeting.

The final version was "to be the preeminent specialty brewer in the Midwest, profitably producing traditional, hand-crafted ales and lagers of the highest distinction."

It may not be as terse as Nike's "Crush Reebok," the unofficial, but oft-heard mission statement in the 1980s, according to **Scott Reames**, senior communications manager at Nike; or NASA's Apollo mission statement "to land humans on the Moon and bring them safely back to Earth." Yet, the Boulevard statement well defines both the market and the scope of the company. You know Boulevard won't be expanding into wheat-grass or papaya juice in the near future, or looking for national distributors.

The bad with the good. If you suggest to Amazon.com CEO **Jeff Bezos** that the mission of his company is to get consumers to buy books, he'll correct you. The real mission is to get consumers to rely on Amazon as the source for buying almost anything. Amazon's decision to include negative as well as positive reviews on books is a demonstration of their efforts to earn customer confidence.

WHAT IS YOUR COMPANY STORY?

Everyone should have a company story that tells the world what your business is all about. It should be a tale of passion, triumph, motivation, and opportunity. It shouldn't have anything to do with your company mission statement (which should keep you focused), or how wonderful your product is.

Your story can be about how or why you started your business or what incident best illustrates what you and your business are all about.

It could be about something that drove you to start your business Or something from your childhood that inspired you to land where you are today.

You may want to ask yourself some of the following questions posed by **John Jantsch**, owner of BrandWorks in Kansas City, as you try to draft your story:

- Looking back in your history what incidents make you proud?

- What funny or poignant or even tragic incidents express the spirit of your business?

- Where were you the day you decided to start your own company?

- What was your state of mind? Your state of life?

- Was there some mentor or influence in your life that led you to this place?

Consultant **Anne Baber** gives some great advice. When someone asks you what you do or what your organization achieves with its existence, tell a success story. Sharing your success as a story allows you to talk about your organization in a way that invites listening. People are much more interested in hearing stories than in being sold on a product, and they are more likely to cast themselves in the plot.

Baber says before you go to your next networking or professional association meeting, plan your success story. As you construct your story, be sure to keep these suggestions in mind:

S = **Short.** Make it no longer than three sentences.

U = **Unique.** Point out what makes you stand out. If you're in real estate, for example, don't just say, "I've been selling lots of houses." That's expected. Say, "Last week, I found a home for a couple who both needed home offices. Both of them wanted first floor offices with outside access, lots of light, and great views. I found just the home, with French doors to a patio just off the driveway." (This story teaches your conversation partner that you can find the unusual home.)

C = **Clear.** Be sure you eliminate all jargon of your profession.

C = **Concrete.** Give a couple of specific details to help your partner get a vivid picture. Notice that you can almost "see" the home described above.

E = **Exciting.** Let your enthusiasm shine through. Use vivid language, an upbeat tone of voice, and a speedy, not "dragging," delivery.

S = **Service oriented.** Be sure that your story teaches how well you serve your customers or clients.

S = **Strategic.** Think about what you want people to know about you or your business, then find or build your story around that point.

You can plan several success stories on several topics, and then use the one that seems most appropriate to the person with whom you are talking.

This model applies to individuals and to companies as well. Think how much clearer the technology-solution ads would be if they followed this model in answering the question "What do you do?"

MY STORY: MOMENTS WHEN MY LIFE CHANGED

Everyone has moments in their lives that touch their souls and make them feel empowered in some way. My first one occurred when I got my first bicycle at 10 or 11. I was living in the suburbs of Philadelphia, and a bicycle was freedom. I could go over to a friend's house by myself. That was a major release of feeling that I was my own person. I had wheels. I didn't have to ask to be driven somewhere. At 16, I got a used Jeepster convertible. To have my own car, that was another level of being in charge of my life. The next two things that happened in my life were going away to college and realizing that I wasn't living at home. I could come and go when I wanted. I was in charge of when I ate, what I ate. I didn't have to answer to anyone. Next came being able to earn a living, to support myself—although this one wasn't as big as the bicycle.

The most important moments in my adult life are being able to indulge my curiosity. When I realized how big an acre was. When I understood about the Union Carbide disaster in Bophal, India, or when I understood how big Versailles was or Angkor Wat in Thailand. The exhilaration of feeling that you understood something, the putting together of the parts, the "ah hah" factor. I put those at the same level as the bicycle, finding out more about what interests me in an invisible way that has no edges to it. It's like flying. I'm grabbing some of this, a little of that. How can I mix them together and form a new relationship? How can I soar through this stuff and learn something that touches me viscerally. I try to design every day so it has a few of these moments in it.

I've described myself at the age of 22 as an empty bucket and my decision that I would put in the bucket only those things that I absolutely understood and could explain to another human being because of my acceptance of my limitations. It's important that the image isn't a full bucket—nor a cornucopia of riches—because you can't put anything into a full bucket. You never know what will spill out.

FINDING THE RIGHT QUESTIONS

All projects start with a question, yet few spend enough time crafting this question. Take orientation programs for new employees. Most grow out of the questions. For example, how can we give new hires as much information about the company in the shortest amount of time? They usually include a session on employee benefits and what forms are required. Some include talks by managers on what their individual departments do.

At the end of the day, the new hires may understand the protocol and even certain aspects of the company, but they are probably still clueless about the kind of information that will help them thrive in the business, which is really what they want to know. They still don't understand the culture or the community.

How? How do you help them formulate the questions they need to survive in your environment? Embedded in every question is a subject, which relates it to a specific category, a memory map that they can take with them to navigate through your organization.

You can always tell when someone didn't find the right question. Have you ever gone into a department store and found it organized in departments with meaningless names like "Today's Woman," "Personal Touch," or "Point of View." Let's say you are looking for a cocktail dress, where would you go? These names give you no indication of what you might find in each department. Now, of course, this would be good if everyone entered a department store with a whole day to spend wandering around, but who has that kind of time?

These department names respond to the wrong question, which is the merchandising consultant's question: How can we come up with catchy sounding names? The right question would have been more along the line: How can we help customers find their way to merchandise that will appeal to them?

> The outcome of any serious research can only be to make two questions grow where only one grew before.
>
> – Thorstein Veblen,
> *The Place of Science in Modern Civilization*

Thousands of Web sites are guilty of asking the wrong questions. That's why you see so many sites organized by divisions in the company. They look like a webmaster took the company org chart and stuck buttons on the different divisions. They instead should have asked: How do customers buy our products?

Another example is the preponderance of time-hogging Java plug-ins and applets. Are they eye-catching and clever? Okay, some are, but who wants to wait while these things download? People want to know what the capital of Myanmar is or the cheapest way to get from Detroit to Dallas. The fact is, many of a site's target audience don't have the fastest processors and Internet connections.

There's a company called Frog Design (www.frogdesign.com) that promises "creative convergence for the eConomy, but only if you are willing to download a few applications just to get the company address. The company's ad in *Fast Company* magazine had a slogan, "More than Eyeballs." This was truly what you needed in order to read the contact information in the ad, which was printed in reverse type in a tiny, slender font. At the bottom, it read: "Frog. Get Vision." However, the ad required that you have great vision just to reach the company.

Dr. Pepper "Makes the World Taste Better," according to its Web site, but its browsing experience sure doesn't leave a very good taste in your mouth. It took more than three minutes to load the splash page on a Pentium III, 500 MHz computer with a 56K modem. While the process was under way, the site had a progress page, which let you know that it was in the process of downloading "splash components, button components, and interface components." Does the customer want to know about the internal workings of the Web site? No. What do customers want? They just want to order a hat or a T-shirt, and they most certainly don't want to wait an interminable three minutes for a splash page.

The trouble is no one gets a course in asking the right questions. I think universities should offer degrees in asking questions or at least offer mandatory courses on the subject. Then, every year, we should get a refresher course in how to ask a good question or hang out with more three-year olds. Questions permeate every aspect of our work and our lives. Life is all about questions. If you stop asking, you stop living.

THE STORY OF *UNDERSTANDING USA*

Questions drive all of my work. *Understanding USA* is a study in questions. It began with a question, was organized by questions, and it raised questions about book production in the future.

Twelve years ago, I had an idea for a book entitled *12 Issues* that would come out during an election year. It was based on one of the most important questions that drives my life: How can I make America more understandable to Americans?

We started the Understanding USA Project with questions, questions that concern us as everyday Americans, questions that we didn't know we didn't know the answers to, questions with answers that belong to the public, questions that affect the public.

Understanding USA is filled with public information, both in its questions *and* answers.

Public information refers to everything that explains our citizenship. Public means everything that we agree should be available to the body politic, but making information public is somewhat less generic. This public means presenting, designing, and structuring this information so that it is accessible, available, understandable, and free. Public means that the simple basic questions in the minds of the American people are easily, readily, and clearly answerable.

Initially, I talked with **Peter Jennings** about a joint project, how we could build doorways of access into complicated issues, and about which questions this book would address. Jennings was negotiating for a new contract, and the network execs didn't want a book clouding the issues of the contract, so the plug was pulled. Four years ago, I tried again, but the timing wasn't right.

Most of the time, we should thank our lucky stars when things don't work out. Mistarts and failures are the key to creative efforts. With the year 2000 approaching, a new century, and a new president around the corner, I decided to try again.

I hosted a lunch at **TED**9 with the **TED** board of advisors to talk about illustrating issues of importance to the public. I invited sponsors, people in media, and members of the **TED** board. They all told me I shouldn't do it. They said I'd never get a publisher or

Life is the first gift, love the second, and understanding the third.

– Marge Piercy

a distributor. It was already February 1999 and I'd never get it out in the year 2000. They said I wouldn't raise money; I wouldn't find the research. How could I narrow it down to 12 issues? Who would make the decisions? What would the criteria be? "Impossible," they said.

Rejection inspires me. At the same moment as I was being discouraged to go forward, I was inspired. The impossibility of something gives me delight.

So many meetings are based on people telling you why you shouldn't do something. We learn too early that the way to protect yourself is to be negative. As an architect, I created Wurman's Law #3: "In recognition that any good idea is a fragile thing, you have to give it a few minutes to breathe—like a good red wine."

We started the book in my office in February 1999. We did research here, extracting data from existing resources. Most of it started with statistical abstracts.

I realized that I couldn't get a publisher because the books wouldn't come out in time. So the notion of a publisher and a distributor went right out the window. I convinced some sponsors to put up good faith money of $5,000 each. I told them, if this works, great. If not, they aren't out much. I promised sponsors I'd put their names on the back of the book and nothing else because it was the right thing to do. I have to say these companies—all different people, different reasons, different ways—they all got it: That this was the right thing to do.

You can use questions to inspire and organize information. The Understanding USA Project came about because of questions. *Understanding USA* is a celebration and a visual demonstration of questions and answers leading to understanding. This book demonstrates the power inherent in understanding and the notion that understanding is power.

The questions became organizing sections. I asked 12 designers all over the world to help me answer basic questions about the United States, everything from government and business to education and the environment. I wanted to create the perfect integration of art and design, question and answer, words and

---

UnderstandingUSA **Sponsors**

America Online
General Motors
Hearst Communications
Intel
The Markle Foundation
Mattel
Olympus America
Ovations/UnitedHealth
SmartPlanet
Steelcase
USWeb/CKS
Xerox

pictures and numbers. I gave each information architect 22 pages. They represented a vast diversity of styles, so a question on each page was used to tie the book together.

We asked illustrators to answer these questions with charts and graphs and text, giving a visual and written representation of the answers. In addition to creating a beautiful book, full of the latest in modern informational art, we created a teaching tool and a learning tool, all in the same package. Have a question? Here's an answer.

The questions hold the book together, and they tie the book to the Web site. This is one of the first projects where a book and a Web site were developed as one package. I designed the book, and my son **Reven** and **Bobby Greenberg**'s amazing company R/GA designed the Web site at the same time. Site navigation was part of the original idea. The questions were part of the original idea.

We forged a new course. We didn't run ads, send out review copies, or solicit blurbs. As 12 different designers were working on the book at 12 different locations, we weren't sure what we would get. Anyone could have dropped out. So, we dispensed with a title page, a table of contents, an index, and even page numbers. Right until the day the book was printed, I didn't know what would be in it. When you don't have a publisher, you can make new rules.

The book got done…on time. It was printed in December 1999—nine months after it was an idea that everyone said was impossible. Would it have been nice to have had page numbers? Yep. A table of contents? Yep. An index? Yep. But, I got it done. That's the art of the possible.

It was sent to every member of Congress, to 3,500 high school teachers, and to people in the design community. The Markle Foundation distributed 10,000. UnitedHealthcare distributed 5,000, and Steelcase 1,000 copies. I gave one to every **TED**ster at **TED**10. I'm trying to market the book by letting people see it and tell others about it. I don't know if it will be considered a success by traditional publishing standards.

The *Starbucks 1999 Annual Report* is organized into sections by questions posed by its own employees. "How do you build an enduring company? How are we impacting these fragile environments where we buy our coffee? Can a Starbucks store change a neighborhood? What about Starbucks remains constant and what can be adapted to different cultures? If you're going to be relevant in the 21st century, where do you have to be?" The questions give you a sense of the people behind Starbucks.

The book is sold through b&n.com and Amazon.com, and distributed by Ingram. The Web site is hosted by the University of Illinois/Chicago. SmartPlanet (ZDNet) developed 138 courses of study, Ask Jeeves developed a series of questions based on the book, and 12 researchers at Federal libraries have compiled sources of additional information. And because we've got it posted on the Internet, you can use the material to answer your questions any time you want to ask them.

Not only is this a valuable tool in a civics class or history class or economics class or social studies class, but it is the perfect demonstration for educators on the different ways in which people learn: visually, audibly, and tangibly.

MAKING AMERICA UNDERSTANDABLE TO AMERICANS

The purpose of *Understanding USA* is not looking back at our past or ahead to our future, but rather to help Americans understand their country at this particular moment. The goal of this project was to make America understandable by restructuring the reference materials that are fundamental to our lives. I think this is the challenge—the gauntlet—of the Information Age.

The following is the introduction to *Understanding USA*, which explains my passion and mission in doing this work:

> *The simple basic questions in the minds of the American people are easily, readily, and clearly answerable. It is our right to question and get answers.*
>
> *This book is a celebration and a visual demonstration of questions and answers leading to understanding.*
>
> *This book demonstrates the power inherent in understanding and the notion that understanding is power.*
>
> *In 1975 I began preparing for a gathering of 5,000 architects in Philadelphia the following year to coincide with the 200th anniversary of the founding of the United States in that same city.*
>
> *As national chairman of the AIA convocation, I entitled it the Architecture of Information and began to call myself an Information Architect.*

This field is a three-way marriage among the information technology corporations, the talent of great American graphic designers, and the abilities of researchers and librarians to focus on making the complex clear.

Now in the year 2000, the focus of this book is on the power of understanding. I hope readers will develop their own intricate road maps of follow-up questions to address our leaders, would-be leaders, each other, parents, friends, and children.

The word "public" shares the same root as publication. So it is fitting to publish this book for the public. The idea has been part of my recurring vocabulary every four years over the past twelve years. Circumstances happily conspired to put off its birth until now—the millennium year.

THE RIGHT TO COPY

UnderstandingUSA isn't copyrighted, either. Anyone can download chapters free from the Web site. On the same page is a link to sites where people can *buy* the book.

This presents an interesting ethical and business model. We are giving the product away for free and telling customers where to go to pay for it.

One of the biggest questions unanswered today in the communication industry is copyright.

The ability to copy—the proliferation of the technology of copying—has turned the nature of copyrights on its head. The whole notion of copyright is threatened when you, number one, can copy everything and, number two, are faced with so much which is available that can be copied.

In 1976, I wrote a fable where the laws of copyright are changed to the right to copy. It recognized that every good idea should be a public idea. The only thing that should be copyrighted are bad ideas. We should be protecting the flow of bad ideas.

Even if you can't find a source of demonstrable bias, allow yourself some degree of skepticism about the results as long as there is a possibility of bias somewhere. There always is.

– Darryl Huff
How to Lie with Statistics

Don't worry about people stealing your ideas. If your ideas are any good, you'll have to ram them down people's throats.

– Howard Aiken

Anybody interested in *UnderstandingUSA* will not download 320 pages and print them in color because it would cost them more to print out than to buy the book, which only costs $25. People joke that the inkjet toner cartridge manufacturers are leading the right-to-copy revolution. If you just want one spread, then it's better to download it. Besides, maybe you'll like it and go back for more or recommend it to a friend who will buy the book for all of his or her friends. That's why grocery stores give away free samples.

We are at the primitive stages of print on demand. Barnes & Noble has a bookstore that doesn't just sell books, it publishes them. It has launched a division that mostly republishes out-of-print books, although it will do some first-runs as well. The company is proceeding gingerly, so they don't get publishers out of joint.

ANSWERING QUESTIONS EQUALS USABILITY

Your customers may know about toothpaste, but have no idea why yours is better than the one they have at home. But what if your product is more complicated than toothpaste? Someone who knows nothing about your product may not even know where to begin asking questions. You must find the question for them. Let's say you owned a camera shop. How do you explain to a novice customer what an f-stop is, if that customer has never held a camera? Can you explain it in such a way as to allow your customer to understand the concept?

Most readers and viewers get interested in reading or viewing because they may know the answer to one of the questions, but don't know the rest. That is what draws people into *UnderstandingUSA*. They might want to know that the U.S. Department of Defense spent $48.9 billion on weapons procurement in 1999, but they also might be drawn in to find out how many weapons you could buy for that amount.

20TH CENTURY CIVILIAN WAR CASUALTIES BY COUNTRY by Kit Hinrichs (*UUSA*)

A chillingly graphic visual
presentation of the horrors of
war by Kit Hinrichs from his section
of *Understanding USA*.

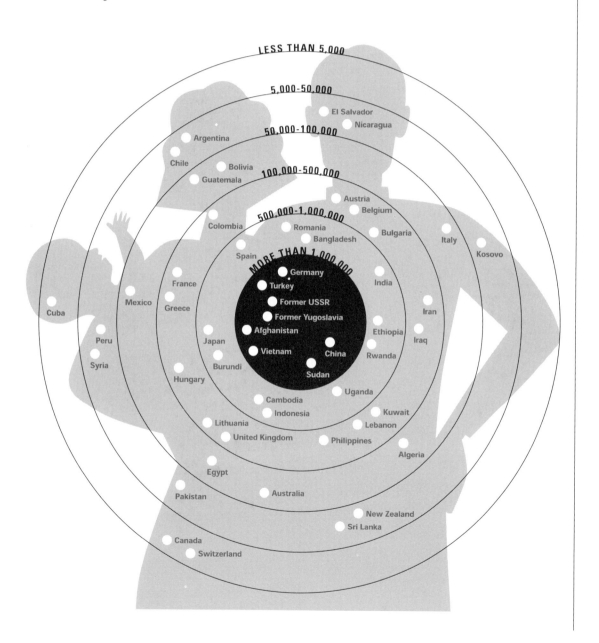

POPULATION DISTRIBUTION by Agnew Moyer Smith (*UUSA*)

Agnew Moyer Smith created this population distribution map by using 1990 U.S. Census figures loaded into MapInfo GIS (geographic information system) to produce a grayscale image, which was converted into a 3D model with FormZ, cleaned up in Adobe Photoshop, and finally overlaid with state boundaries and city labels with Adobe Illustrator.

The population of the United States is not distributed evenly. Instead, we tend to bunch up in communities, leaving the spaces in between more sparsely inhabited. Most Americans live in or near cities; today 53 percent live in the 20 largest cities. 75 percent of all Americans live in metropolitan areas.

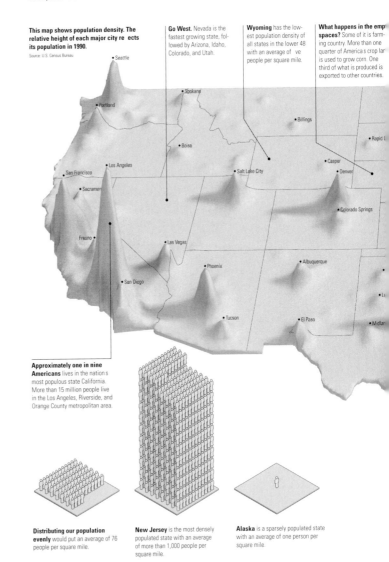

This map shows population density. The relative height of each major city re ects its population in 1990.
Source: U.S. Census Bureau

Go West. Nevada is the fastest growing state, followed by Arizona, Idaho, Colorado, and Utah.

Wyoming has the lowest population density of all states in the lower 48 with an average of ve people per square mile.

What happens in the emp spaces? Some of it is farming country. More than one quarter of America s crop lar is used to grow corn. One third of what is produced is exported to other countries.

Approximately one in nine Americans lives in the nation s most populous state California. More than 15 million people live in the Los Angeles, Riverside, and Orange County metropolitan area.

Distributing our population evenly would put an average of 76 people per square mile.

New Jersey is the most densely populated state with an average of more than 1,000 people per square mile.

Alaska is a sparsely populated state with an average of one person per square mile.

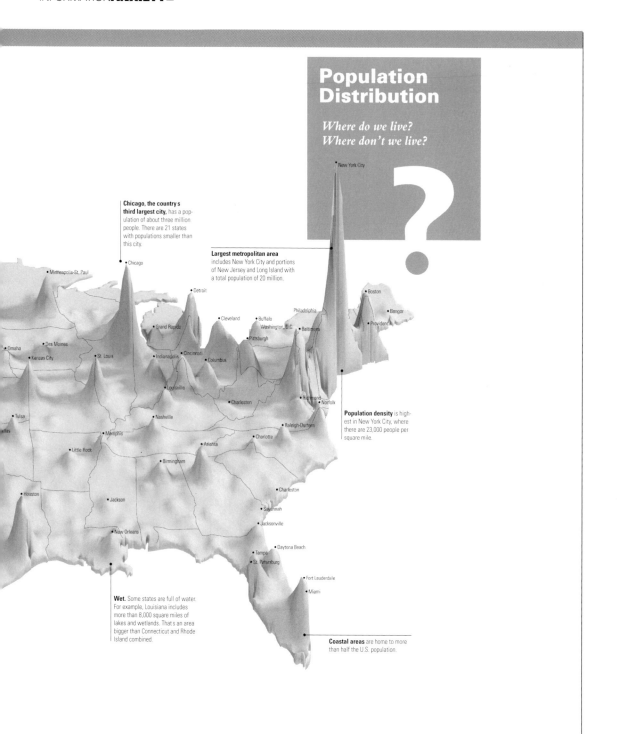

Population Distribution

Where do we live?
Where don't we live?

Chicago, the country's third largest city, has a population of about three million people. There are 21 states with populations smaller than this city.

Largest metropolitan area includes New York City and portions of New Jersey and Long Island with a total population of 20 million.

Population density is highest in New York City, where there are 23,000 people per square mile.

Wet. Some states are full of water. For example, Louisiana includes more than 8,000 square miles of lakes and wetlands. That's an area bigger than Connecticut and Rhode Island combined.

Coastal areas are home to more than half the U.S. population.

New York City
Chicago
Minneapolis-St. Paul
Detroit
Boston
Bangor
Cleveland
Buffalo
Philadelphia
Grand Rapids
Washington, D.C.
Providence
Pittsburgh
Baltimore
Des Moines
Omaha
St. Louis
Indianapolis
Cincinnati
Columbus
Kansas City
Louisville
Richmond
Norfolk
Charleston
Tulsa
Nashville
Dallas
Memphis
Raleigh-Durham
Little Rock
Charlotte
Atlanta
Birmingham
Houston
Charleston
Jackson
Savannah
Jacksonville
New Orleans
Tampa
Daytona Beach
St. Petersburg
Fort Lauderdale
Miami

BECOMING PRESIDENT by Agnew Moyer Smith (*UUSA*)

The Presidential election metaphor of going up the stairs shows it to be a difficult but somewhat orderly task, which requires using many people (even the inclusion of a dog). You can see yourself in the climb. Think about the effect of describing this process in words—it would be boring, and wouldn't leave you with a residual mental map.

One step at a time.
Reaching the White House is a long trip. It may take years. Basically, you've got to convince millions of voters that you know how to run a big, rambunctious country like the United States.
Source: Larry Elowitz, *Introduction to Government*, 1992

This list highlights some of the key steps along the path to the presidency.

1 Raise a few million. To demonstrate that you have broad national appeal, you've got to raise at least $5,000 from small contributors (contributions of $250 or less) in at least 20 different states—that's $100,000 and it's the bare minimum to get started as a candidate. You'll need every penny.

2 Take a stand that will appeal to both the public and people who are active in your political party.

3 Hire some help. Get a handler to make you look good. Professionals are available to help you package yourself so that you'll have maximum appeal. Hire a spin-doctor to package you for the media and help you put the most positive spin on everything that happens. It's vital that you seem credible and attractive to the print and broadcast media. Special consultants can help.

4 Declare your candidacy early enough to become a household name before the first primary. Some candidates now become visible more than 15 months before Election Day.

5 Buy opinion polls to find out what the public thinks of you, your issues, and your opponents. Make changes to increase your appeal.

6 Keep good records. You've got to be able to show where all your campaign contributions came from if you expect to receive matching federal campaign funds. Each candidate must turn in periodic reports to the Federal Election Commission to detail both income and expenditures.

7 Win in a straw poll. Straw polls are trial elections that state parties use for fund-raising and publicity. The results of these elections don't count, but if you make a good showing, you'll get lots of positive publicity. The Iowa caucus is typically the first and most visible straw poll.

8 Eat rubber chicken. Fund-raising dinners will nourish your campaign. Get out and meet people. Impress them with your wit and wisdom. Listen to their concerns.

9 Distinguish yourself from your same-party opponents. Until you emerge as your party's chosen candidate, you've got to flaunt your issues. Separate yourself from the herd. Later you can move to the middle of the road.

10 Win some state primaries to show your voter appeal. A good showing is vital to financial support. The New Hampshire primary is the first and the most visible. It's tiny, but the press loves to cover it. In recent years, it is rare for a candidate to become president without first winning in New Hampshire. In fact, in the last 40 years only Bill Clinton did not carry the New Hampshire primary.

11 Cash Uncle Sam's check. Candidates who receive many small contributions from many people qualify for matching federal funds. The money keeps coming until you gain less than 10 percent of the popular vote in two consecutive primaries and fail to win 20 percent in a subsequent primary.

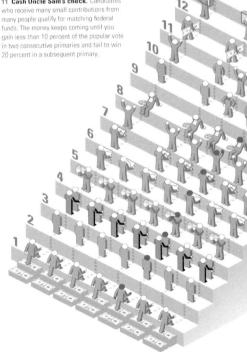

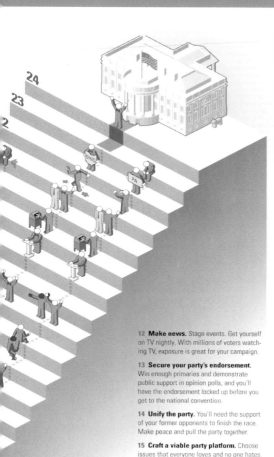

Becoming President

How do you get to the White House?

?

12 Make news. Stage events. Get yourself on TV nightly. With millions of voters watching TV, exposure is great for your campaign.

13 Secure your party's endorsement. Win enough primaries and demonstrate public support in opinion polls, and you'll have the endorsement locked up before you get to the national convention.

14 Unify the party. You'll need the support of your former opponents to finish the race. Make peace and pull the party together.

15 Craft a viable party platform. Choose issues that everyone loves and no one hates. It's harder than it sounds. Be prepared to make some compromises. Move to the middle of the road. Politically, Americans are largely similar. No extreme candidate can win. If you supported extreme positions to win attention early in the campaign, it's time to shift to a more moderate position. Make exciting promises.

16 Choose a running mate who can pull in extra votes, level out platform imbalances, and keep feet out of mouth.

17 Escape mainstream media. Find ways to talk directly to the voters. Appear on MTV or a talk show to avoid distortion of your ideas by news commentators or editors.

18 Debate. Demonstrate your ability to think on your feet and show voters that you are fit to be a president.

19 Get out the vote any way you can. Stimulate volunteer efforts. Mailings, phone calls, and ads are expensive. And priceless. Meet the voters face to face. Do it while the cameras are rolling.

20 Return favors. Support your party's local candidates loyally if you expect party support to keep you afloat. Visit the cities and states where local elections are close to give your party's candidates a boost. Help them and they'll help you.

21 Sling mud but wear Teflon. Disparage your opponent's record and values carefully. Negative campaigning can backfire. Be prepared to counter low blows directed your way.

22 Target swing states. Don't waste time in states where you're likely to lose or where you have a strong lead. Go to the undecided states where electoral votes are plentiful and hit hard.

23 Don't stop running until the last vote is cast. Your official presidential campaign ends on Election Day—the Tuesday after the first Monday in November. Don't plan any time off until the race is over.

24 Get to work. The race was the easy part. Now it's time to make good on your promises so that four years from now, you can win the race all over again.

FEDERAL INCOME/FEDERAL EXPENSES by Nigel Holmes (*UUSA*)

Nigel Holmes illustrates clearly here, based on research by **Meredith Bagby**, Federal income and spending.

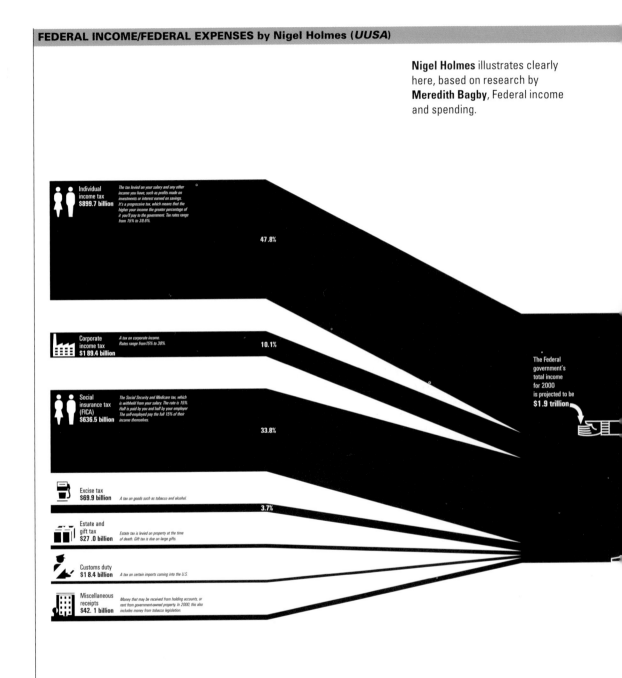

Individual income tax
$899.7 billion
The tax levied on your salary and any other income you have, such as profits made on investments or interest earned on savings. It's a progressive tax, which means that the higher your income the greater percentage of it you'll pay to the government. Tax rates range from 15% to 39.6%.

47.8%

Corporate income tax
$189.4 billion
A tax on corporate income. Rates range from 15% to 38%.

10.1%

Social insurance tax (FICA)
$636.5 billion
The Social Security and Medicare tax, which is withheld from your salary. The rate is 15%. Half is paid by you and half by your employer. The self-employed pay the full 15% of their income themselves.

33.8%

Excise tax
$69.9 billion
A tax on goods such as tobacco and alcohol.

3.7%

Estate and gift tax
$27.0 billion
Estate tax is levied on property at the time of death. Gift tax is due on large gifts.

Customs duty
$18.4 billion
A tax on certain imports coming into the U.S.

Miscellaneous receipts
$42.1 billion
Money that may be received from holding accounts, or rent from government-owned property. In 2000, this also includes money from tobacco legislation.

The Federal government's total income for 2000 is projected to be **$1.9 trillion.**

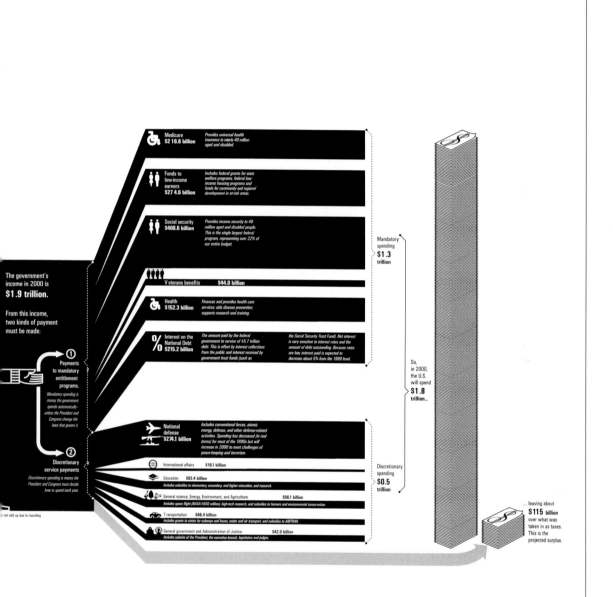

The government's income in 2000 is **$1.9 trillion.**

From this income, two kinds of payment must be made:

① Payments to mandatory entitlement programs.

Mandatory spending is money the government spends automatically—unless the President and Congress change the laws that govern it.

② Discretionary service payments

Discretionary spending is money the President and Congress must decide how to spend each year.

... may not add up due to rounding

Medicare
$2 16.6 billion
Provides universal health insurance to nearly 40 million aged and disabled.

Funds to low-income earners
$27 4.6 billion
Includes federal grants for state welfare programs, federal low income housing programs and funds for community and regional development in at-risk areas.

Social security
$408.6 billion
Provides income security to 48 million aged and disabled people. This is the single largest federal program, representing over 22% of our entire budget.

Veterans benefits   **$44.0 billion**

Health
$152.3 billion
Finances and provides health care services; aids disease prevention; supports research and training.

% Interest on the National Debt
$215.2 billion
The amount paid by the federal government to service of $5.7 trillion debt. This is offset by interest collections from the public and interest received by government trust funds (such as *the Social Security Trust Fund). Net interest is very sensitive to interest rates and the amount of debt outstanding. Because rates are low, interest paid is expected to decrease about 5% from the 1999 level.*

National defense
$274.1 billion
Includes conventional forces, atomic energy, defense, and other defense-related activities. Spending has decreased (in real terms) for most of the 1990s but will increase in 2000 to meet challenges of peace-keeping and terrorism.

International affairs   **$16.1 billion**

Education   **$63.4 billion**
Includes subsidies to elementary, secondary, and higher education, and research.

General science, Energy, Environment, and Agriculture   **$56.1 billion**
Includes space flight (NASA $650 million), high-tech research, and subsidies to farmers and environmental conservation.

Transportation   **$46.4 billion**
Includes grants to states for subways and buses, water and air transport, and subsidies to AMTRAK.

General government and Administration of Justice   **$42.0 billion**
Includes salaries of the President, the executive branch, legislators and judges.

Mandatory spending
$1.3 trillion

Discretionary spending
$0.5 trillion

So, in 2000, the U.S. will spend
$1.8 trillion...

... leaving about
$115 billion over what was taken in as taxes. This is the projected surplus.

THE UBIQUITOUS QUESTION

We find questions everywhere. There's a wonderful site called howstuffworks.com that is all about answering questions. It has a "Question Archive" with questions organized by category, by chronology, and by popularity.

Top 20 Questions

1. The Year 2038 problem?
2. What does WD-40 mean?
3. What causes flatulence?
4. How do light sabers work?
5. How do silencers work?
6. How do jake brakes work?
7. What does 10W30 mean?
8. What are MP3 files?
9. How does root beer work?
10. Is flour inflammable?
11. What is a light year?
12. What is the fastest computer?
13. Will adding more RAM make a computer faster?
14. What is the difference between sites that do and don't require the "www" in the URL?
15. What do they put in hot dogs?
16. How does a DVD work?
17. What do the error messages "fatal exception error," "invalid page fault," and "illegal operation" mean?
18. How does a Lava lamp work?
19. How do Internet cookies work?
20. How do traffic lights detect that a car is waiting?

Curious? Visit the site howstuffworks.com for answers.

The creator of *How Stuff Works* is **Marshall Brain**. Marshall is the author of 10 books (including his most popular—*The Teenager's Guide to the Real World*), and is nationally recognized for his ability to communicate complex ideas clearly. Brain formerly taught in the Computer Science Department at North Carolina State University.

We have learned the answers, all the answers: it is the question that we do not know.

– Archibald MacLeish,
The Hamlet of A. Macleish

8 FINDING THINGS

M ost things can be found in context with a map. A map provides people with the means to share in the perceptions of others. It is a pattern made understandable; it is a rigorous, accountable form that follows implicit principles, rules, and measures.

Maps provide the comfort of knowing in that they orient us to the reality of place. They enable us to make comparisons between places, and they tell us where we are in the grand scheme. Walking through the confusing jumble of streets and alleyways that make up the *souk* (marketplace) in Fez, Morocco, I felt the necessity to know where I was in relation to the market as a whole, to make a mental map. If I had been following a guide, I would never have felt a sense of the place. When you are always a passenger in a car, you are less likely to learn your way around. To comprehend something yourself, you have to have the impetus to make it understandable.

Throughout history, maps have always been equated with power, whether they depicted hunting grounds, trade routes, military sites, or buried treasure.

The South Sea Islanders made maps with shells and twigs. The twigs represented ocean currents and the shells denoted islands. These maps gave them mobility.

Maps have been associated with the unknown and mysterious. They beckon the spirit of adventure in all of us. They distill the environment, giving us just what we need to know to explore new territory.

The mapping of the vast territory known as cyberspace has begun in earnest. Cyberspace maps are being produced by geographers, cartographers, artists and computer scientists. They range from glorious depictions of globe-spanning communications networks to maps of Web information.

Many have no geographical references, instead turning to nature, the cosmos or neuroscience for spatial models. They stretch the definition of a map in their effort to capture, sometimes fancifully, what is sometimes referred to as the "common mental geography" that lies beyond computer screens.

– Pamela LiCalzi O'Connell
"Beyond Geography: Mapping Unknowns of Cyberspace"
New York Times (9/30/00)

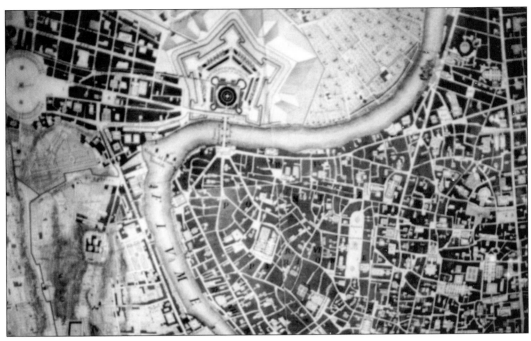

Detail from Nolli's map of Rome

I have always loved maps, and one map in particular—**Giovanni Battista Nolli**'s 1748 map of Rome, La Nuova Topografia di Roma. A few years ago I was able to find a copy of this large, beautifully engraved map, which I now keep in a secondary office that I use for meetings.

While I was trained as an architect, my fascination with maps has shaped my career. I talked my way onto the team that surveyed the Mayan ruins at Tikal, and learned how to survey in the process. My first book presented comparative topographic maps of world cities. My *Access* guides included maps of cities organized by neighborhoods. My *USAtlas* was a road atlas of the United States at a uniform scale designed to show a reasonable day's drive, with the states organized geographically, rather than alphabetically.

MAPS AS METAPHORS

Most people have a fairly limited concept of a map as a depiction of a particular geographic location. To find our way through information, we also rely on maps that will tell us where we are in relation to the information, give us a sense of perspective, and enable us to make comparisons between information.

Maps can take a myriad of forms. A CAT scan is a map of the human body. A grocery list is a map of a trip to the grocery store. A chart of a company's production over a year maps its output. A loan application is a map showing the route from your actual to your desired financial status. You can map ideas and concepts as well as physical places.

Maps enable us to exchange information, whether about Benares or building codes. Maps are virtually synonymous with reference information in that we use them to direct or influence the course we follow in life. The principles of photosynthesis are reference information or maps to a botanist, but not to someone who doesn't own a plant. Maps are the metaphoric means by which we can understand and act upon information from outside sources. A map by definition must per-form, whether it is a multi-million dollar, four-color production of the National Weather Service, or two cans of beer on a counter showing the relationship of a friend's new house to his old one.

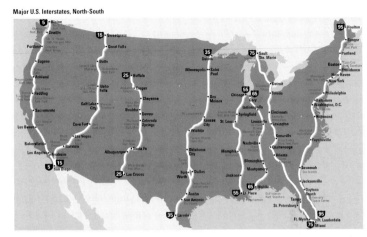

Major U.S. Interstates, North-South

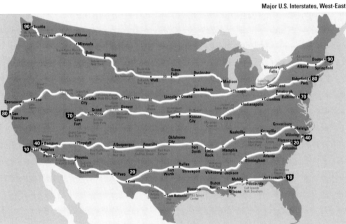

Major U.S. Interstates, West-East

North-South and East-West U.S. Interstate maps from *USAtlas*. Many people today might not realize that the U.S. interstate system was designed and built during the Cold War to evacuate U.S. cities in the event of a nuclear war.

CONCEPT MAP OF SEARCHING THE INTERNET by Hugh Dubberly

A particularly useful map would be a good map of the Internet, which continually expands and extends beyond anyone's ability to keep up. In 1995, Hugh Dubberly created a concept map of the Internet (shown in Clement Mok's excellent book, *Designing Business*.) Later, working with Hugh, Matt Leacock created this map of Internet search.

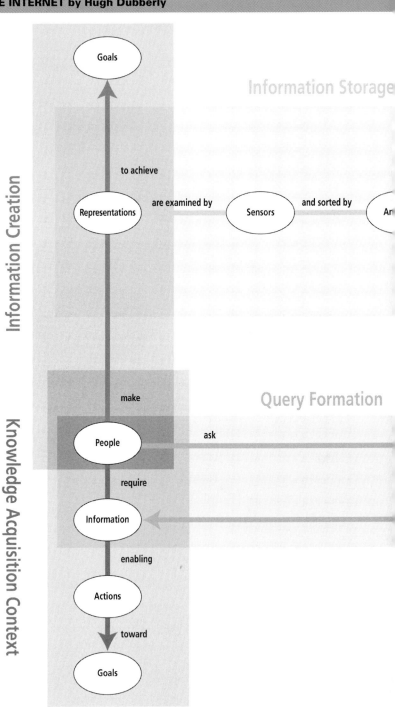

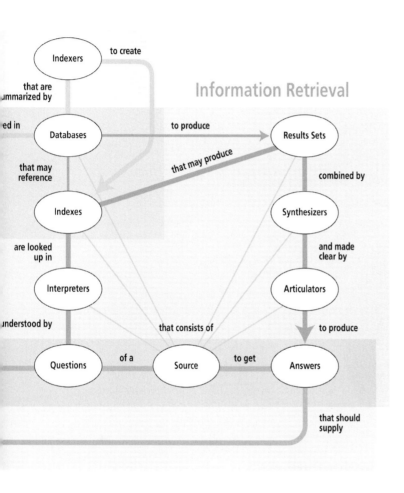

Information Retrieval

Indexers — to create

that are summarized by

 summarized by

ed in

Databases — to produce → Results Sets

that may produce

that may reference

combined by

Indexes

Synthesizers

are looked up in

and made clear by

Interpreters

Articulators

understood by   that consists of   to produce

Questions — of a — Source — to get — Answers

that should supply

nderstanding Internet Search
January 2000

gned by Matt Leacock
ch Core Concept Map, version 1.5

TYPES OF INFORMATION: THE FIVE RINGS

We are all surrounded by information that operates at varying degrees of immediacy to our lives. These degrees can be roughly divided into five rings, although what constitutes information on one level for one person may operate on another level for someone else. The rings radiate from the most personal information that is essential for our physical survival to the most abstract form of information that encompasses our personal myths, cultural development, and sociological perspective.

The first ring is internal information. This consists of the messages that run our internal systems and enable our bodies to function. Here, information takes the form of cerebral messages. We have perhaps the least control over this level of information, but we are the most affected by it.

The second ring is conversational information. It is the formal and informal exchanges and conversations that we have with the people around us—be they friends, relatives, coworkers, strangers in checkout lines, or clients in business meetings. Conversation is a prominent source of information, although we tend to play down or ignore its role, perhaps because of the informality of its nature. Yet this is the source of information over which we have the most control, both as givers and receivers of information.

The third ring is reference information. This is where we turn for the information that runs the systems of our world—science and technology—and, more immediately, the reference materials to which we turn in our own lives. Reference information can be anything from a textbook on quantum physics to the telephone book or dictionary.

The fourth ring is news information. This encompasses current events—the information that is transmitted via the media about people, places, and events that may not directly affect our lives, but can influence our vision of the world.

Cultural Information

News Information

Reference Information

Conversational Information

Internal Information

The fifth ring is cultural information, the least quantifiable form. It encompasses history, philosophy, and the arts, any expression that represents an attempt to understand and come to terms with our civilization. Information garnered from other rings is incorporated here to build the body of information that determines our own attitudes and beliefs, as well as the nature of our society as a whole.

FLYING THROUGH INFORMATION

The late **Muriel Cooper**, who founded and ran the Visual Language Workshop at the MIT Media Lab, made a wonderful presentation with **David Small**, one of her students, at my **TED**5 conference in 1994. Although I've been fascinated with information, and finding my way through information my entire life, until I saw Muriel's final work with the Visual Language Workshop, I had never experienced the dream of flying through information.

I dedicated my book *Information Architects* to Muriel:

> *The wings of triumph and aura of discovery were all around Muriel at the **TED5** Conference. She worked with David Small for three days to assemble together the premiere and single live incident of a presentation which she—hesitantly at first and then with noticeable joy—showed to the extraordinary audience of that conference. It changed forever the visual paradigm of information for all who saw the presentation. As I came on the stage—holding back the tears of joy that come when you've seen something absolutely magnificent, I said "Muriel, I believe we've all had dreams of flying and here you've allowed us to make those dreams a reality as we were flying through information."*

The Visual Language Workshop developed a number of powerful concepts and prototypes, but eventually without Muriel's direction, and with the evolution of research at the Media Lab, was disbanded. **John Maeda**'s Aesthetics & Computation Group (ACG) continues to work on some similar projects. **Ben Fry**, a member of ACG, has been working on the Valence project, which visualizes text in a three dimensional space. On the following two spreads he has produced visualizations of one of the chapters of this book.

See the Visual Language Workshop archive at: **http://vlw.www.media. mit.edu/groups/vlw/**

VISUALIZING TEXT IN A THREE DIMENSIONAL SPACE by Ben Fry

Still images taken from Valence, a software experiment based on "organic information visualization." The pictures here and on the next two pages show different instances in time as the visualization progressively reads chapter 16, with each new word being added into the space, and competing with the other words for more prominent visual positions based on their frequency of use.

The lines connect words that are found adjacent to one another in the text.

For more information, see: http://acg.media.mit.edu/people/fry/valence

Benjamin Fry
MIT Media Laboratory/
Aesthetics & Computation Group

© 1998-2000 MIT

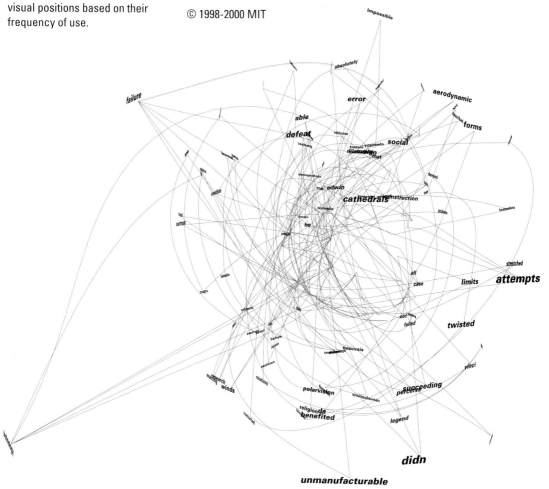

VISUALIZING TEXT IN A THREE DIMENSIONAL SPACE by Ben Fry

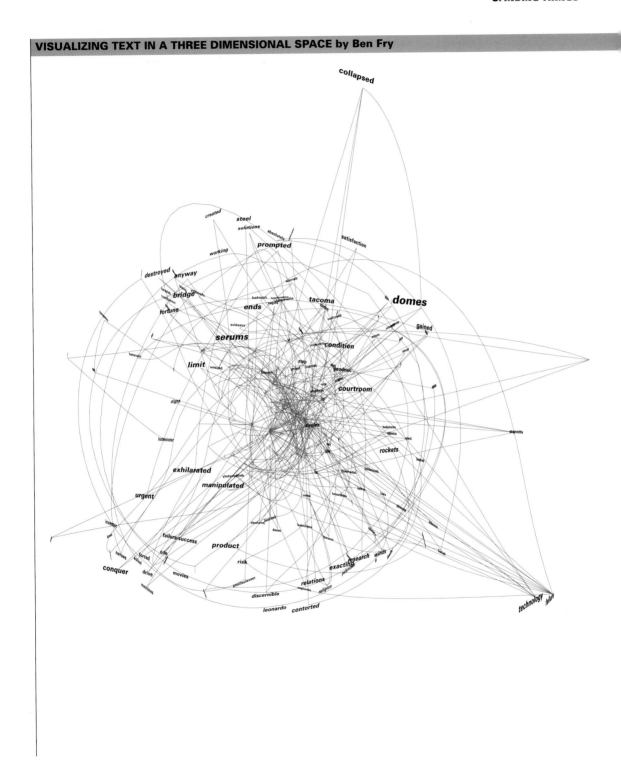

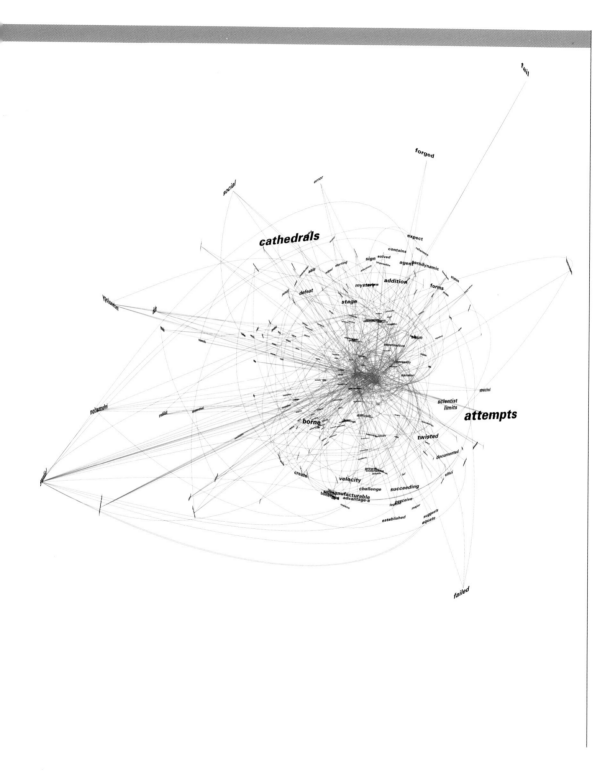

SEE & GO MANIFESTO by Ramana Rao

Some time ago, the graphical user interface became known as the point and click interface. The point being simplicity. Point and click, anybody can do it, but point and click, point and click, point and click, all day long and you have… Windows 95. It would be like calling the file cabinet a pull and grab device, but the file cabinet isn't a device for pulling and grabbing, but rather for storing information.

Point and click, the mechanics, we're being dragged into the machine. The graphical interface is hardly graphical any more; it's become the mechanical, textual, reading interface. It requires going to see if you want to be there. Would you go to India just to see if you wanted to be there?

We can do better.

How can we allow users to attend to the truly important? The problem is not so difficult as it might appear. It is in fact natural for us humans to process large amounts of information. Think of the number of bits we dealt with in the jungle long ago or on the streets of Manhattan today. It was necessary to take in lots of information and select the important for us to survive as a species. We can take advantage of great human skill thus evolved in nature.

Let us design around what we were before we were born. Let us design around skills like seeing red or tracking objects as they move, detecting edges and discontinuities, comparing shapes, noticing motion or changes of light.

> *"Let us design around what we were before we were born. Let us design around skills like seeing red or tracking objects as they move, detecting edges and discontinuities, comparing shapes, noticing motion or changes of light."*

Surround point and click, with see and go. Point and click becomes simply the snap of the finger that says yes, let's go. But first you would have seen that you wanted to be there.

We can achieve in the world of the mouse something as rich and natural as the physical office and maybe beyond. To better something already of great wonder, it is best to appreciate the wonder so its values may be retained, and then to take on the power afforded in the new. The computational tools we have built for interacting with information are more like the file cabinet, a great tool, but not as wondrous as the office that surrounds and includes it. It is no surprise that piles appear in offices; among other reasons, we fear that putting documents into the file cabinet, we will never find them again.

Even as we attend to the great values we must retain, we can aspire to transcend. We have something magical in this stuff called computation, and in striving to use it, we will articulate the laws of a magical realism. And those laws will be consistent with the natural laws of ancient and modern realities.

We builders of interactive tools have learned much on how to do this over the last dozen years of the journey. Many a "wide widget"— new intensely graphical components that scale to large amounts of information—have we built that embody our knowledge.

Seven principles illuminate the path

1. Put graphics first

Seeing graphics is fundamentally different from reading text. If one person stands up in an audience of say a thousand people, I can instantly see him. I can decide whether the event is important, and thus, whether to attend or not. If 1,000 numbers are displayed on a screen, the numbers (like text) require a great deal of mental effort to process and understand. Turn the numbers into a thousand tiny bars and you can see instantly for example that some value sticks out. Or you can see the general distribution of values, or once sorted, you can compare the shape of the distribution to other distributions.

Putting graphics first in a sensible arrangement allows the user to see before going. Furthermore,

Reprinted from "Reflections," *Interactions*, Sept/Oct 1999, © ACM graphical representations can be packed more densely then text, so much more information can be processed in parallel. Effective use of graphical marks—of varying color, light level, texture, shape, size, iconography, so on—and linking or arranging the marks in space allows a large number of objects and relationships to be quickly assimilated. So long as graphical properties that are perceived easily by humans are mapped onto underlying attributes of the information that are relevant to the task at hand, then the human will be able to decide when and on what to attend.

2. Use the "grain of the wood"

Information has inherent structure, a grain. Trees, tables, time, documents, calendars, these are the spines that organize information. By designing tools based on such canonical information structures, they become potentially applicable in a wide range of situations.

Furthermore, these underlying structures are a resource for organizing the interaction in ways that reduce needless mechanical overhead. By spinning, shaking, sorting, and generally rearranging according to the inherent shape of the information, the interaction is at the level of the semantics of the information and thus becomes coherent and meaningful. The focus becomes the information rather than the tool through which we are viewing the information.

3. Provide focus & context

Even using rapidly perceived and denser visual representation, there is still a fundamental limitation on available screen space. There is a trade-off between showing a lot about a little and a little about a lot. One strategy for dealing with this is to switch between overviews (a little about a lot) and more detailed views like a page view (a lot about a little). However, the page view is awful when you want to read a map, and the map is awful if you really want to read.

An alternative strategy is based on seeing that these two types of view really form a continuum. In fact, many well-designed information layouts including magazine layouts and better designed portal Web pages combine the two in various ways. We can show an integrated view that shows a lot about some of the information (focus) amidst a little about much more (context). The focus becomes the area of current attention, and the context provides, well, context for interpreting the current focus as well as the resource for navigating and for changing attention.

4. Animate the transitions

Animating the transitions between one arrangement of the information and another allows the user to connect the before and the after. In well-designed transitions, the user will not wonder what is going on. No conscious effort is spent

since our skills of object tracking and constancy fuse the motion into a coherent, even as it is a magical, reality.

Animating the changes of focus in a wide widget organized by an information spine, in particular, reinforces the coherence of the interactive experience. Animated transitions are another example of exploiting our perceptual skills. Consider the ability of the eye/brain to fuse a series of images together to maintain a sense of object constancy when the images are delivered quickly enough. From our understanding of visual cognition, a speed of roughly 50-100 milliseconds per frame is fast enough.

5. Create stable and consistent spaces

The desktop metaphor from its beginning was based on exploiting our spatial memory and thus the principle of stable and consistent spaces. Arranging information spatially in a way that is consistent across time and across manipulations allows users to improve their performance over time. Because of the intensely dynamic rearrangement of objects and space in a wide widget, this principle requires particular attention. As various warping techniques are used to achieve focus and context, much of the challenge becomes figuring out how to preserve some interpretation of the overall space, and the current arrangement of it.

SEE & GO MANIFESTO by Ramana Rao

Preserving the spatial relationship between an object and some absolute location like a home or root object allows a user to get back to objects from a top or central location. Or alternatively, preserving the relationship between an object and local relatives allows the users to use the widget to navigate relatively. For example, if children of an object are always to the right, then without even looking, a user can navigate down a hierarchy. These two modes of spatial preservation show that the tool can on one hand boost the user's ability to learn how to use the tool regardless of information collection, or on the other, learn how to navigate in a particular information collection.

In any case, spatial constants can lead to tools that achieve a form of bi-directional relationship between amount of knowledge and facility of navigation. Knowledge about the information can speed navigation, or conversely, navigating naturally yields knowledge about the information.

6. Favor interacting directly on the stuff

By supporting direct operations on rendered objects, a level of immediacy is achieved that supports an illusion of transparent interaction with the underlying information. One of the most prominent operations is a means of changing focus from one object to another. Pointing and clicking on objects to indicate interest and initiate changes of focus can eliminate the need for harder-to-perform interaction with distant scrollbars.

Other operations may align well with the structure of the information itself. The branches of a hierarchy or the rows and columns of a table are natural sub-collections to leverage in an interaction. Associating operations with locations that conventionally represent these sub-collections can enhance the fluidity and the memorability of the interaction.

7. Spotlight results of computation in the same space

Given a view of a whole information set, search hits (or items matching by any underlying computation) can be marked saliently so that a user can see where they are and how to get there. Because hits are shown in context, effects like clusters of hits, near-hits, and isolated hits are easily seen.

This is a sharp contrast to getting back a long list of scrollable textual items that must be read. Spotlighting reveals information about the effectiveness of the query, where in the site it might make sense to browse, and unusual hits that may be interesting. All of these revelations allow the user to make better decisions about further use of time.

A more subtle virtue of spotlighting is that it ties search to spatial and visual cues, which are quite persistent in our memories. Imagine searching for something by a name that you just happened to see today in the paper, say the name of a division on a corporate Web site. In a week or two, it is likely that you will have forgotten the name and thus would have lost the ability to search by name. However, had you seen the results spotlighted in a space, it is likely that you will remember that the matches were, say, down in the lower left corner and thereby be able to get back to those pages.

When these seven principles are embodied effectively in an interactive design, a new level of interface experience is achieved. See and go loops back, creating fluid cycles of seeing and going. Neither perceiving nor acting encroaches on the "think" that can now rest calmly between the see and the go. Alan Kay to Mark Weiser have invoked Flow & Wittgenstein. We forget what we are doing as we are doing it. And we blind men begin to see with our canes.

"When these seven principles are embodied effectively…a new level of interface experience is achieved.…Neither perceiving nor acting encroaches on the 'think' that can now rest calmly between the see and the go."

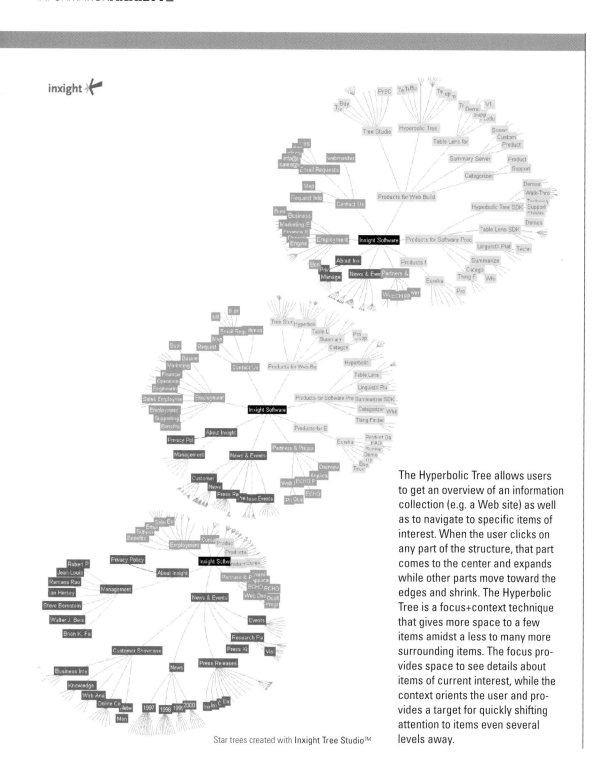

Star trees created with Inxight Tree Studio™

The Hyperbolic Tree allows users to get an overview of an information collection (e.g. a Web site) as well as to navigate to specific items of interest. When the user clicks on any part of the structure, that part comes to the center and expands while other parts move toward the edges and shrink. The Hyperbolic Tree is a focus+context technique that gives more space to a few items amidst a less to many more surrounding items. The focus provides space to see details about items of current interest, while the context orients the user and provides a target for quickly shifting attention to items even several levels away.

TOOLS FOR SEARCHING THE INTERNET

An intriguing part of **TED**8 in 1998 was a series of presentations on search engines and information interfaces. I also had **Walt Mossberg**, who writes the influential Personal Technology column in the *Wall Street Journal* interview **Ozzie Osborne** of IBM Speech Systems and **Janet Baker** of Dragon Systems, then talk about voice recognition technology. I told the audience that voice technology and search engines give you Star Trek. Of course, everyone is still working to improve and extend both of these technologies, but their promise is for simple and powerful access to information.

The cook-off of search engines included presentations by representatives of a number of search engines and related companies. We had a good representation of many of the major players and intriguing start-ups of the time.

Eric Brewer is the Chief Scientist & Co-Founder of Inktomi (www.hotbot.com).

Eliot Christian is a Computer Specialist with the US Geological Survey who has specialized in what is known as Global Information Locator Service (www.gils.org).

Bill Gross is the Chairman of idealab!, who was introducing a new search engine (www.goto.com).

Vinod Khosla is a Partner at Kleiner Perkins Caufield & Byers, the venture capitalists, and was on the board of Excite (www. excite.com).

Scott Kurnit is Chairman and CEO of About.com, which was then named The Mining Company (www.about.com).

Steve Larsen is Senior Vice President of Net Perceptions (www.netperceptions.com).

Max Metral is the Founder and Chief Technology Officer of PeoplePC; he was the Chief Technical Officer and a Founder of Firefly Networks, a software agent company begun by **Pattie Maes** and others at the MIT Media Lab.

Louis Monier is the Chief Technology Officer of BigVine, a barter site; he was a Senior Consulting Engineer at Digital Equipment, where AltaVista was developed (www.altavista.com).

Ramana Rao is Chief Technology Officer at Inxight Software, a spin-off of Xerox (www.inxight.com).

David Seuss is CEO of Northern Light Technology (www. northernlight.com).

Ben Shneiderman was until recently the Director of the Human-Computer Interaction Lab at the University of Maryland (www.cs.umd.edu/projects/hcil).

Lisa Strausfeld is principal of Information Art. She was Design Director and **Earl Rennison** was the Chief Technology Officer of Perspecta, another company that began with work at the MIT Media Lab.

STARTING WITH SEARCH ENGINES

Most search engines take users way beyond where they want to go. How many times have you gone to a Web site where you've entered your question and you get 1,500 hits or more of sites that could possibly be related to your topic? The hardest part about web searching is you've got to think like a search engine. How did the person who wrote that program decide to link up words and phrases? How did the organizations register with that search engine in order that their links would come up first? How do you sort through the advertising links to get to the information you really need?

Some of the metasearch web sites—Highway61, Dogpile, AltaVista, etc.—simply give you those interminable lists. And those lists aren't always complete; most search engines index only a fraction of the content on the web. According to an NEC Research Institute study of 11 search engines, Northern Light indexes one-sixth of the pages on the web, making it the most comprehensive search engine available. After Northern Light, the two most comprehensive search engines are AltaVista and Snap.

But even if those search engines do bring up one-sixth of the Internet, do you really want to wade through that much content? That's why Ask Jeeves has a unique place in the search engine universe. What Ask Jeeves does is help you discover the right question to ask, and it provides the appropriate information, information you may not have realized you really needed to know.

HOW DID TEA COME TO BE?

Its origin as a beverage is lost in antiquity, but Chinese legend provides an answer, saying that tea was discovered accidentally about 3000 B.C. by Shen Nong, the Divine Cultivator. Also credited with inventing agriculture and herbal medicine, he is honored as one of China's three mythical early sovereigns. One day leaves of the tea plant fell into water he was boiling outdoors. He liked the drink, found it to have medicinal value, and tea was born. Another legend says that as an experimental herbalist he sampled various kinds of plants to determine their individual effects. This boldness sometimes resulted in poisoning, and he used tea as an antidote.

– Kit Chow & Ione Kramer,
All The Tea In China

For example, I asked Jeeves what the price of tea was in China. Jeeves didn't give me what I wanted but gave me what I needed. Instead of the price of tea in China, Jeeves gave me a list of questions I could use to examine why I asked my question in the first place. Jeeves gave me the answers to my unasked questions.

Perhaps I really just wanted to know the price of tea in China so I could buy some. Jeeves pointed me to www.tealuxe.com with its question, Where can I buy tea online?

Jeeves asked, Where can I find information about tea in China? The answer was a beautiful article about the traditions of tea in China, kinds of tea, legends related to tea and how tea relates to the *I Ching*.

But the information Jeeves gave me with its questions didn't stop there. One of Jeeves' new questions was, Where can I get a quote for translation services? The answer there was bizbuyer.com. At bizbuyer.com, you can find translation services and a plethora of other business-to-business assistance, from printing to consulting. This would be especially helpful if you needed a consultant to help you import that tea from China.

You've got a topic of interest, and you begin combing search engines for sites related to your topic of choice. What is more horrible, getting 4,000,000 hits or only four? The assault of too much or too little information can be a deal killer. That creates Information Anxiety. We must make the transaction of and search for information via search engine easier. We must improve the design of search engines so that people can find what it is that they're looking for.

We have made some strides in this area. Log onto www.dogpile.com and you can experience a multi-engine, semi-parallel search interface. What does that mean? Simply put, the site automatically searches 20 plus search engines, three at a time for your subject of choice. Or go to www.google.com for the searches at warp speed. Or www.profusion.com and search Yahoo!, AltaVista, LookSmart, Netscape, Excite, web Crawler, InfoSeek, Lycos and Direct Hit for the best three choices, the fastest three or all results.

Or, if you own a Macintosh, they've already done this for you. Sherlock (Sherlock 2 if you use the latest operating system OS 9) automatically searches 12 major search engines for your request and provides links with short descriptions of each site. This across-the-board searching is called metasearching, and it can help users cover more ground in a shorter time span.

In fact, a study conducted by NPD New Media Services beginning in the Spring of 1997 and continuing into this year, shows that users might have to work at it, but they eventually find what they're looking for. Out of 33,000 respondents, almost 60 percent of users reported finding results most of the time while fewer than three percent reported never finding relevant sites.

And nearly 80 percent said they search the same site, using a different keyword search if they don't find the results they're seeking. Further, about 45 percent of those surveyed said they will enter multiple keywords when their second attempt fails. So users don't give up. The problem is that they have to work so hard to find the information they're seeking, and once they find it, they have to wade through scores of sites to find the helpful ones.

Yet the metasearch, although a step in the right direction, can cause information overload. Oftentimes, sites are repeated from search engine to search engine, and popular topics yield hundreds and even thousands of results. So how do you ensure that your web site will be displayed in the top ten results, where most users find the information they're looking for?

This problem begs another familiar question for today's information architects: How do we design for search engines? It's really a matter of process. Some tips from **Danny Sullivan** at www.searchenginewatch.com:

- **Pick strategic keywords.** Ask yourself how you think people will search for your web site or industry. Then choose a keyword for each page of your web site. Pick phrases of two or more words, and you'll have a better shot at success.

- **Next, position keywords.** Make sure your strategic keywords appear in the crucial locations on your site. The page title is the most important place to include keywords. Also place keywords high on the page (i.e. a headline or in the first paragraph).

- **Post relevant content.** Changing your page titles and adding meta tags is not necessarily going to help if the page has nothing to do with the topic. Your keywords need to be reflected in the page's content.

- **Avoid stumbling blocks.** Search engines may see the web the way someone using a very old browser might. Check and see if the search image reads image maps and frames, or the search engine may not index your site.

- **Submit your key pages.** Most search engines will index the other pages from your web site by following links from a page you submit to them. But sometimes they miss, so it's good to submit the top two or three pages that best summarize your site.

- **Verify and maintain your listing.** Check on your pages and ensure they get listed. Once they're listed, monitor your listing every week or two. Pages disappear from catalogs, links get screwy. You never know. Resubmit your pages if you spot trouble.

Also, remember that while search engines are a primary way people look for web sites, they are not the only way. People also find sites through word-of-mouth, traditional advertising, the traditional media, newsgroup postings, web directories and links from other sites. Oftentimes, these alternative forms are far more effective draws than are search engines.

BEYOND SEARCH ENGINES

Many people, as they became familiar with the Web, became comfortable with search engines like Altavista, or Hotbot, or directories like Yahoo or Lycos. The differences between pure search engines and directories of suggested Web links has become indistinct in many cases, as everyone tries to offer everything.

Then, there are specialized search engines, such as those with natural language queries, like Ask Jeeves. Other sites rely on human experts, like About.com, or the experts you can refer to at Brill's Contentville.

Some magazines post the entire content of each issue on-line, while other publishers are timid about allowing access to all their material. Some newspapers, like the *New York Times*, allow you complete access the day or week of publication, but then you have to pay to access archived issues. A few magazines (particularly those that have started more recently) provide free access to all issues online—such as *Wired*, *Business 2.0*, and *Fast Company*.

There are some free online magazines with impressively rich and varied original content, such as *Salon* and *The Atlantic Unbound*, but you have to wonder if they'll be able to afford to continue so ambitiously.

Currently, the greatest amount of both timely and extensively archived information is found on proprietary databases, such as Nexis. These tend to be rather expensive (especially when many people think they should be able to get everything free on the Web). These databases are incredible resources, but tend to be used most by journalists, professional researchers and graduate students. Less extensive resources include online encyclopedias, such as Britannica.

In terms of online information, perhaps the most exciting development is sites like Ebrary, which should launch this fall, with plans to provide free non-subscription browsing and content purchase on a page-by-page basis from a vast library of books, documents and magazines. The test of course, will be how extensive of a library they will be able to arrange to provide.

Finally, software agents are another method of setting searches in motion, perhaps most commonly for shopping online.

MAKING A GLOBAL INFORMATION LOCATOR SERVICE By Eliot Christian

Why is information so hard to find?

This is the Information Age. We ought to have easy ways to find all the information we need. In our daily lives we are constantly taking in and giving out information: a driver asks for directions, a shopper reads a package label, a mother seeks child care advice, a gardener compares pesticide data, an investor evaluates a company's performance. Most of the time, our information comes from sources we have used many times before. We know what we are doing; we know what we are getting.

Problems arise when we need information but we do not have trusted, familiar sources. We may be in a foreign country and dealing with a medical emergency. We may be new parents or exploring new careers. Or, a familiar information source moved to the Internet and we need to learn new ways to get what we need.

This is the essence of information discovery. We need information but we cannot just retrieve it. We do not know who might have it, where it might be, or how to ask for it. Now that information discovery is becoming essential in our daily lives, it just has to be made much easier.

The Internet is not a Library, yet

The Internet provides access to an amazing quantity of information. Internet-wide search services index hundreds of millions of web pages. However, people cannot discover what they need unless the information is somehow organized. One approach is to make a huge pile of all the pages and create a giant index. Many services also classify the pages in various and innovative ways. Yet, few of these

services today actually work with each other. Most Internet services have yet to agree on standards comparable to what libraries achieved many years ago.

Think about how a library helps people find information. Now imagine the Internet with many catalogs and indexes all working together to help us discover information. Anyone could create and operate such catalogs, as simply as we make a Web page. We could focus the catalogs on topics or places we know best, present information in our own language, and design for our choice of skill level. This next generation search strategy would encompass not only Web resources but catalogs and indexes of most of the world's libraries, atlases, directories, and databases. And, anyone who has used a library would be already familiar with how it all works.

The GILS Vision

A catch phrase for this next-generation search vision is the Global Information Locator Service (GILS). Basic standards and technologies for the GILS vision are already mature and deployed widely. The challenge now is to share the vision throughout our global information society.

The GILS vision originated in the context of global change research. We need complex and long-term data sources to understand issues such as climate change and loss of biological diversity. We need a wide array of environmental information from social, economic, and political domains. Formats and media range from field notebooks to genetic libraries to global satellite observations. Potential users include anyone from children to scientists to politicians, communicating in any language and

with diverse needs. In short, we need a true global information infrastructure, including easy-to-use and global tools for information discovery.

Happily, we do have models for this grand vision. Libraries, museums, and archives provide organized access to information far into the past. But, we also know what happens when information is not carefully organized and managed for accessibility over the long term. It is lost forever. Even now, we are losing important information that was on the Internet only a few years ago. Unless we embrace an information infrastructure vision that is long-term and global, the beginning of the 21st century may mark the time when societies begin to lose their memory.

GILS focuses on searching metadata. For example, a searcher may want information having a certain word in its title. The provider then searches only locator records that have metadata mapped to the concept of title. By virtue of this semantic mapping of search terms, just about any information search service can offer a high degree of interoperability.

A single search service can handle locator records that vary across format and language. Records may be distributed across the Internet or even within other catalogs, directories, and databases. To find my local grocery store, an intermediary search service can search across entries in a telephone database, maps in an atlas of my neighborhood, and an index of web pages. Metadata from these different locator records is then presented in esponse to my search request.

Semantic mapping and locator records together make for an elegant and powerful search service. However, a searcher also needs to know the specific set of search concepts actually supported. GILS-compliant search services always support a specific minimum set of search concepts. These concepts relate through semantic mapping to whatever locator metadata is available.

Search concepts in GILS are traditional bibliographic concepts from a long tradition of cataloging. About thirty years ago, bibliographic communities worldwide agreed on the Machine Readable Cataloging standard. They have also created mechanisms to search library catalogs on the Internet. Because GILS adopts its search strategy from these mechanisms, GILS interoperability encompasses the accumulated knowledge represented in many millions of bibliographic records worldwide.

GILS gives a minimum set of common concepts, but there is no limit to extending the interoperability. An information community focused on popular music can supplement their GILS support with online lyrics and directories of artists and events. Searchers may access a Web gateway to search among these various resources. The gateway uses GILS to extend the community's information to related communities and libraries. The community might also extend the gateway with a new search-by-sound feature. This feature would simply co-exist with the GILS interoperability. Later, the community might make this new feature interoperable across communities as well. With GILS as a solid foundation, communities can build whatever interoperability they need.

Organizing an Information Community

Information communities understand and organize their own information. These organizations are in the best position to manage their information over the long term. Yet, intermediaries and secondary users have needs, too. They need to find information across communities.

GILS resolves this conflict. For example, one collection may have hundreds of bibliographic records with precise metadata. Another collection may have thousands of machine-generated Web page metadata that is much less precise. Using GILS, there is no need to dumb-down the more precise metadata to support cross-domain searches.

Using GILS

For information users, GILS provides a standard way to find information resources by their characteristics. That information resource may be a specific document, an information service, a collection of information, or an entire organization. Having a common standard allows searchers to find information across institutions separated by geography, charter, focus, or government. Because GILS adopted standard bibliographic concepts, anyone who understands a book citation or a library catalog already knows the concepts used in GILS.

It is important to understand that GILS defines a search service only at the level of computer to computer communication. The design of user interfaces for searching is outside the scope of GILS and there are no constraints on presenting the service to searchers. GILS simplifies the way an information provider or intermediary offers content to a wider audience and exploits content accessible elsewhere. Most searchers are unaware when GILS is being used. In fact, some searchers are not even people but software "agents" gathering search results for later use.

An Evolutionary Future

Over the long term, the GILS vision must focus on a sustainable information infrastructure that reflects basic values such as unrestricted inquiry, free flow of information, and public access to government information. Certain design choices also follow from such policy considerations. For instance, the policy requirement to support diverse points of view is a strong argument for using decentralized technologies and global, public networks. The policy requirement to encompass traditional bibliographic information requires some way to accommodate the standards already widespread in the bibliographic community.

A vision such as GILS depends not only on addressing perceived needs but also on how the vision can be sustained by diverse communities over the long term. Ultimately, the collective activities of searchers, intermediaries, and providers determine an information infrastructure. There are many helpful initiatives by public and private organizations to marshal resources for GILS and related work. These are especially critical to sustain broad-based and open processes for information policy and standards. As the creative impulses and amazing diversity of our global information society become engaged in such initiatives, we can hope that the beginning of the 21st century marks the beginning of communities based on global information sharing.

MY DREAM

We are at an amazing moment of a **Gutenberg**-level event, with electronic wings able to fly through understandable information of our own choosing. With Velcro claws we collect all the data that warm and answer our inherent curiosity and questions.

I dream of asking a question, a simple childlike question and receiving an answer. What a dream!

The dream is here.

We are at the cusp of the marriage of information technology and information architecture. Our extraordinary ability to store and transmit data will make this dream a waking dream.

Louis Kahn said, "Beginnings, beginnings, beginnings, beginnings —I love beginnings."

This is such a beginning—the primitive formation of a new era.

This is the romanesque before the gothic.

This is the temples at Paestum before the Parthenon.

This is **Cimabué** and **Giotto** before **Piero della Francesca**.

Understanding information is power.

We shall never cease from exploration
And the end of all our exploring
Will be to arrive where we started
And know the place for the first time.

– T. S. Eliot

9 BEYOND PERSONALITIES

Our work environment is still far from paradise: mistakes abound, work needs to be redone, and people operate with different understandings of the same project. If our personalities were the only difficulty we had to surmount in the office, working wouldn't be such a dirty word.

There are universal, insidious, accepted corporate practices that tend to create animosity between management and employees. These practices have evolved in order to manage employees, but more often they confuse, undermine, and complicate the employees' attempts to do their jobs. The practices have little to do with individual personalities, but are inspired by business precepts that have been handed down for centuries and have become too entrenched to eradicate.

These fundamental forces haunt almost all work environments, from boardrooms to the warehouses. They act as dybbuks to create problems of communication and instruction, alienating employees and angering bosses. They are created by management policies, historical business philosophy, limitations of time and resources, and shortcomings of language and communications, and they will sabotage the best intentions of individuals. However, an awareness of their manifestations will help to temper their deleterious effects.

To alienate an employee by a conscious exercise of authority is one thing, but to do it unintentionally is another.

> Authority without wisdom is like a heavy axe without an edge, fitter to bruise than polish.
>
> – Anne Bradstreet (1612-1672)

CONDEMNED TO MAHOGANY ROW

Executives are responsible for setting the policy regarding the exchange of information, thereby setting the instructional policy of their companies. The burden of setting the instructional tone and of pairing the right givers with the right takers rests on the shoulders of those who run companies—those with the authority to hire and place employees. To do this, they need a clear picture of the company and of the personalties who work for it. Effective instructions must be based on accurate information. "As I see it, a healthy flow of information separates winning organizations from losers. Deciding means acting on information. Barring blind luck, the quality of a decision can't be better than the quality of the information behind it," said **Arno Penzias** in *Ideas and Information: Managing in a High-Tech World.*

But a host of factors often conspire to deny executives access to such information.

Top executives are often physically, philosophically, and politically isolated from their employees. They are isolated from their companies by their very position.

The complex chain of command, the distance between the executive suites and company operations, and the amount of time an executive spends outside of the company all serve to distance the CEO. Even CEOs of the gregarious, egalitarian variety, who promenade on the production floor, may not hear what they need to know, for the employer/employee relationship is not conducive to telling all.

It is not the voice that commands the story: it is the ear.

– Italo Calvino

"Communication difficulties are a universal problem in business organizations. All too often, we forget that communicating is a two-way process that involves listening and responding to messages as well as giving them. Too often, real ongoing communication upward to management is obscured, largely because managers won't or can't hear what is going on.

Three conditions must be met before communications can take place successfully. Subordinates must:

- Know what their seniors need to hear.

- Be given the chance to provide this information.

- Work for people who can accept it in a way that will not discourage disclosure."

– **Sherman K. Okun**, "How to Be a Better Listener," *Nation's Business*

Life on mahogany row is complicated further by the reluctance of most employees to bear bad news to bosses. No one wants to be responsible for delivering disagreeable tidings to a superior. So lower-level employees will tend to gloss over negative information. As the information moves upwards in the company hierarchy, it tends to be cast in a more positive light. Information may get so filtered or distorted by fear or even by just retelling, that if it ever makes it to the top, it is likely to be out-of-date, exaggerated, or patently wrong.

While the situation rarely reaches such catastrophic proportions in U.S. companies, executives do make decisions based on information that may be glossed over or tempered for the bosses' consumption.

Here is an example. Howie, who works on an assembly line at Redress Clothing, sees that a pattern-cutting machine isn't working properly. He suspects that it needs to be replaced, but doesn't want to report the full extent of the problem for fear his supervisor will think he hasn't maintained the machine. Howie tells his supervisor that there are serious problems with the Fineline Pattern-Cutter. With the same reservations, the supervisor reports to the factory manager that "there are problems with the pattern-cutter." As the factory manager was one of the people who recommended that the company buy Fineline, he is even more reluctant to report the problem, so he tells the general manager that the machine needs overhauling. The general manager, who knows that the three-year-old machine will cost about $250,000 to replace, doesn't want the company president to think he hasn't been on top of things, so he orders routine servicing and doesn't tell the company president. In only four rungs up the corporate ladder, a piece of equipment goes from being defunct to needing a routine tune-up.

To counteract this positive-rising effect, superiors should encourage those beneath them on the corporate ladder to bring them all relevant information, and they should be equally

improving...

needs adjustment

needs fixing

problematic

bad

Very Bad

Terrible

HORRIBLE

CATASTROPHIC!

The bad news filter

appreciative of negative information. Some people have a tendency to blame the bearer for bad news. Kings used to shoot the messengers who brought them accounts of battle defeats or peasant revolts.

No Surprises. Although CEOs rarely resort to such extreme tactics, shouting and raving after hearing about sagging sales is not uncommon—and it is not going to encourage a manager to rush to the CEO with this kind of information in the future. I think CEOs ought to have a placard behind their desks that reads "No Surprises." Getting the bad news as well as the good means no surprises. Negative news is often what the top brass most needs to know. It is what usually requires immediate action. When business is booming, who needs executive interference?

The lack of computer knowledge also fosters isolation. Computers used to be for engineers. Ten years ago, people could still afford the luxury of being technologically illiterate. They could brag about not being able to turn on a computer, work their voicemail systems, or program their VCRs.

Now they find themselves isolated from their most up-to-date and effective source of information. And while the capabilities of their employees are enhanced by computer literacy, their own skills are diminished. Also, without an awareness of the limitations of computers, executives run a greater risk of asking employees for work that can't be done or is inappropriate, time-consuming, and costly to be done by computer.

Consequently, computer proficiency is becoming mandatory at higher levels of management. Techno-competence has become a prerequisite to functioning in society, and computers are commonplace in the CEO's office. Executives with access to computers can stay informed of sales, production, and inventory figures. Stacks of unread, accordion-folded printouts gathering dust on desktops don't count.

Executives who are the last to know have only themselves to blame. They hold the power to encourage information upward from their employees.

Always mystify, mislead and surprise the enemy if possible.

– Stonewall Jackson

Be Prepared…the meaning of the motto is that a scout must prepare himself by previous thinking out and practising how to act on any accident or emergency so that he is never taken by surprise…

– Robert Baden-Powell

A computer terminal is not some clunky old television with a typewriter in front of it. It is an interface where the mind and body can connect with the universe and move bits of it about.

– Douglas Adams

NEARER TO GOD ARE WE

Instead of taking pains to combat executive isolation, management often compounds it by resorting to unnecessary, sometimes even subconscious, displays of corporate muscle. Exercising your power is a heady temptation, especially if you've got it. However, exercised wrongly, it can work against managing your employees. While some distance may be necessary between management and labor, at some point it becomes the fodder for unrest, hostility, and recalcitrance— none of which are likely to produce quality labor.

Often, these ill-advised displays of authority are small and insidiously subtle, such as using the word "we" when "I" is more appropriate. Perhaps management fears that the opinion of one is not enough to impress the wayward employee with the gravity of the situation. More often than not, the use of the big-brother "we" does little but raise employee dander. When a superior tells an employee, "We are not happy with your work," that employee is liable to start looking around to see if there is someone else in the room. If there isn't, the employee will either suspect the superior of hallucinating or be set on edge for no purpose. Use of the word "we" when communicating with employees is authoritarian and threatening. Such a show of communal muscle is bound to annoy an employee and unlikely to predispose him or her to following an instruction. The use of the corporate "we" should be reserved for attempts to raise *esprit de corps*, not used to impress employees that the eyes of the company/community/ society are peering unfavorably upon them. Other offensive tactics include:

- **I'm the Boss, That's Why.** Using your authority to explain why a subordinate should do something is a counterproductive use of power. Your employees may forget to give you phone messages, send letters, and remind you of meetings; they will never forget that you are the boss. Therefore, reminding them of this fact is unnecessary. And if you use it as justification for an order or instruction, you will make them suspicious that you have no other reason for the request. Humoring the boss may be a valid reason for performing a task, but it is not a satisfying motivation for a subordinate. Subordinates need to know the real whys before they can comprehend a task fully.

A man's intelligence does not increase as he acquires power. What does increase is the difficulty of telling him so.

– D. Sutten

- **If at First You Don't Succeed, Scream Louder.** Many employers foolishly think that if their instructions don't succeed the first time, they can try, try, try again in a louder voice. Unless employees have hearing problems, this is not a constructive approach. If someone didn't understand an instruction communicated at a civil decibel level, it is unlikely that hearing it shouted will add to its clarity. Before raising the decibel level, try to figure out why your directions weren't followed correctly before resorting to delivering them again in a louder voice.

- **Always Test Their Loyalty.** Ask them to do frivolous favors for you outside of their work duties. Try coffee first, then move on to more time-consuming favors. It's four o'clock, and you have a craving for Ben & Jerry's hazelnut ice cream. Send your secretary or assistant for a cone. If they are willing to do that, then try asking them to babysit your children. Let your employees know that you consider these tasks beneath you and that is the reason you hired them.

> Leadership is a two-way street, loyalty up and loyalty down. Respect for one's superiors; care for one's crew.
>
> – Grace Murray Hopper

Everyone who has risen up the corporate ladder, especially those who have outlived the tyrannical despots who once clung to the rungs above them, feels that he deserves to be relieved of all those annoying errands that he once grudgingly performed for someone else. Resist the temptation. The animosity you breed won't be worth the antebellum thrill of feeling like you are surrounded by indentured servants. Go get that ice-cream cone yourself. It's good to get out of the office. You may have a brilliant business idea on the way.

If you can't resist asking for these favors, try turning the situation around once in while. Get coffee for your secretary. Answer the phone yourself. Your staff will be less likely to accuse you of abusing your power if they see that you don't consider these tasks beneath you.

GROUP VS. INDIVIDUAL GOALS—THEM AGAINST ME

People toil in the workplace for different reasons. Some can be motivated by the promise of money or power. Others need intellectual stimulation or adventure. Everyone is driven by different forces. Yet the workplace is united by corporate goals.

All of these diverse individuals must somehow be encouraged to labor toward these group goals.

In ideal situations, group and individual goals will be compatible. Let's say the president of a computer company finds out that he has to have his gallbladder removed during the time of an important industry convention. So he asks an ambitious vice president to attend the convention in his place. I bet the VP will oblige happily, for the VP will rise in status and thus meet his or her individual goals. And the corporate goal of maintaining a presence in the industry will also be met by having someone in attendance.

Let's say that the executive assistant to the same president calls in sick. So the president asks the same VP to make some phone calls for him. The VP is going to resent being asked to perform tasks that might be perceived as status-diminishing, even though the tasks might be necessary to meet the corporate goals of conducted business.

Invariably, there will be times when individual goals will be inconsistent with those of the group. Individuals may be asked to do a job that runs contrary to their own goals.

While management cannot avoid these situations altogether, much can be done to minimize their occurrence.

- Wherever possible, management should try to assign tasks to those employees who might find them consistent with their own individual goals.

- When this isn't possible, management should explain the reason that an employee is being asked to perform a task.

- Management should make sure that employees understand just what the corporate goals are.

MISSING THE OBVIOUS

While some instructions fail because they are perceived as orders, others fail because they weren't perceived at all. Even if you recognize the instruction content of your communications, you have to make it clear to the taker. People can't follow your directions if they don't know that is what you are giving them. **Nigel Holmes**, the information architect, had a suggestion for

> Most human organizations that fall short of their goals do so not because of stupidity or faulty doctrines, but because of internal decay and rigidification. They grow stiff in the joints. They get in a rut. They go to seed.
>
> – James A. Garfield

starting instructions that was brilliant in its simplicity. "Good instructions involve letting someone know that the conversation you are having with them *is* instruction and not just idle chatter."

Because instructions run the workplace, perhaps people don't see the need to announce them. Consequently, their subordinates must guess or interpret messages, a condition of uncertainty that could get in the way of understanding.

> I deal with the obvious. I present, reiterate and glorify the obvious— because the obvious is what people need to be told.
>
> – Dale Carnegie

You might think this sounds a bit silly or at least unnecessary, but you would be surprised at how much work doesn't get done because an instruction-giver didn't make this clear. You may have asked Johnson to get you the debt-to-capital ratio for that chemical company you are trying to buy, but Johnson might think you were musing on what you were going to do after lunch. He didn't read the message as an instruction.

Everyone needs to know what is expected from them.

PROMOTION: A DEADLY REWARD

The foundation of most businesses is to reward good workers by promoting them. In most workplaces, promotion, with its concomitant raises, is the sole reward for effort. In this way, so the theory goes, the cream will rise to the top. The only trouble with this idea is that business is not butter.

> I'm way overdue for a promotion. I've made so many lateral moves, I'm beside myself.
>
> – Gary Apple

The oracle of American business has declared that monetary compensation should be on par with one's management level, and so it is. Workers don't make as much money as foremen, foremen get less than managers, managers get less than directors, and so on. Therefore, to reward workers with more money, accepted business practice dictates that they must be promoted. This pervasive practice is often counterproductive for it places people in positions that they may not want or may not be prepared to handle.

THE COMPETITIVE DREDGE

Instead of encouraging people to do their personal best, many managers make a sport of pitting employees against each other.

The foundation of the American economy is built on the principle of may-the-better-product win. This can be a healthy motivation to spur market effort. But this belief in competition as cure-all has entrenched itself within companies so that not only is product pitted against product, but people are pitted against people. And competition isn't always healthy. Keep in mind that this is tantamount to heresy in many U.S. companies.

In a society that worships winners, intramural competition has become the key motivation to many employees who pursue victory with the zeal of Olympic athletes. Crushing your opponents, even if they are also your office mates, has become almost synonymous with success. Most managers believe that among their responsibilities is the training of their employees to be competitive. Then management wonders why these hungry-for-the-kill employees show more concern for their own advancement than for the advancement of company business.

The demise of teamwork induces office paranoia, so employees are less likely to take risks, to suggest unorthodox approaches, or to do anything that might expose them to failure. The Center for Creative Leadership in Greensboro, North Carolina, ranked internal competition as one of the ten most frequently cited obstacles to creativity.

INFORMATION IS NOT THE FINAL PRODUCT

A high value is placed on information in the workplace. Having the most current figures, the most comprehensive data, and the inside sources is better than a corner office when it comes to having an asset that everyone else will admire. Information, in all of its forms, is eating up megabytes of computer space, filling up file cabinets, obscuring desktops, and overstuffing the bounds of briefcases throughout the world.

The managerial mania for acquiring information has become such a hobby horse that few have stopped rocking long enough to ponder what good information is if it can't be communicated. What matters is the ability—through instruction—to transfer information from the mind of one person to another.

In larger companies, if you asked managers what kind of communication program the company had, they might tell you about internal publications, staff meetings, and interoffice mail systems. These are information programs, not necessarily

> Competition brings out the best in products and the worst in people.
>
> – David Sarnoff

> Making duplicate copies and computer printouts of things no one wanted even one of in the first place is giving America a new sense of purpose.
>
> – Andy Rooney

communications programs, and the only thing they can be guaranteed to do is add to interoffice clutter. In themselves, they carry no intrinsic properties that will add to the communication or understanding of information.

INSTRUCTIONS ARE NOT THE GOAL

In an ideal office, there would be no need for instructions. Everyone would understand her job so well that her actions wouldn't need directions.

Because we are so far from this ideal, there is a tendency to forget that giving instructions isn't the purpose of working; instructions are a means of getting the job done in an imperfect world.

The limits of human communication will never make instructions obsolete, but improving their quality can reduce employees' reliance on them. The means to the end might be to communicate directions in such a way that employees understand their role so clearly they can perform their duties on their own.

This requires altering a deeply held belief that instructions are a means of control, a means of conscripting someone else to do work that you don't want or don't have time to do.

The best instructions are actually the opposite. Ideal instructions should liberate both the giver and the taker. They should empower subordinates to do their work, and they should free up time for superiors. Instead of spending time putting out fires, superiors might look in the future to long-range planning instead of short-range emergency services.

In much the same way that industrial designers—at least the good ones—try to create products that don't require as much instruction, employers should try to cultivate employees who don't need as much direction. Really good products should tell you how they want to be used—so should a good employee.

This ideal isn't so farfetched. Managers can move toward this state by changing their view of the role of instructions and by looking more closely at the role of management.

WHAT DO MANAGERS MANAGE?

The accepted answer in most companies is that managers manage people or information. These tasks require focusing on the past, in that they involve keeping track of what people have done, how well they have done it, and whether information about past business activities is accurate, and then correcting inappropriate usage of resources—human or otherwise.

These activities aren't superfluous, but they distract managers from the real essence of management: directing the future action of a company through instructions.

In an article by **Fernando Flores** and **Chauncey Bell** in *Computer Technology Review*, the question was answered as follows: "Managers are paid to discover what is missing in the work that is already going forward and to bring that into being.…The effective manager's first concern is future action. However, most office systems and accompanying technology focus on the recording, manipulation, and presentation of historical data."

For example, if you manage the new products division of a toothpaste company, and you decide that the market is ripe for new flavors, you might study research on acceptance of new flavors in the past, current market conditions, costs of production, etc.—all information from the past. Let's say based on your research, you decide that arugula-flavored toothpaste would be a market-buster. You present your idea with the documentation and research to your superiors. You convince them that your judgment is sound and reliable, so they encourage you to proceed.

But nothing has really happened until you instruct the people who work for you on how to proceed to develop this product. This linguistic communication initiates action. To translate corporate policies into plans for action in the future is the heart of management, not the recording of past events. Management's mission is to bring about action through the expression of words, not to document it after it has happened.

> Effective managers live in the present—but concentrate on the future.
>
> – James L. Hayes

> Management is efficiency in climbing the ladder of success; leadership determines whether the ladder is leaning against the right wall.
>
> – Stephen R. Covey

ATTITUDE OVERHAUL

Bosses are not the enemy—frustration is the enemy, and it comes from instructions that are constructed badly or given carelessly without regard to the follower. Frustration also arises from being ill-prepared to receive instructions.

It arises from a lack of awareness of the larger problems of communication.

In this book, I have tried to make my case for the importance of instructions and have outlined the larger issues with which we all must wrestle in the giving and taking of them. These issues can be summarized as follows:

- Instructions are a major component of communications.

- Instructions in the workplace must be understood within the larger context of current affairs and the economy.

- The transformation from an industrial-based to an information-based economy broadens the role of instructions.

- Changing demographics will make the communication of instructions a more challenging task.

- The first step toward meeting the challenge is understanding what kind of instruction-giver and instruction-taker you are. What about the people with whom you work?

- The next step is understanding the forces at work beyond individual personalities who alter the perception of instructions and obstruct the flow of information.

> Preconceived notions are the locks on the door to wisdom.
>
> – Merry Browne

Most of the prior material has focused on the nature of work and the workplace, and it behooves us to keep these in mind when formulating or following instructions. But we come to work with preconceived notions and biases toward certain modes of thinking that make it harder for us to understand each other. An examination of how we learn and use language will provide more insight into the intricacies of instructions.

10 EMPOWERMENT: THE WORD OF THE NEW CENTURY

Empowerment is what enables employees to go beyond the instructions they are given. Empowerment means to give rights and responsibilities to employees by giving them a say in their work as well as in company business in general. It recognizes and rewards their input. It is a movement designed to nurture human resources and replace the manager-as-warden mentality with the manager-as-aide-to-action approach.

The difference between an adequate instruction and an inspired instruction is that the latter empowers the takers so that they feel possession of the results of their efforts.

Empowerment is about feelings; it isn't an issue of dollars and cents. Feelings historically have not been the stuff of business. In fact, you were supposed to respond to them in the same way you would a drop in earnings: chagrin, embarrassment, and a promise that it won't happen again. Empowerment has assumed cause status. It is a word that was developed to express feelings that may have existed for a long time, enabling the concept to take root and people to focus on the idea.

> Commonplace minds usually condemn what is beyond the reach of their understanding.
>
> – Francois LaRochefoucauld

"Empowerment is a concept that has gained the sanctity of motherhood and apple pie in corporate America. Indeed, in the years to come your career may well fade or flourish on the basis of how well you master the art of empowering every single individual who works for you," said **Peter Block** in his book, *The Empowered Manager.*

Empowerment depends on the will and determination of both management and employees. Empowerment must be both granted and encouraged by the empowerers (or instruction-givers) and assumed by the empowerees (or instruction-takers), who must recognize that their mission isn't just to realize the dreams of others, blindly following orders like sheep, but to derive their own satisfaction from the instruction-taking process.

THE AGREEMENT

When I was a high school student, I realized that I was only listening to the teacher by my agreement. The teachers couldn't get me to do anything unless I agreed to do it. What could they do if I said I wouldn't go to school? Could they shoot me, put me in jail? We are all educated with the fear that we must do things because we must. When we walk down a crowded street, we walk to the right and avoid bumping into oncoming people. When we miscalculate, most of us say, "Excuse me." There are no punishments for violations of this rule.

Unless society can inflict pain or punishment for violating the rules, people follow them only because they agree to follow them. This agreement is the glue of civilization.

Most people make agreements with society. They promise to make certain compromises—to whisper in the library, wait patiently in line, let a car into a line of traffic—in order to enjoy the company and goodwill of others. I've always wondered how those agreements came about. It seems to me that many of the breakthroughs in the arts and sciences have come about because someone broke the agreement. **John Cage** broke the agreement as to what constitutes music. Radical alternatives are produced by not going along with the rules.

Recognizing that you are the one who agrees to the rules means that you are the one who can choose to disagree as well. Recognizing that you are the one who decides what rules to follow gives you a sense of power. You are the one who makes the choice. I believe that we all have that right.

You don't have to go to work every day. You go because you want something that work gives you—whether it is monetary, emotional, or social satisfaction. I believe that people do what they want to do; they don't always recognize this though. You might dread going to a party and complain about having to go, but maybe you want the chance to meet new people or establish business connections, so you go. If you find yourself starting a lot of sentences with "I have to...," keep in mind that you probably don't. There is probably some reason why you "want to." "Want to" is more liberating than "have to."

> Civilization had too many rules for me, so I did my best to rewrite them.
>
> – Bill Cosby

This right to follow or to break the rules also gives us the right to ask for what we want. To get what we want, though, means being able to instruct others in our wishes. You can't be upset about the table you get in a restaurant, the benefits you get at work, or even the gifts you get from a spouse unless you have made it clear through instructions about what you wanted in the first place.

I am on planes a lot, and I try to make the experience as comfortable as possible. When I fly at night, I like a window seat so I am not disturbed by other passengers getting in and out of their seats. During the day, I like an aisle seat because there is more room, and you can get up without disturbing others. I was taking the red eye from San Francisco to New York, so I asked for a window seat as far forward as possible. The airlines complied with my request and gave me a seat in the third row. It turns out that there were only three rows in first class, so I got the seat in front of the bulkhead, which doesn't recline as much. I didn't get what I wanted, which was to go to sleep, because I didn't communicate the right instructions.

All of us could have our way more often if we knew how to communicate our desires. Each of us has the right. What we need to develop is the ability to ask for it.

In a restaurant you have the power to get what you want. You are the boss. Most restaurants, especially the better ones, are willing to entertain your specific instructions for food and liquor or substitutions of ingredients. One of the drinks I like is similar to a vodka Gibson—but not exactly the same. I like Grey Goose Orange with only 2 rocks and a wedge (not a peel) of lime and extra onions. To get what I want, I have to give these instructions. A lot of people don't get what they want. Most people would just order the vodka Gibson. Many restaurants, especially Japanese and Italian, allow you to tailor meals. You can order half portions or full portions, a few pieces of sushi, or a platter.

> Power can be taken, but not given. The process of the taking is empowerment in itself.
>
> – Gloria Steinem

My wife, **Gloria**, likes chili with a lot of beans. Before she orders it, she will ask the waiter or waitress, "Does it have a lot of beans?" Thinking that she doesn't like beans, sometimes the person will respond, "No it doesn't have too many beans." So she doesn't order the chili, which she would have liked, because she didn't give the order in a way that enabled the server to give her what she wanted. All she would have to say is "I like a lot of beans. Does your chili have them?"

TO OBEY OR NOT TO OBEY?

Along with the freedom and right to get what you want, empowerment brings responsibilities. Employees have the freedom to act or not to act, and they must bear the consequences of the choice. Choice carries responsibilities. An article in *Time* about how East Germans are adjusting to West German ways of business reported that they were overwhelmed by the number of choices and reluctant to make decisions about what to buy.

> Any fool can make a rule. And every fool will mind it.
>
> – Henry David Thoreau

The article, "Speeding over the Bumps," by **James O. Jackson**, stated that "One reason for Eastern docility in the face of aggressive Western sales forces is 40 years of Communism. 'It's hard to imagine what the central command system did to people,' says Stahmer (**Ingrid Stahmer**, West Berlin's deputy mayor in charge of housing and social services). 'Too many of them just sit and wait for instructions. They lack initiative and judgment. It's a crash course, but they are learning fast.'"

Throughout history, subordinates have attempted to exonerate themselves from guilt by claiming that "I was just following orders."

The Nazi holocaust, the massacre of civilians at My Lai during the Vietnam War, the Iran-Contra affair, the misappropriation of millions in the Department of Housing and Urban Development, and the Exxon Valdez oil spill are only a few episodes that were colored by the "following-orders" defense. Throughout history, some variation of this has been used as a defense for wrong actions in almost every field of endeavor. And, time and time again, it has come up short as a justifiable excuse. It drives home the message that at some time in your life, it might be better to *not* follow orders. Making this decision opens a Pandora's box of conflicting emotions and ethics. Do we follow our conscience or our desire to please? The line where a responsibility to obey transgresses into the territory of unethical behavior must be moved toward individual accountability. No instructions should be followed blindly. Just because you are working under the authority of someone else doesn't mean that ill-conceived actions can be absolved by claiming that you were just following orders.

SPHERE OF VISION

Empowerment doesn't mean granting absolute freedom. The boundaries of empowerment are set by the sphere of vision of the instruction-givers. What are the limits of your own vision? Make sure that the people to whom you give instructions understand how far they can go. Then give them the freedom to work within these boundaries.

You have to have a clear vision of your sphere. The trick is to define your sphere so that it is meaningful to employees, large enough not to inhibit your employees' creativity, and small enough so as not to overwhelm them with options.

All of my work has my mark, yet I do little hands-on work. The people who work for me have changed over the years, but the imprint of my work has not. This is possible because I empower people to do their work, and then I give the instructions for it to be done. I'll put my work on the line to prove it. It may sound silly and arrogant, and it's probably not something you're supposed

A vision is not a vision unless it says yes to some ideas and no to others, inspires people and is a reason to get out of bed in the morning and come to work.

– Gifford Pinchot

to say—that I don't do any work—but it's true. **Lee Iacocca** didn't build cars, but his vision gave birth to a renewed Chrysler Corporation almost two decades ago.

I make a living by doing the opposite of the way other people do things. I look for the patterns in what doesn't work. I find the pattern in failures. Why can't I use the dictionary properly, the telephone book, the *TV Guide*, the *Official Airline Guide*? I'm not self-conscious about saying things that sound simple. This frees me. I have stripped myself of the pressure of having to sound smart. I can be the professor of ignorance.

As to the creative work that gets done—the phone books, the *USAtlas*, the *ACCESS* city guides—I've done well because I have less and less to do with producing things that have more and more of my mark on them. Because I've allowed people the freedom to be creative, they have an identity with the projects. I try to give happy limitations so that the projects fall within an acceptable range of the ideas I have for them.

I allow people to be proud of what they have done, to feel that they have ownership or possession of the task. This enlists their energies to produce a better product. I may not sit in front of the computer and do illustrations, yet they are all my inspiration. There is no doubt that my employees create work better than I could. This book is an example.

I empower people by giving them a creativity allowance. I find people who can do better than I can do, but I make sure their work does not pierce the sphere of my vision.

WHAT GOOD IS EMPOWERMENT?

> I'm slowly becoming a convert to the principle that you can't motivate people to do things, you can only demotivate them. The primary job of the manager is not to empower but to remove obstacles.
>
> – Scott Adams

The possibilities of empowerment outweigh the responsibilities for instruction-givers and takers. An empowered workforce benefits individual employees as well as groups and organizations.

Empowered employees are more likely to be motivated. Motivation is a higher form of instruction. Motivation can move mountains. Motivated people do exceedingly complex work, which they enable themselves to do by interest. People follow complex pattern instructions because they want to make a dress, but will claim they are baffled by electronic equipment. We learn to do those things we want to do. If I'm on a private plane and the pilot has a heart attack and dies, I'm going to be quite interested in learning how to fly a plane. As long as the pilot is doing his or her job, I really don't care.

Empowerment can reduce the reliance on instructions and thus minimize the possibility of misunderstanding them. Giving freedom to employees encourages them to act on their own. By acting on their own, they liberate their superiors (instruction-givers) from having to spell out every detail of every task.

Empowerment encourages the generation of creative ideas. And the most desirable response to instruction depends on creative ideas. As we move toward an information-based rather than a product-based economy, the business community is awakening to the importance of ideas in the marketplace. Ideas aren't as predictable as materials; they cannot be produced with formulas, and they require a more flexible atmosphere.

> I am a man of fixed and unbending principles, the first of which is to be flexible at all times.
>
> – Everett M. Dirksen

JUST SAY "YES"

Empowering employees can be done without risking life and limb, without any sporting equipment at all. After all, empowerment is an attitude. At the 1990 International Design Conference in Aspen, **Ken Brecher**, currently Executive Director of the Sundance Institute, talked about former first lady **Nancy Reagan**'s "Just Say No" campaign against drugs as the antithesis of empowerment. Telling people to "Just Say No" to drugs is authoritarian; it doesn't empower people to make decisions for themselves. Empowerment means telling people that "You could say 'yes' or you could say 'no.' The choice is yours."

The problem is how to get executives to give instructions that will enable their employees to go beyond the status quo, to follow instructions to their own satisfaction and growth, yet still realize the ideas and dreams of their bosses? Employees are empowered by the following circumstances:

> Status quo is Latin for the mess we're in.
>
> – Jeve Moorman

- Having the option of making decisions about their work and about the company as a whole.

- Being informed about company business—the bad as well as the good.

- Feeling that they own their work. They receive the credit, the criticism, and the praise.

- Having the comfort of knowing that they can make mistakes, which are inevitable on the road to success.

- Understanding corporate goals and the ways those goals can be applied to their work.

- Understanding their superiors' sphere of vision.

Empowerment depends on the practice of participatory leadership, which recognizes the power of employees and promotes a climate of cooperation.

There are no limits to our future if we don't put limits on our people.

– Jack Kemp

The applications of empowerment are almost universal. It can be employed to improve office morale, personal relationships, and even political and economic conditions. **Jack Kemp**, former secretary of the Department of Housing and Urban Development under President **George H. Bush**, suggested that empowerment was the way to solve the homeless problem in this country by allowing tenants to run their own housing projects.

I predict that leaders will look toward empowerment to solve some of the problems facing the business and political communities today. They will abandon hiring policies that look for "yes" men and instead look for people who are allowed to do a better job than their leaders. More leaders will recognize that those who can encourage self-esteem in their employees will get higher quality work than those who are driven by a desire to keep their employees under their thumbs.

I predict that, inevitably, the empowerment movement will redefine the role of leaders in many organizations.

11 INSTRUCTIONS: THE DRIVER OF CONVERSATION

Every successful communication is really an instruction in disguise—from love letters to company brochures.

When you tell your date that beets make you queasy, you are giving instructions. In the words is an implicit instruction that, if you want to show me that you care, you won't serve me beets when you invite me for dinner. If you are paying attention, you will remember this. We've all had experience when someone doesn't do what we wanted or disregards our requests. The tendency is to write the person off as inconsiderate or incompetent, but just perhaps, the real problem is that we didn't give very good instructions.

Good instructions involve letting someone know that the conversation you are having with them *is* instruction and not just idle chatter. The instruction or "how to" is what attracts people to information. It's what promises (although not always delivers) to help them do what they want to do.

Only teachers and trainers think of themselves as instructors, yet we are all instructors every time we communicate. And, the more we think of communicating as *instructing* versus *informing,* the more satisfaction we're likely to find in the process.

Exploiting the instructive component of information is the best strategy for making sure your message attracts an audience. When you start thinking of yourself as an instructor as well as an informer, your power base expands. You become not just someone who *tells*, but someone who *leads* people to action. When you start designing information around the intended action, your communications become more powerful.

> Knowing where you are going is all you need to get there.
>
> – Carl Frederick

THE POWER OF INSTRUCTIONS

Most people want to follow instructions. When you're walking down the street and someone behind you yells, "Stop!" that's what you'll probably do.

Ad campaigns succeed because they have given great instructions. Think about AT&T's "Reach out and touch someone" campaign, which sent millions of people running to their phones. Another powerful instruction is Nike's "Just Do It."

Conversely, Apple has great ads, but they don't sell very many computers. They're often missing the instruction, the component that lets the audience know just how this product is going to help run their lives. Surveys after the splashy dot-com ads that ran during the 1999 Super Bowl showed only a third of viewers could remember the name of a single dot-com company whose ads they saw.

Good directions are dynamic. They can get you from Paris to Istanbul, from your house to mine, from inertia to action. They can get customers to buy your products and services and employees to follow company directives.

Instructions are creative.

- Composers don't give us music; they give us the instructions for making music.

- Architects don't build buildings; they give contractors the instructions to build a building.

- Generals don't win wars; they give the instructions for victory.

- Publishers don't print books; they give printers the instructions for printing them.

INSTRUCTIONS ARE EVERYWHERE

Most of our work involves giving instructions to employees or customers on how to…

- Comprehend different aspects of the organization and its products and services.

- Engage in teamwork.

- Understand how one department's work affects another.

> Life is a perpetual instruction in cause and effect.
>
> – Ralph Waldo Emerson

- Buy-in to company practices.

- Instill corporate culture.

- Reach business goals.

That means that all our communications with customers are also instructions. When we fail to communicate these, we have instruction problems.

The business of understanding is vastly more important than the business of persuasion. I don't think that fact has occurred to advertisers. The business of making things understandable is more important than the persuasion business. Most car companies exhibit their products racing down roadways at speeds that no driver will ever reach. Drivers would rather be able to understand and operate all the technology in their cars than navigate a barrel course in the Mohave Desert. The OnStar system in the Cadillac, for example, isn't made understandable enough to consumers, nor is that the focused goal of the ad—a product for understanding, communication, and reduced anxiety. You see the car with the sun dazzling off the fender, but you have no idea how the OnStar system works.

> Following instructions is one of the most difficult comprehension tasks encountered in daily life.
>
> – H. A. Simon & J. R. Hayes,
> *Understanding Complex Task Instructions*

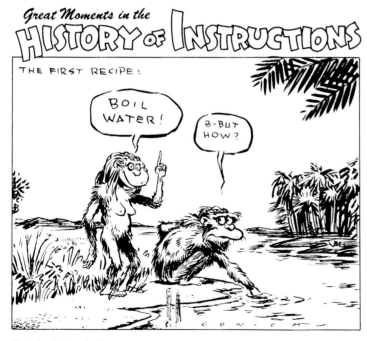

Illustrations by Larry Gonick

Consumers are more likely to buy something if they can understand, install, and use it. Online retailers have only begun to recognize this. Many e-commerce sites require a software developer to navigate. The success of Amazon certainly doesn't depend on its product lines, but on the ease with which you can acquire them. You don't need computer skills to find and buy a book on the Amazon site. You can feel the hand of someone who thought about how people shop.

BETTER INSTRUCTIONS MEAN BETTER COMMUNICATIONS

When all else fails, read the instructions.

Just how effective communications are depends in large part on how well they instruct. The quality of information is judged not only by its accuracy and clarity, but by the impact it has on its audience.

- Is it useful and relevant?

- Does it have meaning or is it merely facts?

- Is it feedback to the audience's question?

- Does it have the power to change or expand the audience's knowledge?

■ Does it help the audience move forward or take some action?

To build more actionable instructions, you have to look at how they are structured. What are the basic components and how can you put them together to build sound instructions?

You have to go back to the fundamentals. You can't build a tall building without understanding triangulation—that the structure stiffens and passes on stresses in a significant way. I don't think you can give or follow instructions without understanding the underlying structure. When your education starts, you learn the alphabet, then words, then sentences, then paragraphs. There is a progression. You can't miss a step and expect to get terrific results. The education system has missed out on a significant part of our communications.

We have neglected and even avoided the fundamentals. To me, our society is a lot like French cooking. The French appear to care much less about the essential ingredients and more about the sauce. We tend to focus on the dressings, the forms, the features of things, and not the essential thing.

Let's say you are sitting in a cave trying to plan a basic course in instruction construction. First, you'd want to know what are the different kinds of instructions? How do they differ? What are the building blocks? Are the instructions for making a flint spear essentially the same as the instructions for operating a flour grinder?

You'd want to look at just the content of an instruction—independent of the other parts of the instruction system, independent of the channel in which it is delivered, the personality of the giver or the taker, the context in which it is set. In the cave, you'd want to know about the most essential component in the system—the content.

These are bread and water concerns. This is not about semantic translation of the Samoan language. It's not esoteric; it's not brain surgery. It's fundamental and pervasive.

> [Knowledge is] the small part of ignorance that we arrange and classify.
>
> – Ambrose Bierce

Illustrations by Jo Mora

Joe Mora, in a long out-of-print book *Trail Dust and Saddle Leather* (Charles Scribner's Sons, 1946) clearly outlines some complex procedures, much less common now than in his time.

ALL GAUL IS DIVIDED INTO THREE PARTS

Despite the myriad different versions of instructions, there are roughly only three different types.

- **Those that involve the past**, as in transfer of knowledge that occurs in school where students learn history, geography, biology, and mathematics. Aside from memorization and regurgitation for tests, past-oriented instructions are usually passive; they don't require any immediate action. When you learn about the Battle of Waterloo, you won't have to fight it.

- **Those that involve the present**, such as operating and assembly instructions. "Push this button if you want to send a message." "Turn left at Route 66." Present-based instructions include those for all equipment instructions, as well as directions from one place to another, recipes, and assembly manuals. These instructions demand immediate action.

■ **Those that are future–oriented**. This is the realm of interest in the workplace and in social relationships. When a boss instructs you to reduce spending in the marketing department, she is asking you to do something at some future point. It may be next week, next month, or next year. When a company president talks about corporate goals, he may be giving implicit instructions that will dictate future actions. The explicit and implicit instructions that we give to our friends and relatives fall into this category, whether it be "Pick up a quart of ice-cream on your way home" or "I hate to dance," which carries the implicit instruction, "Stop suggesting that we go dancing."

Each of these can be oriented in a goal–based or a task-based manner. Goal-based instructions give the end product. Task-based instructions give the steps that will move you toward the goal. "Increase sales by 20 percent" is a goal–based instruction. "Schedule a meeting," "hire a consultant," "write a report" are task-based instructions.

Goal-based instructions tend to inspire imagination. They allow the taker to invent the tasks that might realize the goal.

In a task-based instruction, the goal is implicit, but the steps are spelled out. The goal can be played down, existing only as an implicit objective. In a fax manual, the goal is to make the user proficient with the technology, but what the user needs are the steps to make this possible.

Task-based instructions limit imagination by defining the path to the goal, but they also give necessary information. The information to be delivered should determine the orientation.

Depending on what you need to do, a goal-based instruction can be inspiring or frustrating; a task-based one can be helpful or humiliating.

Certain tasks call for certain instructions. If you are going to bake a cake, you probably want step-by-step instructions. You want to know that you should preheat the oven to 425 degrees and whether the butter should go in before the baking powder. You wouldn't be too happy to open your recipe book and find an instruction to "Combine tasty ingredients to bake a delicious cake," with only a photograph of the final product.

Directions for carrying out tasks often contain two qualitatively different kinds of information. The first might be termed component step information, the specific enumeration of the actions needed to perform the task. Another kind of information might be termed organizational information, information about the overall structure and organization of the task. Organizational information indicates how the component steps are related to each other and how they go together to accomplish the task at hand.

– Peter Dixon, "The Processing of Organizational and Component Step Information in Written Directions," *Journal of Memory and Language* (Vol. 26, 1987)

Whether they are aware of it or not, most people began to make a mental plan to execute any instruction, breaking it down into a hierarchy of tasks. Let's look at a fairly simple task like changing a tire. At the top of the list is the goal, which is to have a working car. That means changing a flat tire. That can be broken down into: taking the old tire off of the car and putting the new one on. Within each of these tasks are more specific ones—jacking the car off the ground, unscrewing the lug nuts.

– Peter Dixon, Jeremiah Faries, and Gareth Gabrys "The Role of Explicit Action Statements in Understanding and Using Written Directions," *Journal of Memory and Language* (Vol. 27, 1988).

In other realms, step-by-step instructions can be stultifying. A photographer working for a client doesn't want to hear what stop and shutter speed he should use. He needs to have the goal. "Take a picture of this interior so that it shows off the built-in furniture." Takers tend to respond to a goal-based instruction by developing their own mental plan composed of tasks that might be expected to accomplish the goal.

This plan hierarchy operates at more complex levels of accomplishments. When your boss tells you to tighten up spending in the advertising department, you begin to translate the goal into a plan based on performing certain tasks—reviewing current expenses, assessing the value of certain media, making plans to cut back spending. Then you might turn each one of these into a subgoal, from which you might develop tasks that are more specific.

The goals focus on states of being, and the plans focus on actions that might produce these states.

If you are giving a goal-based instruction, keep in mind that the taker will start to formulate a plan, so make sure that the overall goal is delivered up front.

In delivering instructions, you should keep in mind how you orient your own instructions. Task-based ones yield more uniform and predictable results (although this depends somewhat on their quality). As the margin for interpretation widens with goal-based instructions, so do the possible results. Often, instructions contain both goal-based and task-based messages.

Both goal-based and task-based instructions can be either implicit or explicit. "Get George Sherman on the phone for me" is explicit and task-based. "When you've got George Sherman on the phone, tell him that the meeting has been rescheduled" only implies an instruction to call him. It is the measure of explicitness that determines the clarity of an instruction, not whether it is goal- or task-based.

Goal-based instructions aren't bound by definition to be vague; they can be quite explicit. One of the most complete extensive examples of goal-based instructions is architectural drawing.

Architects work with ideas of space, color, materials, and joinings, and transform them into goal-based instructions. The working drawings don't tell the contractor how to dig a hole or make the concrete forms; they show him what the goal is—with words, pictures, and numbers. Every element of the building is defined by size, shape, and material. The building is shown at different scales and from different vantage points—the section, plan, elevation, axonometric, and isometric. A full set of construction documents also includes specifications for measuring quality and spelling out how much stress particular elements should be expected to bear. Architects give their plans to craftsmen/carpenters who in turn develop more detailed instructions in the form of shop drawings outlining the specifications of how something will be built.

> Our plans miscarry because they have no aim. When a man does not know what harbor he is making for, no wind is the right wind.
>
> – Seneca

Contractors are then free to use their own knowledge and imagination on how the goal is to be accomplished, how the production should be staged, what the timing should be, how equipment should be brought to the site.

Architectural instructions are a model for all kinds of instructions. They define a goal, and then offer the components that will help people to realize it.

BUILDING BLOCKS OF ACTIONABLE INSTRUCTIONS

All instructions should be built with certain components—or structural members, to use the vocabulary of architecture—to enable the takers to use their own skills in following them. No matter what form the instruction takes or what kind of instruction it is, including these components will facilitate understanding by minimizing the general problems of communication and enabling the taker to visualize the instruction.

The components are:

- Purpose (Reason)

- Objective (Destination)

- Core (Procedure)

- Time (Duration)
- Expectation (Anticipation)
- Failure (Error)

To define these components, I am going to use the example of instructions to go someplace because we've probably all had experiences where we gave instructions to someone else who promptly got lost trying to follow them, or where we tried to follow someone else's directions, cursing all the way. The principles of geographic instructions work for all kinds of instructions, though.

You can use this road model for instructions to tie your communications to business goals, to help your employees understand what you expect of them, to tell someone how to find your office, to create more effective communications, or to get your husband to do what you want.

We'd like you to come to our house next Friday. (**Destination**)

We're having a dinner party to celebrate our anniversary. (**Reason**)

Our address is 1015 Forest. Get off at the Oak Park exit on the Eisenhower Expressway. (**Procedure**)

The whole drive should take about 35 minutes in moderate traffic. (**Duration**)

On the expressway, you will pass Central Avenue and then Austin Avenue before you come to Oak Park. (**Anticipation**)

If you see the exit for River Forest, you have gone too far. (**Error**)

When you forget the destination, you can wind up with some pretty ineffective instructions, like this one that appears at voting precincts around New York:

YOU CAN BE ASSISTED IF YOU CANNOT READ.

Do you think a lot of blind or illiterate people made it to their destination?

OBJECTIVE: WHAT'S THE DESTINATION?

All instructions should have a goal that is made clear when the instruction is given. If you were giving someone directions to your house, you would tell them the address—reaching that address is the objective. This defines the scope of the instruction and helps the taker make necessary decisions along the way.

Shad Northshield, a seasoned instructor as the senior executive producer of CBS News, stressed the importance of the objective in empowering instruction-takers. "You don't tell people to do something unless you make it clear what it is you want to achieve. That takes into account their own creative facilities. Instruction-giving should be a kind of enlightened autocracy. Let them make an investment; out of that comes great respect and affection. When I ask an editor to do something, I'm dealing with a person who is very creative. At the same time, he is a technician. My instructions work best when they understand what I want and why. Often, they don't do what I suggested. Very often they do something better, but it still fulfills a need I had."

Where do you want your audience to go? How can you get them there? Amazon.com's CEO **Jeff Bezos** keeps the destination in mind when he tells people that the company's mission isn't to sell books, but to help customers make book-purchasing decisions. That's what colors many of the decisions made on the Web site, such as printing bad as well as good reviews and the one-click technology that makes it easy to act on your decisions.

If you cry "forward," you must make it plain in what direction to go.

– Anton Chekov.

Do you want your Web site to be a place where you interest consumers in your product or explain how to use it? Is it brochureware or documentation or a sales tool? Each objective will color the choices you make.

Having an objective gives you a natural place to measure success. How many users or customers reached the objective? Is it to attract eyeballs to your Web site or to prompt calls to your sales department? It's amazing how many people don't think about this before sitting down to create communications materials. They are thinking how can we make something that looks fabulous, that wows the boss, that looks jazzier than anything on the market, but the most important question is what is the objective? A brochure could win every design award, but it wouldn't be much use if no one could understand what it was selling. When you know what the objective is, you can create criteria to measure how many people reached the objective.

You can always tell people aren't thinking about the objective when they come up with patently misguided measurements of success. How many customer service departments measure success by the number of people the reps can handle in an hour. What if the reps are pissing off 20 people an hour instead of 10? It would be better if they only handled 5 calls an hour. If the objective of customer service is to get customers' issues resolved, wouldn't the number or successful resolutions an hour be a better measure of success?

By asking the questions "Where do we want our audience to go?" and "What is the rationale for taking them there?" and "What steps do they need to take to act?", new and creative ways of instruction might appear. An organization in Kansas City, the Stop Violence Coalition started a campaign. They wanted to start a kindness movement, so they printed thousands of buttons that said "Kindness Is Contagious—Catch It!" Each person who got one was told to pass it on whenever they met a kind person. The buttons have spread all over the world.

Instructions are so powerful that just adding an instruction to be creative can lead people to solutions that are more creative. Psychologist **Melba A. Colgrove** conducted a study at the University of Michigan with 475 students who were asked to find solutions to time-scheduling problems on a subassembly line. The

Great Moments in the
HISTORY OF INSTRUCTIONS

1842: COMMODORE THOMAS A.C. JONES, U.S.N. PACIFIC FLEET, HAS INSTRUCTIONS TO SEIZE CALIFORNIA **IF** WAR BREAKS OUT. BUT HOW TO KNOW? MESSAGES FROM WASHINGTON TAKE 4 MONTHS TO ARRIVE! SO — ON OCT. 19, JONES INVADES MONTEREY, ARRESTS EVERYONE, REALIZES HIS ERROR, AND LEAVES AFTER 30 HOURS.

SO SORRY... I COULDN'T KNOW... LET'S HOPE I DON'T HAVE TO REPEAT THE BLUNDER...

GONICK

students were divided into two groups and were both given identical instructions to suggest a work schedule that would produce the best results. One group received an additional instruction—"Be Creative."

In the group given the standard instructions, only 39 percent arrived at what was deemed the highest quality solutions. In the group that received the instruction to be original, the rate was 52 percent.

PURPOSE: FOR WHAT REASON?

The purpose explains why an instruction is being given. You want to invite someone to your home for dinner, so you extend an invitation and give him or her your address. Dinner is the reason; reaching your home is the destination. The reason should be given first, and it should be distinguished from the objective. In this way, the takers know what to expect, they know why they are being asked to reach a destination. This sounds simplistic, because in giving road directions, the purpose is usually given, but it's surprising how often the purpose is left out of other instructions or confused with the objective.

The purpose should inspire how the instruction-taker performs. In the crash of the Avianca jet liner, the pilots didn't make it clear to the air-traffic controllers that the purpose for their request to land was that they were running out of fuel. The air-traffic controllers—assuming that all pilots have a safe landing as their objective—made them wait because of crowded skies. The controllers didn't recognize that the Avianca pilots had an emergency, special request.

Hearing the purpose first will diminish the tendency of people to confuse the channel or form with the content, to become distracted by the forms and neglect the spirit of the instruction. Let's say that you own an advertising firm and are asked by a museum to publicize a new exhibit of beer steins. When you are instructing employees, tell them that their work should be focused on bringing people to the exhibit and ensuring that their tour is pleasurable, instead of saying, "We have to design a poster or some advertising for a beer stein exhibit." This already orients them toward an objective—the specific production of a poster or print ad. Maybe the best solution would be to send up hot-air balloons or produce radio ads or sponsor beer tastings. The purpose could be accomplished in a variety of ways, so predisposing employees toward a particular objective will limit the imaginativeness of their solutions.

Having a purpose helps people prepare and weigh the importance of the instructions. Having a purpose is liberating. It inspires more creative outlets for information. Odetics, a technology firm in Anaheim, wanted employees to have more fun at the company. That was the reason that inspired the Fun Committee. Members plan hula hoop contests, bubble gum blowing contests, and telephone booth stuffing. Instead of putting puzzles in your newsletter, maybe you should hold a contest to see which team can peel a watermelon the fastest, bake the best dessert, come up with the most disgusting screen saver.

The objective and the purpose of the instruction prepare the taker for the core instructions by giving a frame on which to organize them. They can either limit or expand the imagination of taker.

CORE: WHAT'S THE PROCEDURE TO FOLLOW?

The procedures are the meat of the instruction toward which all the other components are oriented. "Drive three miles, then turn north. Take the Eisenhower Expressway for about 10 miles, then turn off at the first Oak Park exit..." The type of instruction influences the significance of the core. In a task-based instruction, all other components serve the core. In a goal-based instruction, the core may only be suggested.

Surrogate fingers. An image to think about when you envision the core of an instruction is the pointed finger. The core should lead you to a specific place along the path to comprehension. When you ask someone how to get to someplace and they point their finger, that is an unmistakable direction. When someone is describing a place to you and they point to it on a map, you know

Keeping Tabs on Your Stock

At first glance, stock listings look like an endless sea of numbers. This has more to do with the volume of listings and the use of small type than with the complexity of the information.

To read the listings, remember that stock prices are given in fractions of dollars. Thus $8^1/2$ **equals $8.50;** $8^1/4$ **equals $8.25. The fraction** $1/8$ **refers to** $12^1/2$ **cents; and** $8^1/8$ **equals about $8.13.**

Highest and lowest prices of the stock are shown for the last 52 weeks. Stocks reaching a new high or low for the year are marked with an arrow in the lefthand margin. These figures show you the **volatility** of a stock – an indicator of both profit potential and risk. The percentage gain or loss is often more significant than the dollar gain or loss: a $5 change in a $10 stock indicates more volatility than a $5 move in a $30 stock.

For instance, Harcourt Brace Jovanovich, Inc. was more volatile over the past year (swinging $9^1/2$ points, or 71%, between $13^1/4$ and $3^3/4$) than was Harris Corp. which moved $18^1/8$ points between $40^1/8$ and 22, or roughly 45%.

Cash dividend per share is given in dollars and cents. A dividend is a payment to shareholders of part of a company's profit. This figure is an estimate of the anticipated yearly dividend per share. Hartmarx's yearly dividend is estimated at $1.10 per share. If you owned 100 shares, you'd receive $110 in dividend payments each year, probably in quarterly payments of $27.50.

Sometimes the dividend column for a company is blank, indicating that the company doesn't pay cash dividends.

P-E Ratio, short for price-earnings ratio, refers to the relationship between the price of one share of stock and the annual earnings of the company. (Since earnings aren't given here, you can't calculate this figure yourself from this chart.)

For La-Z-Boy Chair Corp., the price-earnings ratio has been derived by dividing the **closing price** of $15.37 by the company's **earnings per share** (about $1.39) to arrive at 11. It's useful to read the P-E ratio as follows: *The price of a La-Z-Boy share is 11 times the company's earnings per share for the most recent four quarters.*

The P-E ratio is a critical piece of information because it expresses the value of a stock in terms of company earnings rather than selling price. The P-E ratios of different stocks can be compared to assess their relative values.

It's important to remember that there's no perfect P-E ratio. Some stocks which have lower earnings will have higher P-E ratios; these are usually growth stocks. On the other hand, an income stock which pays consistently high dividends will tend to have a lower P-E ratio.

Net change compares the closing price given here with the closing price of the day before (given in the previous day's paper). A minus (-) indicates this closing price is lower than the previous day's; a plus (+) means it's higher. This figure shows you what's happened to the stock's price in the last day. Since La-Z-Boy Chair Corp., closing at $15^3/8$, was down $1/8$ point; you can infer that the closing price quoted the previous day was $15^1/2$.

Stocks that show a price change of 5% or more are shown in boldface type. Landmark Bancshares Corp.'s move of $1^1/8$ represents a change of 8.1%

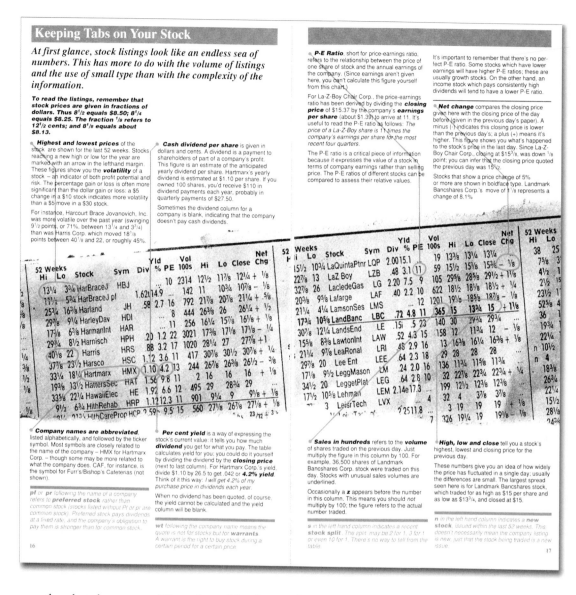

Company names are abbreviated, listed alphabetically, and followed by the ticker symbol. Most symbols are closely related to the name of the company – HMX for Hartmarx Corp. – though some may be more related to what the company does. CAF, for instance, is the symbol for Furr's/Bishop's Cafeterias (not shown).

pf or *pr* following the name of a company refers to **preferred stock** rather than common stock (stocks listed without Pf or pr are common stock). Preferred stock pays dividends at a fixed rate, and the company's obligation to pay them is stronger than for common stock.

Per cent yield is a way of expressing the stock's current value: it tells you how much **dividend** you get for what you pay. The table calculates yield for you; you could do it yourself by dividing the dividend by the **closing price** (next to last column). For Hartmarx Corp.'s yield, divide $1.10 by 26.5 to get .042 or **4.2% yield**. Think of it this way: *I will get 4.2% of my purchase price in dividends each year.*

When no dividend has been quoted, of course, the yield cannot be calculated and the yield column will be blank.

wt following the company name means the quote is not for stocks but for **warrants**. A warrant is the right to buy stock during a certain period for a certain price.

Sales in hundreds refers to the **volume** of shares traded on the previous day. Just multiply the figure in this column by 100. For example, 36,500 shares of Landmark Bancshares Corp. stock were traded on this day. Stocks with unusual sales volumes are underlined.

Occasionally a **z** appears before the number in this column. This means you should *not* multiply by 100; the figure refers to the actual number traded.

s in the left-hand column indicates a recent **stock split**. The split may be 2 for 1, 3 for 1 or even 10 for 1. There's no way to tell from the table.

High, low and close tell you a stock's highest, lowest and closing price for the previous day.

These numbers give you an idea of how widely the price has fluctuated in a single day; usually the differences are small. The largest spread seen here is for Landmark Bancshares stock, which traded for as high as $15 per share and as low as $13^3/4$, and closed at $15.

n in the left-hand column indicates a **new stock**, issued within the last 52 weeks. This doesn't necessarily mean the company listing is new, just that the stock being traded is a new issue.

16

17

exactly what they mean. There is nothing better than a finger for pointing out people and locations, for identifying, for stressing a point. In a written text, highlighted paragraphs, bold type, arrows, etc., all act like fingers to point the way. Instructions should be like surrogate fingers. They should offer the security of being able to have a point clarified, to have something repeated, to know that there is somewhere to turn for more information.

Never be afraid to repeat yourself either. If you were on life support in a hospital, you would be happy to know that the hospital has redundant power systems in the event of a failure. Phone companies have redundant networks in the event of storm damage. As informers, we are taught that redundancy is evil. Don't repeat yourself. But, most great instructors know that redundancy is essential to learning. **Albert Mehrabian** in his book *Silent Messages*, wrote that people exposed to an idea once, at the end of 30 days, retained less than 10 percent. When exposed six times at intervals they retained 90 percent in the same period. Microsoft really exploits this. They give you multiple ways to do almost everything whether to save a file or format a font. There are quick codes or, if you forget, there are drop-down menus. If you forget one way, there's always another.

In the summer of 2000, there was an exhibit on early Syrian civilization at the Musée de la Civilization in Quebec City. Yes, the show had all the basic poster board panels printed with information about how the Syrians who settled in the Fertile Crescent and were able to live by agriculture instead of having to roam as hunters became the earliest true stable civilization. So, for those who like to read, the show got high marks for informability, but the exhibit designers didn't stop there. They had fabric panels printed with images and information, which repeated key ideas from the poster boards. The swaying panels also gave people the feeling of living in tents. In the background, a tape played of the sounds of the time you might expect to hear. Therefore, you had information coming in visually, intellectually, and aurally. The multiple channels left a memorable impression. Had I just read the text, I wouldn't have remembered half as much.

Stoplights in Quebec also take advantage of the right of ways. They use shape and time as well as color to convey information. The red light is a square, the green a circle, and the yellow a triangle. This way, even someone who is color-blind could drive safely. When the green light is nearing the end of it's cycle, it starts blinking to alert drivers that a yellow caution light will soon appear.

I used to think if I could just get information in the perfect form, I would be a success. But, when it comes to communications, everyone needs a different level of information and likes to get

their information in a different way. Some people like to get their explanations verbally, others like to read them, others like to learn by example. Use different components to reiterate messages. The more variety of forms you offer, the greater your chance of inspiring action.

TIME: WHAT'S THE DURATION?

The estimated time or effort it will take to carry out an instruction should be built into an instruction, whether you're telling someone how to get to Grandma's house or how to load a communications program on a computer. This gives the instruction follower cues that something is amiss and prevents unnecessary investment in fruitless or misguided attempts. If you have an idea of the time an instruction will take, you reduce the anxiety of feeling like you are wasting your time on the wrong path.

You are in Los Angeles and some friends invite you over for dinner at their house in Santa Monica. They give you directions. They tell you to take the San Diego Freeway and get off at the Santa Monica Freeway. If you have no idea how long you should drive before your exit, you could wind up in Mexico before realizing you have overshot the mark (although your error might be somewhat tempered by southern California traffic). However, if your host tells you that the Santa Monica Freeway should appear after about 45 minutes of driving in moderate traffic, and you have driven on the San Diego Freeway for one hour, you will be alerted to the fact that something may have gone wrong.

The Internal Revenue Service has really mastered the time concept. Most of the tax forms state how long it should take to fill out. When you fill out a form in 15 minutes and see that it should have taken two hours, you can probably figure that you didn't do something you should have.

Knowing the time something should take saves wasted effort. It keeps you from investing too much energy in the wrong direction. If employees are told how long the task is expected to take, they have some measure against which they can compare their own efforts—whether you're telling them how to get to Grandma's house or how to take advantage of a new purchasing program.

Estimating the time a task takes also influences the importance an instruction-taker will give to a task. "Will you write a report on what happened at the meeting in the next half hour?" will be accorded less weight than "Write a report on the meeting, and I want it in a week."

EXPECTATION: WHAT CAN I ANTICIPATE ALONG THE WAY?

Anticipation is the reassuring element of instructions. This is what the taker can expect to encounter while carrying out the instructions. Anticipation helps correct misperceptions in time and ill-defined goals. Knowing what you can expect to see along the way reassures you that you are proceeding correctly. You should drive until you see the red brick church and take a right. When someone has told you that the drive will take 20 minutes and you drive for 30 before seeing the first landmark, you shouldn't panic about the time estimates.

Road instructions are usually good in the anticipation department. You will pass Sam's Feed Lot and when you get to Belly-Up Savings and Loan, turn left. Even electronic equipment manuals often tell you what to anticipate along the way. "If a red light flashes, then you have installed the battery correctly." The lack of anticipation is most often found in informal instructions. If you tell your secretary to "Get Snead on the phone for me," and neglect to tell her that Snead doesn't want to hear from you, she may give up with the first call. If she anticipates his reluctance, she might call again or try another route.

Are You *Sure*? Unfamiliarity breeds anxiety. Most people are apprehensive about going someplace they've never been. My wife, Gloria, sits next to me in the car and asks, "Did you ask them how long before the Santa Monica Freeway? Did you bring their telephone number? Are you sure? Are you sure?" Of course, I'm not sure; I've never been on this road in my life. How do I know whether I've gone too far? It drives me crazy, so the ride seems like it takes an hour. Then coming home seems so fast. It's because I don't have the anxiety of wondering how long the ride will take. You can never completely remove the anxiety of going to a place for the first time, but you can reduce it.

Anticipation is comfort. It's like having your own sherpa. Knowing what you can expect to see along the way reassures you that you are proceeding correctly. The anxiety of feeling that you are on the wrong track can be alleviated, if not eliminated, by getting a pat on the back as you reach points in the process.

FAILURE: HOW DO I RECOGNIZE AN ERROR?

This is the part that's most often missing from directions, yet is probably the most effective way of reducing frustration on the part of the follower. All directions should have in them the indications that you have gone too far, the warning lights to turn back. In other words, if you see a second Mobil station, you have gone too far.

What are the signs that you've screwed up? You learn more from failure than from success. I believe that the troubleshooting sections should be the most important part of any manual. Usually, they are stuck in the back in an appendix, but this is always the information that people desperately want. Failure is the warning light to turn back or a number to call for help.

One wrong button, and you're out $16 million. A London brokerage house found out how critical it is to build an error component into its training program that would alert new hires

when they pressed the wrong button in executing trades. A young stock trader-in-training pressed the wrong key during a training session last year and moved from the training module to the market, unintentionally launching a $19 billion trade, the largest single transaction in German futures. The trade cost his employers an estimated $16 million. I can't imagine it would have been as costly to build an alert into the system that would have caused a box to pop up and say: "Warning, you are about to enter the actual trading system. Do you *really* want to execute a trade?"

The junior trader who thought he was still on simulated training software, posted an offering of 130,000 German bond futures contracts, worth at least $19 billion. The button he pressed actually delivered him to the online system for real trading, and the trade went through.

Computers have one of the most meaningless ways of telling you that something has gone wrong: the "fatal error" message. Who came up with this name? The first time I saw it I thought my computer had died. It sounds so permanent. It's so meaningless that it's inspired a host of prank programs and even poetry.

THE ROAD TO EVERYWHERE

Attention should be paid to the order in which the instruction content is given, for it will affect the order in which it is followed. You probably wouldn't give someone road directions in random order, but you might give an assistant instructions for the day without thinking about their order. This applies to the building of a particular instruction, as well as to offering several instructions at once.

Your directions will be understood more easily if they are given in sequence—the purpose of the instruction, the desired objective, the core instructions, the estimated time it should take, what can be anticipated along the way, and the signals that indicate mistakes or failure. Each step will add to the taker's ability to understand and make decisions about the next step. The purpose will help the takers see the motivation for the objective and maybe even inspire them to suggest other ways of meeting your objectives. With an awareness of purpose and objective, the takers can isolate core instructions that don't make sense in light of the purpose and seek clarification.

RELATIVE AND ABSOLUTE INSTRUCTIONS

In the same way that words can be placed on a continuum from concrete to abstract, instructions can be plotted on a line from relative to absolute depending on their degree of specificity. The instruction "Let's get some light in here" could be interpreted to mean "Open the drapes," "Turn on all the lights," "Turn on a particular light," "Let's call in some experts to shed some light upon a subject." The performance of the instruction is highly relative to the taker's interpretation.

The range of possible interpretations increases as the instructions move toward the relative end. Depending on the task at hand, the width of the interpretation range can be either desirable or deadly. If you are trying to put together a futon bed, you need a high degree of specifics. You want to be told in no uncertain terms. If you are a competent salesperson, you might be insulted if a sales manager starts specifying how you talk to a potential client on the phone. A more relative instruction to "Increase sales" might be more effective, for it could inspire a variety of actions.

ERROR MESSAGE HAIKU

A file that big?
It might be very useful.
But now it is gone.

– David J. Liszewski

Windows NT crashed.
I am the Blue Screen of Death.
No one hears your screams.

– Peter Rotham

The code was willing,
It considered your request,
But the chips were weak.

– Barry L. Brumitt

Server's poor response
Not quick enough for browser.
Timed out, plum blossom.

– Rik Jesperson

Aborted effort:
Close all that you have.
You ask way too much.

– Mike Hagler

Chaos reigns within.
Reflect, repent, and reboot.
Order shall return.

– Suzie Wagner

No keyboard present
Hit F1 to continue
Zen engineering?

– Jim Griffith

Serious error.
All shortcuts have disappeared
Screen. Mind. Both are blank.

– Ian Hughes

(catdance.home.mindspring.com/haiku.html)

On the other hand, a highly relative order to "work harder" might not give you enough clues as to how the goal might be reached.

The chances for clarity increase as a message becomes more absolute, but so do the constraints. The search for perfect instructions requires finding the balance between clarity and constraint, between the relative and the absolute. There is magic in the ambiguity of the relative, but there is also confounding mystery.

You can spell out all of the details of what you want at the expense of stifling the imagination of your employees. You can also be so vague that they have no idea what you want.

The level of control and dependency varies among different types of instruction. Assembly instructions involve careful adherence to each step. A dictionary on the other hand is an instruction book for words, but it is not necessary to read it cover to cover.

I want people to feel a sense of propriety in their work, the freedom to create, to do things beyond my suggestions. I don't want someone to feel constrained by what I'm asking. I want them to go beyond, but not impinge upon, my vision. I define only the boundaries in which they can work.

The following are questions to ask yourself while composing the content of an instruction:

- Have you made it clear to the taker that you are giving an instruction?

- Have you explained the purpose or the need for the instruction?

- Are you clear on the reason? What is it that you want to get done? Don't answer too quickly. It's easy to say, "I want a report on the return of merchandise." But maybe what you really want to know is how well your products compare to a competitor's products as far as returns go. Maybe you don't need a report, maybe a table or a chart might better answer your questions.

- Have you identified the items to be covered by the instruction? Don't just tell someone to plan a meeting; include the ancillary instructions—who should be notified, what special considerations there are, what kind of record you want for the meeting?

- Have you ordered the instruction in such a way that the taker will understand the sequence in which it should be carried out? What are the most critical aspects of it? What can be ignored if time and resources are constrained?

- Have you included what the taker might anticipate finding as he or she performs the instruction?

- Have you allowed for failure? Takers need to know the signs that they have gone astray in following the instruction. The sooner they understand the mistakes, the sooner they can correct them.

The most instructive communications…

- Lead to defined actions.

- Can be tied to business goals.

- Have a measurable return on investment.

- Are organized for understanding.

- Expressed in a form appropriate to the message.

What were they thinking?

Actual instructions printed on various products:

BAG OF FRITOS
You could be a winner! No purchase necessary. Details inside.

BAR OF DIAL SOAP
Directions: Use like regular soap.

FROZEN DINNER SERVING SUGGESTION
Defrost.

HOTEL-PROVIDED SHOWER CAP IN A BOX
Fits one head.

TESCO'S TIRIMISU DESSERT
Do not turn upside down. (Printed on the bottom of the box.)

NYTOL (A SLEEP AID)
Warning: May cause drowsiness.

KOREAN KITCHEN KNIFE
Warning: Keep out of children.

SAINSBURY'S PEANUTS
Warning: contains nuts

CHINESE-MADE CHRISTMAS LIGHTS
For indoor or outdoor use only.

- Give the audience alternative ways of access.

- Can be visualized in concrete ways.

THE TREASURE HUNT APPROACH

When you go on a treasure hunt, you are given a first clue or instruction. When you solve the first clue, you get an affirmation. "You did a great job. Now you can proceed with step two." Most communications don't give you this kind of encouragement along the way. They don't pat you on the back when you fall off the bike and say, "Good, you've fallen off the bike and didn't hurt yourself. That's a sign that you are learning, because everyone falls off the bike learning balance, and you have learned how to fall without hurting yourself."

Reassurance should be an aspect of every instruction. Instructions to perform a task or find a place can be constructed with affirmations along the way. "When you go under the turnpike, you are halfway there; when the screen says Transmit, the fax is being sent." Any kind of instruction will benefit from this approach. Let your audience know that they are on the right course, and they will pursue the task or goal with more joy and diligence.

I've a set of instructions at home which open up great realms for the improvement of technical writing. They begin, "Assembly of Japanese bicycle require great peace of mind." At first I laughed because of memories of bicycles I'd put together, and, of course, the unintended slur on Japanese manufacturers. But there's a lot of wisdom in that statement. Peace of mind isn't at all superficial, really. What we call workability of the machine is just an objectification of this peace of mind. The ultimate test is always your own serenity. If you don't have this when you start, and maintain it while you're working, you're likely to build your personal problems right into the machine itself.

– Robert Pirsig, *Zen and the Art of Motorcycle Maintenance*

12 TALKING ON THE JOB: SEEING INSTRUCTIONS IN THE CONTEXT OF WORK

What makes work so bad? Most executives imagine their employees complaining they don't get paid enough, their office partitions aren't high enough, their bosses aren't nice enough, and too much is expected of them. But at the top of most employees' gripe lists are problems in communication—not understanding what is expected of them, feeling excluded from important information, working under people who give vague and confusing instructions. When employees see their superiors as their main roadblock to getting their jobs done, the culprits are likely to be irrational or incompetent instruction-givers.

A table in *Corporate Communications: A Comparison of Japanese and American Practices* by **William V. Ruch** reveals that the most important job elements to an employee were rated as the least important to their foremen who were asked to predict what their people viewed as important. The top three were: "Appreciation of work done, feeling 'in' on things (full information), and help on personal problems." The foremen assumed that "Good wages, job security, and promotion" would be the issues dearest to their employees' hearts.

PERCEPTION GAP

The difference between what management and employees think is important represents a staggering gap in most American businesses. When management has a distorted picture of how their employees view their jobs and what is important to them, miscommunications, inefficiencies, mistakes, and ill-will are bound to result.

According to **T. Harrell Allen** in *The Bottom Line: Communicating in the Organization*, "research indicates that 50 percent understanding between supervisor and subordinate on job descriptions is about the best level of understanding that is generally reached."

The situation in most offices never reaches 50 percent. Ask most subordinates to define their job duties, major obstacles to getting their work done, priorities, and future requirements of the job; then ask their supervisors the same questions, and you might wonder if both of these people are working for the same company. Yet these are the aspects of most jobs that should rate the highest

Importance of Job Elements, as Seen by Employees and Foremen

Job Element	Employee's Rating	Foreman's Rating
Appreciation of work done	1	1
Feeling "in" on things (full information)	2	2
Help on personal problems	3	3
Job security (steady work)	4	4
Good wages	5	5
Interesting work (belief in importance of job)	6	6
Promotion	7	7
Management loyal to workers	8	8
Good working conditions	9	9
Tactful disciplining (respectful treatment)	10	10

Source: Merrihue, Managing by Communication, *p. 42, as reported in* Corporate Communications: A Comparison of Japanese and American Practices, *by William Ruch*

levels of understanding between subordinates and their bosses, for job duties and requirements are often written out in detailed employee handbooks. How much agreement is there in your office between employees and their bosses as to job descriptions?

In-depth interviews conducted by the American Management Association found a high level of discrepancy between middle-managers and their upper-management bosses in basic job descriptions and requirements, even when the superiors were allowed to hand select the subordinates with whom they worked most closely.

More than 75 percent of the 222 pairs studied received a rating of 2 or lower on a scale of 1 to 4 (the highest degree of agreement). The only category in which superiors and subordinates agreed slightly more than they disagreed was in job duties.

When management and employees don't see eye-to-eye on such basic issues as job duties, the communication gap is likely to manifest itself in other areas as well. If your boss doesn't have the same view of your job as you do, all of her instructions will come filtered through this disparity. When you think you are the company bookkeeper and your boss thinks you are her private secretary, neither of you will perform at full capacity.

What most companies fail to realize is that even if all employees are adequately trained to perform tasks and operate machinery, the problems are only half-solved. The day-to-day operations will require constant communication between staff and management. The main component of these communications is instructions. The communication of instructions is how management tells employees what to do—to translate its vision into products and services. It is the means by which work gets done.

Poor communications mean more than just Joe in quality control not informing Sam in pattern cutting that fly fronts are showing up in the trouser backs. It means that essential instructions are not getting through, or they are misunderstood and misinterpreted.

The workplace runs on instructions, but they are of little value if they cannot be accurately communicated. Poor communications can affect every area of operation. Often employees must labor under the ill-formed instructions of their superiors, who perhaps have erroneous ideas about their underlings. These workers don't lack in abilities; they lack in instructions because too many bosses are incapable of making their employees understand just what is expected of them.

SEEING LABOR AS PEOPLE

The importance of communication and instructions in the workplace has little historical precedent. In an industrial economy, employees were looked upon as physical equipment, like drill presses or forklifts, and prevailing management philosophy called for them to be treated as such, oiled and tightened up as little as was necessary to ensure their continued operation. This policy worked adequately in an industrial society, where products were manufactured on an assembly line by people who performed single tasks. Employees did not require sophisticated information or instruction. Job training consisted of sitting down at your new job and having the guy next to you say, "You're supposed to drill a quarter-inch hole in this piece of metal and send it down the line." The margin for misinterpretation of the instructions was minimal.

In 1927, researchers from Harvard University conducted a study at the Hawthorne Works of the Western Electric Company in Illinois. They found that productivity increased when workers were moved to a room with more lighting, when additional breaks were permitted, and when the lunch hour was lengthened. The researchers weren't too surprised until they conducted further tests. They reduced the lighting, the number of breaks, and the length of the lunch hour, and they found that productivity increased in this case as well.

They determined that this resulted because, for the first time, the employees were being treated like human beings, and they responded to the attention by increasing their efforts. Thus was born the human factor in management philosophy.

The human relations school didn't really catch hold until after World War II, when the business community discovered the idea that attention to communications might serve some practical, economical purpose. As jobs grew more complex, groups and committees were formed where work once was done by an individual. Groups, by their nature, had to deliver messages, share information, and reach a consensus to fulfill their commissions.

In a workplace that was becoming increasingly complicated, communications began to rise in importance.

Organizational communications became a buzzword in the 1960s, when material was generated on the subject from almost every discipline—sociology, business management, psychology, anthropology, linguistics, and even the hard sciences. Communication was examined not as a linear process, "but in the context of a changing environment in which communication is an interactive series of behaviors fraught with error," stated Ruch. "Special attention began to be paid to informal communication, communication barriers, non-verbal communication, and international and intercultural communication."

Unfortunately, many companies are still towing a grossly inadequate, Neanderthal attitude toward management communications—a philosophy forged on the assembly line. Looking toward employees as a valuable source of information on business operations still remains a radical idea in many American businesses—and they are paying a high price for their reluctance to change.

INSTRUCTIONS WILL BECOME EVEN MORE IMPORTANT

Improving the quality of office instructions involves an understanding of the context component in the system—in its broadest application. The particular work environment in which instructions are given, the state of a particular industry, and the current economic situation in general will affect the creation and interpretation of instructions. Numerous economic and cultural forces are at work that will expand the role of instructions in the workplace and require a higher caliber of communications. The following forces are also going to make instructions harder to communicate.

- The more sophisticated communication needs of an information-based economy.

- Corporate instability and the concomitant rise of anxiety in the workforce.

- Increased job-hopping.

- Greater consequences of poor instructions in a high-tech society.

In the 1950s, attention turned to choice of effective media, written or oral, and the respective advantages and disadvantages of each. Particular methods began to be recommended for communicating information from management to employees; employee handbooks, company newspapers and magazines, and bulletin boards.

…Also in the 1950s, methods of upward communication received great attention: attitude surveys, suggestion systems, and interviews among them. Management began to realize that employees have ideas for improvement of their own work methods, the basis for the quality circle, which is growing in use and popularity today.

– William V. Ruch,
*Corporate Communications:
A Comparison of Japanese
and American Practices*

- New demands on companies to communicate in different languages and tailor their products to different cultures, as a result of the globalization of markets.

- Changing demographics of the workforce.

- Illiteracy in the workplace.

In the last 20 years, the transformation from a product- or industrial-based economy to a service- or information-based one has become complete. More than 50 percent of all businesses deal not in tangible products but in information. Information is now the dominant base of our economy, and with it comes a concomitant need for communication. Dealing with people— that is, customers, clients, salesmen, and co-workers—requires more sophisticated skills than working on an assembly line.

Emphasizing communication is no longer an avant-garde option; for forward-thinking companies, it is a necessity.

When the product is information, humanity becomes a factor. In a world run by ideas, people are the resources. Work is affected by the ability of bosses to communicate tasks, by the employee's interpretation of the instruction he gets, by the moods and personalities of the people in the office.

American executives devote 94 percent of their time in communication-related activities, according to **George Plotzke**, market manager of AT&T's technology group. Oral communication accounts for 69 percent of that time, with 53 percent spent in face-to-face meetings and 16 percent on the telephone. Dealing with written material and mail accounts for 25 percent of their time, and problem-solving, planning, and idea work accounts for three percent. Middle managers spend somewhat less time communicating—80 percent for middle managers and 70 percent for first-line managers.

> I can't tell you how many companies I've called and had someone say, "Well, we're in the midst of an internal re-organization and we'll be able to give you what you want once we get organized." I think *eternal* reorganization might be more accurate.
>
> – Richard Saul Wurman

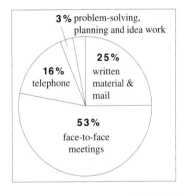

American executives' performance of communication-related activities.

FEAR AND LOATHING IN THE OFFICE

The very vocabulary of corporate America is dispiriting to employee imagination and establishes a poor atmosphere for creatively carrying out instructions. The word executive has violent connotations, sharing a root that means to put to death. Executives fire orders, command respect, and marshal the troops. It is a word of intimidation, designed to instill fear, not inspiration, conjuring up pictures of wrathful despots who delight in throwing their weight around. Phrases like dominate the market, crush the competition, butt heads with rivals, and run it up the flagpole are common parlance in boardroom bandying. Sometimes it seems that the language of enterprise was lifted directly from the army or the football field—neither an arena noted for its imagination or creativity.

Today's business climate fosters anxiety and defensive responses. With takeovers, mergers, unstable business climates, and widespread job migrations, people are robbed of the freedom of being able to admit they don't understand, to ask questions, or to disagree with a superior. This promotes an atmosphere of insecurity and mistrust. Our lives are more complicated, run by more machinery, and demand more knowledge; anxiety proliferates during an age that demands a more assured response.

In a stable office environment, co-workers are more likely to cooperate, to share information, and to help each other. In a more volatile one, the likelihood is higher that the person next to you may be after your job. This dog-eat-dog attitude in the office reduces the incentive to share information or to instruct your office neighbor in company protocol. Yet this is the bedrock of corporate life and the economy increasingly relies on it.

AT&T's official 150-page downsizing manual referred to the firing of 40,000 workers as a "force management program" aimed at reducing an imbalance of forces and skills. Employees not invited back are labeled "unassigned" and a dismissal notice is an "involuntary offer" to work elsewhere. Human Resources VP James Meadows warns that "People need to look upon themselves as vendors who come to this company to sell their skills." Jobs, he says, are being replaced by "projects" and workers need to see themselves as "contingent."

– *New York Times*, (2/15/96)

Microsoft has been under criticism for exploiting temporary workers by hiring them for what really are long term positions and then keeping them on for years at the lower temp wages. Recognizing the problem, Microsoft has announced a new policy they believe will help clarify to "contingent" employees their true status. From now on, temporary employees will simply leave their jobs for a month after a year's employment, as a reminder that they are temporary or contingent....

Sharon Decker, director of contingent staffing is quoted as saying, "The change is intended to strengthen temps' relationship with the employment agencies that are their employers of record."

– *Seattle Times*, (6/24/98)

Anxiety and fear inhibit constructive response to instructions. By their nature, they dominate other emotions and are the last feelings you want to evoke when giving important instructions. They are paralyzing; they pave the way for errors and misunderstandings. When the primary emotion toward your job is the fear of losing it, you are likely to be too anxious to follow orders.

Feeling that your job is always on the line also brings back test anxiety—the fear from your years in school that your future will be determined by your performance. Only the most well-adjusted or the most oblivious perform at their peak when the weight of their future hangs in a perpetually tenuous balance.

Fear tends to get in the way of listening. It evokes a flight response. The instruction-bearer becomes the dreaded one. You try to second-guess the instructions, to demonstrate your task–fluency by exclaiming your understanding prematurely in an attempt to escape an uncomfortable situation. This fear is picked up by the instructor and, most likely, will make her uncomfortable as well.

Your chances of understanding the spirit of an instruction are slim to none if your first response to it is to fall into a morass of anxiety and self-doubt, wondering, "What happens if I make a mistake, what are the liabilities, how can I do this without causing any trouble, what could go wrong, how can I protect myself from problems, could it lose money, could someone sue me, could I wreck the equipment?"

The motive becomes stalling not solving, hedging your bets instead of making decisions. Then, if you feel a decision is imminent, you can always call in expensive consultants with the thinly veiled task of supporting the decisions rather than reacting genuinely to them. "Let's cover our asses. Maybe we'd better do a mall-intercept study in Des Moines." Research should be inspired by a need to know, not used to spread the blame in case something goes wrong.

People fear failure, because they don't see it as the road to success. By getting wound up in anxiety about failing, people often make more mistakes, because they are so busy fearing that they are going to make them.

When I teach, I tell my class, "What I want is difficult and most of you are going to screw up." When I hire an assistant I say "whatever you do, it's not going to be good enough. But I won't hold it against you, therefore, don't hold it against yourself."

I want to take away the fear of failure, by saying it's okay to fail. I want them to know that they will make mistakes. Few people are permitted this knowledge. Instead they carry the solitary and private fear that they are going to screw up, sure that everyone else knows how to do what they can't.

LET THEM MAKE MISTAKES

A friend of mine used to work at Rizzoli Bookstore. Sometimes, books that have been on the shelves for a long time lose their price tags. The book clerks usually call down to the stockroom and ask for a price. But these are invariably the books for which records have long since disappeared. So the stockroom manager will spend 15 minutes looking for something that probably doesn't exist anymore, and the fearful book clerk who has been indoctrinated into blindly following the rules has to tell the customer that there is no price, which is tantamount to saying, "We cannot sell this book." My friend gave up on this fast. She reckoned that if she made up a reasonable price and the customer bought the book, she could increase store profits by freeing up space on the shelves for books that sold more quickly. Soon, she got a reputation in the store as the one to ask if you needed a price. No one ever questioned where she got her information; they were all delighted to give up on the fruitless calls to the stockroom. They were absolved of responsibility because they had checked for the price.

If she feared not following the rules, the books would still be on the shelves gathering dust and many customers would have walked out thinking: Does this store really want to sell books?

WHICH WAY TO THE EXECUTIVE SUITE?

The increasing rootlessness of people also plays a role in the importance of instruction. People used to spend their entire working careers at one company where they could learn the ropes gradually, following a natural apprenticeship program. But today, jobs have become as disposable as diapers. People jump from job to job, often from one industry to the next.

According to a report by the Center for Creative Leadership in Greensboro, North Carolina, most white collar workers will have from eight to 20 bosses during their careers—depending on their rising speed. Owing to the number of corporate takeovers, buyouts, and restructurings, these bosses will often have less experience with the company than the employees do. If you haven't been on the job long enough to figure out what you're supposed to be doing, you'll have a tough time explaining duties to an underling.

Many companies have a turnover rate of 20 to 30 percent a year, so more people have to be trained more quickly.

HIGH-TECH SKILLS REQUIRED

The glut of information that must be perused further taxes human capabilities—whether it be about developments in the field or new equipment in the office.

According to **Robert Horn**, president of Information Mapping in Waltham, Massachusetts, the typical manager wades through a million words a week. "Not surprisingly, several problems result from this kind of information gridlock—high error rates, low recall, inordinate demands on supervisors, expensive rewriting of documentation, and a constant need for retraining people."

And the skills that the workforce has to master are harder to teach. The advent of telecommunications, robotics, and sophisticated computer systems has complicated the workplace, requiring even more science and math skills. The ability of one person to affect many has risen exponentially. In the financial world, billions of dollars can go through the hands of one person in a day. In the medical world, the machinery that sustains life requires more expertise to operate. People have to be taught how to operate and maintain complex equipment, sometimes in an afternoon, and then make decisions that may affect millions of people.

DUTIES ONCE REMOVED

The complexity of business today makes the big picture harder to grasp—how do the efforts of one person affect the whole? Workers have become distanced from their duties—figuratively and literally. In an agrarian society, a farmer plowed furrows in a field, planted seeds, and knew that corn would grow in the summer. Even in an industrial economy, workers on an assembly line got to see the finished product, even if their only contribution was to drill a few holes.

This luxury of proximity and familiarity is denied many workers today. The finished product is often information—a commodity whose real life is abstract. A recommendation, a report, a file has little tangible value in its paper and ink. The value is the ephemeral information itself, information that may have been compiled by hundreds of people from hundreds of sources.

The scope and reach of companies has scattered company functions around the world. Corporate offices can be in one country, the factory in another. Management, which might not be doing a great job communicating with employees working in the home office, must now communicate with people of different countries, whose differing languages and cultures increase exponentially the difficulty of giving understandable instructions.

The scattering of functions around the world also makes it harder for people to stay informed about different parts of a business. People work for companies in which they never see the product. A commodities trader could spend his lifetime dealing with grain and never see a stalk of wheat. A garment executive might never feel the nap on a roll of velour.

This distancing of people from products does more than induce poetic longing or nostalgia. It complicates describing a product (tangible or not), understanding company business in perspective, comprehending the totality of an issue, and giving instructions that take into account the big picture.

"Whether as citizens, as family and neighborhood members, or as workers and professionals, the vast majority of us now live in a context affected on a daily basis by international forces. This fact poses profound and far-reaching challenges....Our nation has been steeped in the history, traditions, arts, religious practices, political ideologies, and bureaucratic philosophies of Western Europe.

"We have a long way to go to equip our citizens, our labor force, and our leadership to function in a world where the Orient, central Asia, and Latin America represent major economic and political forces."

– Kerry A. Johnson and Lin J. Foa, *Instructional Design: New Alternatives for Effective Education and Training*

M ESCOLATE PIANO, con un cucchiaino, il caffe, in modo che il caffe sgorgato per primo, più denso, si mescoli con quello meno denso, sgorgato successivamente.

M É LANGUEZ LE CA- FE LENTEMENT à l'aide d'une cuiller, de façon à ce que la café débité d'abord, qui est plus dense, se mélange avec le café moins dense débitépar la suite.

R UHREN SIE DEN KAFFEE LANGSAM mit einem Loffel um, damit der anfangs ausgetretenen Kaffee, welcher starker ist, sich mit dem nachher ausgetretenen gut vermischt.

S TIR THE COFFEE SLOWLY with a spoon, so that the first part of the coffee to ooze out, which is more concentrated, is mixed with the weaker, last part.

GLOCALIZATION: TAILORING PRODUCTS TO MARKETS

Surviving in the worldwide marketplace demands not only that companies must be able to communicate to people of different countries, but also that they must understand their cultures enough to tailor products to meet the needs of different populations.

The international marketplace has become so crowded that the ones who succeed will be the ones who can adapt their products and their marketing to local cultures. The ability of international companies to create products that recognize the preferences and needs of individual markets requires a competence in multicultural instructions as well.

This means that companies will have to design their products with instructions that can be customized to different languages and perspectives, as well as instruct their own suppliers who may be located around the world. A product or marketing approach that works in one country cannot be counted on to work in another.

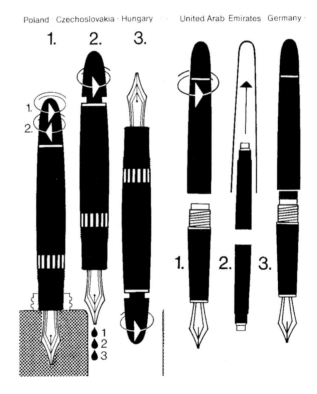

13 EDUCATION IS TO LEARNING AS TOUR GROUPS ARE TO ADVENTURE

Contrary to **Voltaire**'s Dr. Pangloss, we are not living in the best of all possible worlds. Not only are we overwhelmed by the sheer amount of information, most of us are also hampered by an education that inadequately trains us to process it.

School is the place where our information habits are formed, yet most of us graduate ill-equipped to handle the avalanche of new information that we will have to continuously acquire. We suffer from information anxiety primarily because of the way that we were, or were not, taught to learn.

Theoretically, the goal of our educational system is learning, but it is bound by the limitations of any bureaucracy, in that the demands of administering the system often take precedence over the initial purpose of the system. A principal objective of any operational system is to keep operating, to maintain the status quo. But this is often done at the expense of the people who move through the system.

It's a bureaucratic Catch-22, similar to the one that operates in the healthcare system. Being awakened at 2 A.M. to have your temperature taken is not conducive to healing, nor is being awakened again at 6 A.M. to have the bed sheets changed, breathing airborne contaminants, or having to make yourself available to well-meaning but sadistic friends and relatives for four hours every day because the hospital has proclaimed this time for visiting. This schedule is primarily conducive to the hospital administration.

Educational Reform that Works /
John Doerr, TEDX presentation

- **NOT PCs in classrooms**

- **Smaller classes & schools, longer school days & years**

- **Teachers with time, incentives, preparation**

- **Innovation (eg. charter public schools)**

- **Accountability, end social promotion**

- **Choice; competition; leadership**

- **Parental involvement**

Thus the day-to-day demands of administering the educational system distract from the quality of education and inhibit learning. One has only to look at the way the educational system is covered by the press. The headlines are about teachers' salaries, crime in the schools, reading levels, prayer in the classroom, test scores, and building improvements. The quality of education and joy of learning are in fine print.

GIN-RUMMY MEMORY

The single most counterproductive element of our educational system is the importance placed on puzzle solving and memorization. The predominant measure of success is the test; thus the mission of schools is to raise students' test scores. Across the country every day, teachers are saying, "He's such a bright boy, but he doesn't test well," and shaking their heads with the tragic somberness you might expect from a doctor telling a patient to get his affairs in order.

This places extraordinary emphasis on short-term memory, at the expense of long-term understanding. How much can you cram before tomorrow's test? This doesn't further your understanding of things, and you will remember what you learn this way about as long as you will a gin-rummy hand. It is garbage in and garbage out. Students are forced to compete against other students rather than against their own aspirations.

While the debate rages on about what makes an intelligent student and educators scramble to compile lists of facts that everyone should know, we lose sight of the fact that the lists are arbitrary and the judges are biased.

SACRED BULL FIGHTING

Our education system is riddled with sacred bulls that we take with us into our lives after school. They affect the way we conduct our lives and perform in our careers, and most of us would increase our productivity if only we weren't afraid to question them. Do these truths sound familiar?

What are we giving up if we convert schools into test preparation and test administering institutions? What are the contents of these tests and how important are these kinds of learnings? Most important, if we were to substitute quite different kinds of tests (I prefer the term "assessments"), how would students fare?

One of the most dispiriting findings of recent years is that students scores decline significantly when a somewhat different test is used; one has to ask, are the students acquiring skills, knowledge, understandings of some generality and flexibility, or are they just being trained to succeed on a certain kind of instrument? And what kinds of individuals would be attracted to a profession in which the training of seals is the prototype?

– Howard Gardner, from videotape interview, *Re-inventing our Schools: A Conversation with Howard Gardner*

■ **If only everybody could read well and get high scores, everything would be fine.** Of late, educational theorists have come to realize there are two kinds of intelligence—one academic and one practical. They have found there is little to indicate that doing well in one will assure the same success in the other. The neat structure of school, with only one right answer to every question, bears little relation to the ambiguity we face outside. More educated students won't necessarily produce more successful human beings.

■ **The one who always has the right answers wins.** In school, we are measured by our ability to answer questions and, in one form or another, this occupies most of our time. What we need to know is how to ask the questions. Most of us are surrounded by answers and solutions in our lives. Our adeptness at asking questions will determine how we reach the solutions.

■ **Classes should have thirty students and last for one hour.** This precept has given birth to the inflexible rule that is responsible for a good many of the unproductive business meetings taking place around the country every day. People feel cheated unless the meetings last for an hour, yet an hour is a highly arbitrary unit of time. Because this is the way we are taught, we assume that this is the way things should be. Just as there is no such thing as an ideal class size or length, there is no such thing as an ideal meeting size or duration. Some subjects could be best addressed by a few people in fifteen minutes, others by five hundred people in an hour. As the size of meetings will change the character, the subject should determine the time and amount of people involved.

■ **Students should be stuffed with facts like sausages.** Facts are meaningful only when they can be attached to ideas. Unless students are taught a system for learning or processing information, facts are of little use to them. Several books have come out in the last two years about what students know, don't know, or should know. Some have even attempted to make lists of what a person needs to know to qualify as a culturally literate human being. In addition to the sheer presumption of making such a list, these books tend to distract readers from the real issues as they try to memorize lists.

Traditional school activities do not generally allow children to make authentic presentations of their thoughts and opinions to their peers. Students are required to hand in their work to be read over, but usually this is done to get it "corrected," not to communicate something the students care about to the teachers. Similarly, answering questions which a teacher asks is generally an exercise to demonstrate knowledge, not to share it. Shauna, a fifth-grader, explained her view of how students in her class "get in trouble" when the teacher asked questions:

"She yellin' at you, she, we, we be like…she know we don't like readin' our book…and she know we don't know the question, and she lookin around, and she say, "Shauna", and she know I don't know the question, I read the book, but the book…it's not a good book."

– Michele Evard
Epistemology and Learning Group
Learning and Common Sense Section
The Media Laboratory, MIT

Classes should be held during the day and homework done at night. Just as some people learn faster by reading, by trial-and-error, or by example, people learn more easily at different times of the day. Everyone should pursue their education in the manner that best befits their learning preferences—in their own time. In this way, homework will become homejoy.

Halls and corridors are nonspaces for lockers. Circulation space accounts for more than any single other space in schools, yet it is treated as a throwaway. Instead, hallways could be great arcades where people meet, talk, learn, and fall in love.

Senior faculty teach senior classes, junior faculty teach the freshmen. This is backwards. Freshmen are more impressionable than seniors. Their educational future is more fragile and needs the benefit of the most experienced faculty. By the time students have spent four years in college, they should be more able to direct themselves.

SEEING, HEARING, EXPRESSING

If we are lucky, we learn reading, writing, and arithmetic, but what we need to learn in the Information Age are seeing, hearing, and expressing. We need to know how to make connections from one interest or subject to the next. In an ideal system, teachers shouldn't be expected to be fact machines, police officers, or psychiatrists. They should be guides down interest paths, with special insights about the path-to-path and interest-to-interest connections.

But it is not the best of all possible worlds, after all. So if we have been hampered by our education, it is incumbent upon us to develop our own models for learning.

FEAR OF LEARNING

Learning involves nurturing an interest. The greatest threats to learning are guilt and anxiety. Guilt and anxiety are parent and child, and they stop interest cold. They stop the movement of information into memory, into utilization, and into communication. They stop you from genuinely committing to your interest, which is what gives you a sense of ownership of the information and enables you to use and communicate it.

Much traditional teaching is based on the model of a pipeline through which knowledge passes from teacher to students.

The name "constructivism" derives from an alternative model, according to which the learner has to construct knowledge afresh every time.

Jean Piaget, the most influential advocate of constructivist education popularized the slogan: "to understand is to invent."

The role of the teacher is to create the conditions for invention rather than provide ready-made knowledge.

– Seymour Papert,
The Connected Family Web site

You feel guilty that you haven't kept up your college French course and fear that your verb conjugations may be slipping, so you don't admit to being able to speak the language, and thus you close off a chance to exercise your skills and improve at a subject that once interested you.

A widely held myth, fostered by the regimen of school, is that people should learn continuously. But when do people really learn? We learn at moments rather than continuously, and it's the acceptance of moments of learning that allows you to make full use of them. If you believe you're supposed to learn continuously and you don't continuously learn, then you'll be full of anxiety and guilt. You'll be distracted from learning because you're too busy worrying about not learning.

Our educational system doesn't have exclusive rights on the guilt and anxiety associated with learning. Learning inherently involves some trauma; it requires a certain amount of exertion and implies giving up one way of thinking for another. Added to this is the puritanical attitude that we are put here on this earth to suffer and that suffering is good for us; therefore, learning shouldn't be too pleasant.

Given this, it is inevitable that learning is regarded somewhat like cod-liver oil, as something that might taste pretty bad but may do some good in the long run. Learning is invariably perceived, to varying degrees, as a source of anguish.

Fear of learning is endemic in our culture. **Carl Rogers** notes that although humans have a natural potential for learning, they approach the process with great ambivalence because "any significant learning involves a certain amount of pain, either pain connected with the learning itself or distress connected with giving up certain previous learnings."

To avoid suffering the pain of learning, people will go to great lengths to trick themselves with sugar-coated approaches to knowledge in much the same way that those who are fearful of the unknown approach travel: They try to make the trip as easy as possible by having every moment planned in advance, by turning over the arrangements to someone else, by trying to turn travel into a neat package. This deters the traveler from ownership of the experience. And while the tour-group approach to travel can make a trip easier and reduce the

Many people don't realize that honesty is one of the most important values in learning.

When a software product advertises itself as "so much fun she won't even know she's learning," that product is telling you that the only way your child will learn is if you lie to her.

Children are not dupes, they know when you are lying to them.

– Seymour Papert,
The Connected Family Web Site

anxiety of the unknown, it is not always the best way to explore new territory. It is a defensive response and is done from a position of fearfulness. The same can be applied to learning: trying to turn knowledge into a neat package or, worse, trying to protect yourself from new information won't foster learning; you will succeed only in making yourself more anxious.

DEFENSIVE EXPENDITURES

Friedrich Nietzsche, in *Ecce Homo*, discusses how destructive this anxiety can be. "The rationale is that defensive expenditures, be they never so small, become a rule, a habit, lead to an extraordinary and perfectly superfluous impoverishment. Our largest expenditures are our most frequent small ones. Warding off, not coming close, is an expenditure—one should not deceive oneself over this—a strength squandered on negative objectives. One can merely through the constant need to ward off become too weak any longer to defend oneself."

LEARNING ABOUT LEARNING

Defensiveness is unavoidable in a test-based system founded on reward and punishment. We spend our years in school trying to zero in on the information that will reward us by raising our grades or test scores and avoiding the extraneous that may distract us from our goals, even though it may well be relevant to our own interests.

Corroborated by the findings of such people as **Ivan Pavlov** and **B.F. Skinner**, psychologists have long espoused the theory that we learn only by reinforcement or reward. But this is a limiting, overly rigorous concept, restricting of creativity and of those divine leaps that the human mind is able to make from simple observation to global idea. If we are dependent upon reward, we are also dependent on someone else's vision of success.

In *The Society of Mind*, **Marvin Minsky** calls for new ways of learning. "The answer must lie in learning better ways to learn. In order to discuss these things, we'll have to start by using many ordinary words like goal, reward, learning, thinking, recognizing, liking, wanting, imagining, and remembering—all based on old and vague ideas. We'll find that most such words must be replaced by new distinctions and ideas."

The key to improving our instruction is to know what methods of instruction to use when....Perhaps the most important aspect of the situation is the kind of learning that is to be facilitated. Knowing about the kinds of learning helps us to do a better job of teaching them. The most basic distinction is Benjamin Bloom's three domains:

• Cognitive learning (thoughts), such as teaching someone to add fractions.

• Affective learning (feelings, values), such as teaching someone to not want to smoke.

• Physical or motor learning (actions), such as teaching someone to touch type.

– Professor Charles M. Reigeluth
Instructional Systems Technology,
Indiana University

LEARNING FANTASIES

An ideal school would be like a smorgasbord. You could take large or small plates and eat fast or slow. You could construct the meal going forwards or backwards, and you could start again. You would be given permission to have dessert first, and the people who fill up the plates would have conversations with you. You could pick up a plate called fancy cars and have somebody advise you that this salad here, the road system and mode of transportation, go with it.

But most of us don't have that kind of experience with school. In an attempt to overcome any shortcomings in my education, I try to create learning environments in my life. I have developed a list of imaginary courses that I thought would be good courses and would inspire me. They inspire me to look at the world differently.

- **Learning About Learning.** For me, this should be the only course taught for the first six years in school.

- **The Question and How to Ask It.** Asking questions is the most essential step toward finding answers. Better questions provoke better answers.

- **What Do You Want.** We don't pay enough attention to the old adage: be careful what you wish for because all too often it will be exactly what you get.

- **A Day in the Life.** Studying in intimate detail a day in the life of anything—a truck, a building, a butcher—would not only provide a memorable understanding of what it means to be something else, but would also permit us a better understanding of ourselves in comparison.

- **What Are We to Ants.** This would be an advanced version of A Day in the Life. The whole idea of how a thing relates to something else is often left unexamined in school, yet it is the essential doorway to knowledge.

- **Time, Fast and Slow.** If you studied all the things that take place in a minute or a day, or a week, or a year, or a thousand years, you would have a new framework for understanding and for cataloging information.

Education is learning what you didn't even know you didn't know.

– Daniel Boorstin

The chief object of education is not to learn things but to unlearn things.

– G. K. Chesterton

Creativity is the power to connect the seemingly unconnected.

– William Plomer

Commonplace minds usually condemn what is beyond the reach of their understanding.

– Francois LaRochefoucauld

At the national spelling bee in 2000, home-schooled children swept the top three spots. Of 248 contestants, 27 were taught at home, compared to 178 who were taught in public schools.

– Anjetta McQueen.
"Home-Schoolers Sweep Spelling Bee"
Associated Press, (6/1/00)

The Institute (National Home Education Research Institute) says 1.3 million to 1.7 million, or about 3 percent of all 53 million school-age children, attend school at home. And the numbers of these children are growing 7 percent to 15 percent a year, far faster than the school population.

– Peter Kilborn
"Learning at Home,
Students Take the Lead"
New York Times, (5/24/00)

- **The Five-Minute Circle.** What could you do or see in five minutes from where you are sitting?

- **The Five-Mile Circle.** What could you do, see, and understand about sociology, the fabric of schools, urban life, and systems within five miles of where you are sitting?

- **This Is Your New World.** If you were king of this five-mile world, how would you run it, change it, understand it, communicate with it?

- **A Person Course.** You could have a course on **Albert Einstein**, **Louis Kahn**, or **Yasir Arafat**.

- **Hailing Failing.** More learning is possible by studying the things that don't work than by studying the things that do. Most of the great technological and scientific breakthroughs are made by examining the things that fail.

- **Wait-Watching.** We spend a great deal of time waiting—in checkout lines, in ticket lines, in doctors' offices. How could we better occupy this time?

- **How to Explain Something So Your Mother Could Understand It.** The recognition of someone else's ability to understand is essential to all communication, yet it is something we rarely think about. We assume that others can understand the same things we can.

- **The Difference Between Facts and the Truth.** Facts are only meaningful when they can be tied to ideas and related to your experience, yet they are offered in place of the truth.

- **The Obvious and How to Hug It.** In our zeal to appear educated, not only do we often forget the obvious, we avoid it. Yet it is in the realm of the obvious that most solutions lie.

PARALLEL LEARNING

Everyone should have his or her own imaginary course list, which would function as a way to encourage learning in one's own life. There are always opportunities for education if you keep in mind that your life is the place for learning.

Researchers are beginning to recognize that the kind of intelligence rewarded in school may have little to do with the wits that will determine how well one will fare in life. We've all met people who can't balance their checkbook and think that the classics are a series of golf tournaments, but who can turn hot-dog stands into multimillion dollar businesses.

Heretofore, most scales of intelligence were measured by a standard known as IQ, or intelligence quotient. But this only measures certain mental processes that have to do with vocabulary, logic, reasoning, and numeric skills. These tests don't recognize people skills, creativity, or even the practical intelligence that seems to propel some people through life.

Howard Gardner at Harvard describes eight different types of intelligence: visual/spatial, bodily/kinesthetic, musical, interpersonal, intrapersonal, and naturalist. His theory of multiple intelligences is the basis for curriculum and teaching strategies at the popular Key Learning Community, a K–12 school which is part of the Indianapolis Public School system. Other researchers, such as **Robert J. Sternberg** at Yale, divide intelligence into categories such as practical, experiential, and mental.

These theories acknowledge the role of street smarts in intelligence for the first time. Dr. Sternberg demonstrates that while standard IQ tests are fairly good for predicting how people will do in school, they have a very low correlation with job performance.

The tests are composed of questions for which there are only right or wrong answers. They measure a person's ability to perform within a limited arena where all problems can be solved with black-or-white solutions. In the workplace, situations are rarely so unequivocal or even so quantifiable. Yet employers often require their staff to take these intelligence tests.

Not only are the tests an inaccurate indicator of career success, they brand a person for life with a number that they must either live up to or live down. This discourages people from acquiring new skills and new learning that might be defined as beyond the accepted reach of their intelligence rating.

Because our educational system is based on cultivating the kind of intelligence that can be measured in IQ tests, the responsibility of cultivating street smarts lies with the individual.

I have argued very strongly that the purpose of education is to increase understanding. Understanding means that you can take knowledge, facts, concepts, and apply them in new situations—situations you haven't already been coached on—and that if we really tried to do this we would have to change our educational system very very radically. So one area that I think has been neglected is the purpose of education, and how would we know if we've achieved it.

– Howard Gardner

The teacher pretended that algebra was a perfectly natural affair, to be taken for granted, whereas I didn't even know what numbers were. Mathematics classes became sheer terror and torture to me. I was so intimidated by my incomprehension that I did not dare to ask any questions.

– Carl Jung

As I was growing up, my parents fostered the concept of parallel or applied learning that happened outside our schooling. We were encouraged to pursue subjects outside of the classroom. They indulged any reasonable interest that we expressed by buying us books on the subject, finding special courses for us, and, most importantly, taking us places.

I became interested in art as a child. From the first grade on, my drawing was the best in the class. Yet despite the fact that art was something of an anathema in our family, my passion was encouraged. When I was in high school, my father got special permission for me to take courses at the Stella Elkins Tyler School of Fine Arts at Temple University, where he knew the dean.

I was also interested in design as a teenager. So when I was about fourteen, my parents gave me the attic as my bedroom. I separated the space into two rooms—one for working, which I painted white, and one for sleeping, painted black. In my work area, I designed sloping bookshelves that weren't parallel to the floor. The lower end of each shelf acted as a bookend, so the books didn't tip over.

I have tried to encourage my own children's interests, even when they departed from my own. My son, Josh, got half of the family freezer for storing his insect collection.

TERROR AND CONFIDENCE

Everyone should develop personal tests for information. Exercise noncomplacency. How can you apply it to your life? The best kind of learning occurs in situations, not in the classroom.

Throughout my whole life, I have created tests that determine how well I have applied information. Until I was eighteen, I had a comfortable, middle-class upbringing. I decided then that it was important to put myself in jeopardy to understand what kinds of things terrified me. I thought that if I found out what my fears were, I would function more comfortably as an adult. I didn't expect to overcome my terrors, just to know about them and about myself. My first expedition was to go across the country with a friend, a sleeping bag, sixty dollars in my pocket, and a topless, doorless old Army Jeep that had a front seat made out of

> The alternative to giving far more attention to envisioning the future is to squander resources on vainly trying to use new technologies to solve the problems *of school-as-it-is* instead of seeking radically new opportunities to develop *school-as-it can-be*. The conversation about technology in schools is trapped in the wrong subject. The talk is all about "does the technology work" as a fix for the old. It ought to be about developing and choosing between visions of how this immensely powerful technology can support the invention of powerful new forms of learning to serve levels of expectation higher than anything imagined in the past.
>
> – Gaston Caperton and Seymour Papert
> *Vision for Education—*
> *The Caperton-Papert Platform*

a plywood board with two cushions on it. We begged our way across the United States and kept to our pact never to sleep under anything.

From this trip, I made the important discovery that not everyone is afraid of the same things. My most terrifying moment came in Chicago. We were filthy; our limited apparel had begun to decay; and we had perfected the look of vagrants. I wanted to see **Mies van der Rohe**'s twin apartment buildings on Lake Shore Drive. The idea of talking my way into those elegant buildings by claiming I was a former tenant terrified me, but I did it. Looking like the wrath of God didn't bother my friend at all.

My next expedition was to spend a few months on an island off the coast of North Carolina with two friends. We slept on the sand and lived off what we caught. It was a time devoid of decision making because the regimen of survival determined all of our activities. The experience taught me something about mental relaxation, and I probably ate more crabs and clams than most people do in a lifetime. Despite this, I still love them.

After this, in 1958, I ingratiated myself to the director of an archaeological museum at the University of Pennsylvania. Claiming that I knew how to survey, I convinced him to send me on a dig in Tikal, Guatemala, the site of the largest and oldest Mayan city. I didn't know the first thing about surveying, but by the time the team discovered this, it was too late to send me back, so I learned—in five days—and spent six months there.

These trips were all tests; I use these trips even today as measuring devices against which I gauge fear and panic. By putting myself in unpredictable situations for which I was ill-equipped, I was forced to discover new ways of accomplishing things. Often I discover that there is a simpler, clearer way which I didn't know before I committed myself to the test.

The fundamental lesson of my travels and travails has been learning that without prior knowledge, without training, you can find your way through information by making it personal, by deciding what you want to gain from it, by getting comfortable with your ignorance.

God is in the details.

– Ludwig Mies van der Rohe

The psychological impact of the Information Revolution, like that of the Industrial Revolution, has been enormous. It has perhaps been greatest on the way in which young children learn. Beginning at age four (and often earlier), children now rapidly develop computer skills, soon surpassing their elders; computers are their toys and their learning tools. Fifty years hence we may well conclude that there was no "crisis of American education" in the closing years of the twentieth century—there was only a growing incongruence between the way twentieth-century schools taught and the way late-twentieth-century children learned. Something similar happened in the sixteenth-century university, a hundred years after the invention of the printing press and movable type.

– Peter F. Drucker, *Atlantic Monthly*, "Beyond the Information Revolution," (October, 1999)

While I thought that I was learning how to live, I have been learning how to die.

– Leonardo da Vinci

Learn to listen to your own voice and to balance your confidence and your terror.

These two forces have driven my life. Confidence propels me to try new things and terror keeps me from getting too cocky. The balance of these two—arrogance against assuredness—enables me to conquer the fear of not knowing, of the unknown, of the new. Confidence is the belief that this can be accomplished, giving yourself permission to try.

Applied learning outside the formal structure of the classroom is likely to result in the possession of long-term understanding based on information acquired from interest and not from anxiety. This kind of learning permits an essential sense of ownership.

INFORMATION OWNERSHIP

Interaction with information is what enables possession. By putting yourself *in situ*, you will create a conversation that will permit learning. You can ask questions, correct mistakes, and adjust to new ideas in an active environment.

This doesn't necessarily mean that you must apprentice yourself to a woodworker if you want to learn about woodworking. It can also mean taking the time to look up a word or term when reading through a text, finding out about the history of wood joints, asking a few questions about new information with which you are confronted, or just repeating something you have heard to someone else.

All of these will allow you to personalize the information in some way that is likely to make it more valuable to you in the future.

14 LEARNING IS REMEMBERING WHAT YOU'RE INTERESTED IN

Learning can be seen as the acquisition of information, but before it can take place, there must be interest; interest permeates all endeavors and precedes learning. In order to acquire and remember new knowledge, it must stimulate your curiosity in some way.

Interest defies all rules of memorization. Most researchers agree that people can retain only about seven bits in their short-term memory, such as the digits in a ZIP Code or telephone number.

Learning can be defined as the process of remembering what you are interested in. And both go hand in hand—warm hand in warm hand—with communication. The most effective communicators are those who understand the role interest plays in the successful delivery of messages, whether one is trying to explain astrophysics or help car owners in parking lots.

Multi-level parking garages are generally pretty threatening places. They conjure up frightening images—a favorite site for nefarious activities, clandestine meetings, rapists, and mob hitmen, to say nothing of the fear of remembering on what level you parked your car.

In downtown Chicago, I recall there was a multi-level parking garage that used the names of countries instead of numbers to denote each level. In the elevator, the buttons were labeled France, Canada, Greece, Turkey, Germany, etc., each in a different typeface. In the elevator lobby on each floor, the national anthem of the country was broadcast through an intercom. While parking garages don't seem to inspire the imagination of the public, foreign

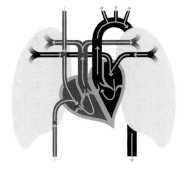

Obviously, someone who had become intrigued by human anatomy would find it much easier to remember the names of the different parts and functions of the heart.

countries do. People didn't forget where their cars were parked, and many left the garage smiling.

The developer of this parking garage took a mundane thing and not only made it work, but made it into a cultural learning center as well. This parking garage exemplified the principle that we learn only if we are interested in the subject.

In his book *Freedom to Learn*, **Carl Rogers** states that the only learning which significantly influences behavior is "self-discovered, self-appropriated" learning. Only when subject matter is perceived as being relevant to a person's own purposes will a significant amount of learning take place.

Information anxiety results from constant overstimulation; we are not given the time or opportunity to make transitions from one room or idea to the next. No one functions well perpetually gasping for breath. Learning (and interest) require way-stations where we can stop and think about an idea before moving on to the next.

> One thing life has taught me: if you are interested, you never have to look for new interests. They come to you. When you are genuinely interested in one thing, it will always lead to something else.
>
> – Eleanor Roosevelt

INTEREST CONNECTIONS

The idea that you can expand one interest into a variety of other interests makes your choices less threatening. You can jump into a subject at any level, and not only can you follow the subject to greater levels of complexity, but you can follow it to other subjects.

If a computer company wanted to develop an exhibit that would make computers less intimidating to the public, they could start at a basic level with the idea of opposites, which could move into on and off, then into binary numbers, the workings of a circuit panel, and into computers themselves. Everyone can identify with the idea of opposites. Its simplicity and universal appeal aren't threatened with self-limitations or exclusivity. They form a path to new interests and higher levels of complexity.

Part of the trauma of decision making is the fear that you must eliminate alternatives that you fear may have been more viable than the one you selected. But when you realize that one interest can always be connected to another, you dispel that fear. If you choose to study automobiles, it doesn't mean you can't study history as well.

DISCRIMINATING BETWEEN INTERESTS AND OBLIGATIONS

The problem with interests is less one of making choices than one of distinguishing interests from obligations. Many people can't distinguish their genuine interests from the subjects they think would make them more interesting as individuals—true interest versus guilt or status. The trick is to separate that which you are *really* interested in from that which you *think* you should be interested in. The pursuit of the first will provide pleasure; the pursuit of the second will produce anxiety. Are you memorizing football scores so your husband will talk to you or because of a genuine interest in the sport? Are you living your life with the idea that you are going to have to take a test?

Sometimes, it is easy to separate interest motivated by genuine curiosity as opposed to guilt, responsibility, or status seeking. But other times, the distinctions are not so clear. They may become clear in time, or they may require asking yourself some questions:

■ Do you find yourself compelled to read every line of a book or magazine despite the fact that your mind keeps wandering off to what you are going to wear tomorrow? Chances are you are probably reading only because you think the information gleaned will improve your cocktail-party ratings and not because you really want to know the information.

■ Do you change your opinion about movies after having read reviews of them?

■ Have you ever asked a teacher, "Will we have to know this for a test?"

■ Have you ever asked a teacher, "Are there other books I could read on this subject?"

■ When someone mentions a PBS program, do you get a queasy feeling remembering that you were watching *Who Wants to be a Millionaire* at the time?

■ Or worse, do you quickly switch the television channel to the PBS station when you hear someone approaching? Do you listen to classical music only when you have company?

■ Do you look forward to the destination or the journey? Do you have a cod-liver oil attitude toward a trip, anticipating how good you'll feel when it's over, or do you relish the process with joy?

• Americans buy more than a billion books a year.

• 43 percent of Americans read five or fewer books a year, while 7 percent read more than 50.

• Fifty thousand new titles are published each year, and a million and a half books are in print, from 20,000 different publishers.

• Books are a $23 billion dollar business.

– Ed Gray,
"The Truth About Fiction,"
US Airways Attaché, (August 2000)

In the education of children there is nothing like alluring their interest and affection, otherwise you only make so many asses laden with books.

– Michel De Montaigne

Your only obligation in any lifetime is to be true to yourself. Being true to anyone else or anything else is not only impossible, but the mark of a fake messiah.

– Richard Bach

Once you have determined your interests, you can develop your potential for curiosity by maximizing the connections between your interests. How do you move from your interest in Ming vases to Chinese history and then to your job as a claims adjuster? How does the word interest figure into your daily life? What do you pursue in any planned way to increase your involvement in these interests? Your work should be an extended hobby.

The most creative project that we can undertake is the design of our lives, so I set to work to redesign mine in such a way that my curiosity could manifest itself in my career. It was sort of an adaptive or reuse project. I followed my path of interests into graphic design and into the architecture of information.

ACCESS® GUIDES

My interest is in the future because I am going to spend the rest of my life there.

– Charles F. Kettering

Literate people possess the means to organize their surroundings and establish personal connections with what they see organized before them. Personal relevance depends on organization and perception.

The fact that people learn in different ways and have varied interests was the inspiration behind the guidebooks to cities, sports, medicine, and finances that I published for a number of years. We structured them so they could be read and used selectively and unpredictably. We wanted readers to feel nothing was being asked of them. We gave them permission not to read from beginning to end. They could skim, concentrate on one section, look at the pictures, do whatever seemed comfortable. We provided traditional background information that I believe a number of people who used the books never read. But it was there for those who did.

You never know till you try to reach them how accessible men are; but you must approach each man by the right door.

– Henry Ward Beecher

The ACCESS® guides to cities were the first I developed and were perhaps the clearest examples of my principles of organization. To describe them in a sentence, one could say I mixed up the pieces as they exist in a traditional guidebook and put them next to each other, as they exist in the city.

When you're visiting a city, you either are someplace or you're going someplace. If you are someplace, you want to see what's around you. If you're going someplace, you want to know what you'll pass by.

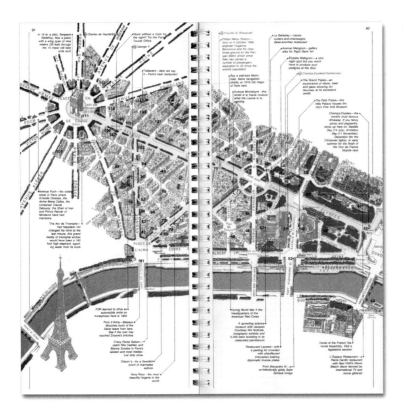

From *Paris Access*, 1987.

The guides were about adjacencies that often seem serendipitous. I learned from drawing maps that categories of information can be indicated by color, so I transferred that to the city guides.

The format involved the use of color to categorize text: red for restaurants, blue for architecture, black for narrative, museums, and shops, green for parks, gardens, and piers. Each city was divided into areas, with brief entries on the topics listed organized according to their location and proximity to each other.

Deciding how to break a city down into manageable pieces was a vital part of our process. The division into areas and their geographical relationships decided how our data was collected and our maps drawn. This breakdown was based on research—reading, talking to people who live in the city for sensible ideas about shopping, etc., finding areas that are already known as cohesive entities, and reacting to what other books portrayed. In planning area divisions, we also considered landmarks that help people orient themselves when switching from one area map to the next.

The strongest human instinct is to impart information, the second strongest is to resist it.

– Kenneth Grahame

Individual sites were described or graphically represented not by any set formula, but by whatever means seemed appropriate. I would ask myself, "What is the key to this particular space or place? Is it a section diagram, a floor plan, an elevation drawing, a story, an anecdote?"

One vital link in an interest-connection chain is familiarity. In our New York guide (and in the Washington, D.C., and Tokyo books) we accomplished this partly via cartoons by well-known local artists, by listings of songs and movies about the locale, by contributions from famous citizens about their city. On the one hand, this provided a familiar flavor. On the other, it surprised readers in what we hoped was a delightful manner. You never knew what you were likely to find on any page.

We didn't have the inside track on information. But we provided a unique format and way to gain access to it. In other guides, you seldom get to know the fabric. Fabric is an important part of understanding a city or any subject. How are the parts woven together in a cohesive whole? Fabric involves overlaying layers of use—neighborhoods, sports facilities, or hospitals—the way they are used, rather than arbitrarily delineating them into sections for the sake of convenience.

Cities would be far less interesting if they were arranged the way most guides are arranged, with all the restaurants in one area and all the hotels in another. More than the space shuttle or any other new technology, the city is man's most complicated invention. It is a mix of a jewelry store next to a restaurant next to a bookstore next to an office building.

GETTING PERMISSION TO LEARN

A good facilitator or teacher, says **Carl Rogers**, tries to "organize and make easily available the widest possible range of resources for learning." One way to learn, Rogers found, is to state your own uncertainties, to try to clarify your puzzlements, and thus get closer to the meaning that your experience actually seems to have. My guidebooks attempt to facilitate learning by allowing free interaction with as close a mirror of a given environment as a reader is likely to get on a printed page.

You have to leave the city of your comfort and go into the wilderness of your intuition. What you'll discover will be wonderful. What you'll discover will be yourself.

– Alan Alda

Poor is the man whose pleasures depend on the permission of another.

– Madonna

I believe that people cannot enjoy an overly structured city. City planners who design rigidly are not really thinking humanely. People do not walk in straight lines, except when they are running for a train. Our guides attempted to offer multiple paths to learning.

Unity of concept is important to any creative endeavor. An architect must form a clear concept of a project in human and social terms before beginning. Then shapes, scale, color, harmony, ornament, rhythm, dominance, subordination, and other devices are used to enhance the basic concept.

My work has to do with overcoming the thoughts with which I have discomfort. My own understanding or lack of it is enough. Committee meetings and market research are not part of this process. I don't believe in using such methods to determine what subjects or cities to tackle. Having confidence in your own understanding, acceptance of your ignorance, and determination to pursue your interests are the weapons against anxiety.

THE IMPORTANCE OF BEING INTERESTED

If my premise is correct that you only remember that in which you are interested, then interest becomes a key word in assimilating information and reducing anxiety. Yet interest is cast in at best a supporting role in our lives. It is tinged with the insignificance of a hobby. A category that is disappearing from resumes is "Interests." They have become "Outside Interests." They have almost become something people are not supposed to have— distractions from your ultimate purpose or mission. We should all look closely at what the word interest means to us. I think all interests should be inside interests. We should figure our interests into our activities every day, into our reading habits, into the news to which we pay attention, into our personal relationships.

The concept of interest may be simpleminded, but I believe that because of this, it should be a word of special delight, because it represents a way to get in touch with clarity.

The happiest people are those who think the most interesting thoughts. Those who decide to use leisure as a means of mental development, who love good music, good books, good pictures, good company, good conversation, are the happiest people in the world. And they are not only happy in themselves, they are the cause of happiness in others.

– William Lyon Phelps

It has all been very interesting.

– Lady Mary Wortley Montagu, last words, 1762

Many fans are interested enough in the major spectator sports to make themselves knowledgeable about detailed statistics and esoteric trivia.

Americans in particular, do not generally have much interest in what we would consider minor sports, particularly sports such as archery, and to a lesser degree, running and swimming.

In the *Olympic Access* book, I attempted to provide a broad understanding of both the fundamentals as well as trivia of all the Olympic sports of the time.

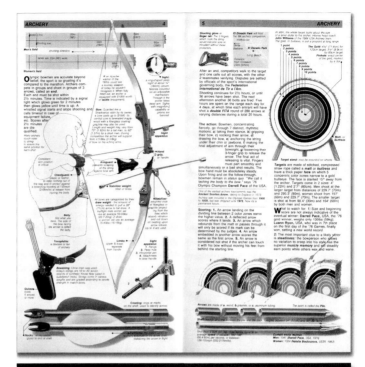

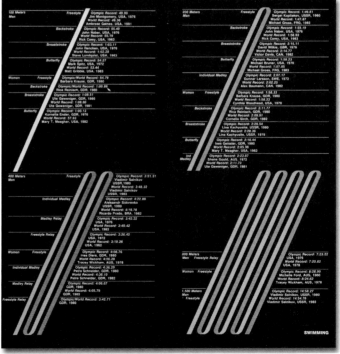

15 YOU ONLY LEARN THINGS RELATIVE TO SOMETHING YOU UNDERSTAND

The origin of the word Eureka is attributed to **Archimedes** on discovering the principle of specific gravity. As the story goes, he was sitting in the bathtub and, as the water ran over him, the idea came to him, and he shouted, "Eureka, I understand!"

We all live for those moments of clarity, but the amount of information with which we must wrestle is making them fewer and farther between.

In the fourth century B.C., **Aristotle** observed that a person's memory of a given item of knowledge was facilitated by associating that idea with another, either in contiguity, in sequence, or in contrast.

Comparative learning, making connections between one piece of information and another, is a concept from which I derive my first law: *You only learn something relative to something you understand.*

Among learning theorists, this is known as *apperception*, which was an idea first put forth in the nineteenth century. It is defined as "a process where new ideas associate themselves with old ones that already constitute a mind," in *Learning Theories for Teachers* by **Morris Bigge**.

Apperception is based on the work of the seventeenth-century English philosopher **John Locke**, who wrote the ambitious treatise *An Essay Concerning Human Understanding*. Locke believed that through chance, habit, or natural relationship ideas become

> I don't understand you. You don't understand me. What else do we have in common?
>
> – Ashleigh Brilliant

> Man knows much more than he understands.
>
> – Alfred Adler

associated in our minds. These ideas "always keep in company, and the one no sooner at any time comes into the understanding, but its associate appears with it…This wrong connection in our minds of ideas, in themselves loose and independent of one another, has such an influence, and is of so great a force as to set us awry in our actions, as well moral as natural, passions, reasonings, and notions themselves, that perhaps there is not any one thing that deserves more to be looked after."

A mind is constantly forming and changing, and the ideas with which we come into contact can redefine our minds.

The theory of apperception differed from the previous view of the mind as an already formed substance that could be nurtured or trained. Apperception implies that the mind is like a framework on which ideas can be hung. Thus, teachers function like architects and builders of children's minds rather than as merely trainers of predetermined mental faculties.

This theory reached full flower with **Johann Herbart**, who believed that ideas combine and recombine in the mind like chemical elements.

By looking into his own mind, Herbart thought that its "chemistry" could be observed and described. His theory held that all perception involves apperception—new ideas relating themselves to the store of old mental states. Memories in the subconscious theoretically helped one to interpret experiences of the moment. Indeed, Herbart felt that without a background of experience "any new sensation would mean almost nothing at all."

MOTIVATING MODELS

For teachers, this meant that pupils could not be regarded as "clean slates," and that they must start with experiences their pupils had already had and then enrich and build upon them.

In *Mindstorms*, **Seymour Papert** talks about how his childhood passion for the workings of gears helped him learn multiplication tables and math equations. "By the time I had made a mental gear model of the relation between x and y…the equation had become a comfortable friend." Papert, who developed the computer-programming language Logo for children and adults

---

Our subconscious minds have no sense of humor, play no jokes and cannot tell the difference between reality and an imagined thought or image. What we continually think about eventually will manifest in our lives. Unfortunately most of us are completely unaware of this fact and we do not monitor our thoughts with the care needed so that we can create in our lives the results we say we want. Since the great majority of people do not feel worthy and deserving of abundant good fortune, radiant good health and total success in all areas of their lives that overriding thought pattern controls the results people get. The first order of business of anyone who wants to enjoy success in all areas of his or her life is to take charge of the internal dialogue they have and only think, say and behave in a manner consistent with the results they truly desire.

– Sidney Madwed

with limited education, maintains that a fundamental fact about learning is that "anything is easy if you can assimilate it to your collection of models. If you can't, anything can be painfully difficult."

THEME AND VARIATIONS

For this reason, I love collections of things. What is only a fact alone can be information if it is collected with other facts. Knowledge is gained by understanding the theme and variations. If I put a cabbage in front of you, you would think that cabbages are round, green, and leafy. That is a fact. But if I showed you a red cabbage, a green cabbage, and a Chinese cabbage, you would begin to understand the essential characteristics—the smell, texture, and density—that define cabbage. That is information. Together, you can understand much more about each of them, by seeing the relationships between them, the variations on a theme.

The designer **Charles Eames** used to talk about change ringing, the traditional English art of ringing tower bells where the goal was to explore all possible sequences or changes of tones. The number of possible changes was calculated using the mathematical formula of permutations, by multiplying the number of bells together. With three bells, only six changes, or variations, in the order can be produced (1 x 2 x 3).

"Einmal ist keinmal," or "once is nothing" as the Germans say. For an idea or a thing to be meaningful, there must be more than one of it.

I tend to buy things in threes. With only two objects, you can see the differences; with three, you begin to see the patterns.

In Rome there is a room in a church with 10,000 human skulls. One skull is kind of frightening, but 10,000 are spectacular. You begin to see the structure of the human head, how much it can vary and still look like a human form. This is valid with ideas as well. People waste so much energy looking for the best example of their point, when their point might be better made with three mediocre examples.

Common sense is the collection of prejudices acquired by age eighteen.

– Albert Einstein

A little and a little, collected together, become a great deal; the heap in the barn consists of single grains, and drop and drop makes an inundation.

– Saadi

LEARNING MEANS MAKING CONNECTIONS

I am convinced that the grouping of ideas is vital to communication. One number in an annual report—for example, gross sales—doesn't tell you very much. Even a timeline that shows the figures over the course of 10 years does not tell you what you want to know. You want to know the profits every year, and how the profits of one company compare to the profits of another in the same industry.

Eugene Raskin notes the impact on architecture on minds "crowded with ideas and associations in a way that may be likened to a random card index file...cross-referenced way down into the subconscious." A person viewing a building must find in his mental file a card that says bank or church or store. The design should evoke recognition, "otherwise, he will be forced to fumble through his file at random; his chances of achieving any perception of unity will be slim indeed," states Raskin, a professor of architecture at Columbia University.

Scale in architecture has to do with easing perception by establishing the relationship of a building's units (doorways, windows, ceilings, etc.) to man. The simplest means of achieving this is to offer things that are familiar in size. As Raskin says, a person "knows the size of railings intimately, because he has walked beside them innumerable times. He knows just how far he bends his arm to put his hand on them, and just where on his hip he would feel the pressure should he lean on them. He knows stairs, too, from his first disastrous encounters with them during infancy. He is familiar with doors and windows...with units of construction he had handled, such as brick...You must give your observer things that he knows."

Just as all architecture is making connections—the way that two rooms are connected, the way the floor meets the wall, the way a piece of wood meets a piece of metal, the way a building meets the street—so is all learning.

In teaching or communicating anything, we have no choice but to make connections between a new idea and that which is already known. The only alternative is to fool ourselves, which happens all the time. When we gloss over what we don't understand, when we fail to question it, we're lying to ourselves. It is unconscionable,

Noble life demands a noble architecture for noble uses of noble men. Lack of culture means what it has always meant: ignoble civilization and therefore imminent downfall.

– Frank Lloyd Wright

Architecture is the art of how to waste space.

– Philip Johnson

yet pervasive to read a word, not comprehend it, and continue reading. These become surface words that peel off and disappear from memory. If you don't remember something, it never happened.

We test communication by conveying a message and having the recipient understand it, be interested in it, and remember it. Any other measure is unimportant and invalid.

Failing to make connections between the known and the unknown prevents us from grasping new ideas and new opportunities.

HOW BIG IS AN ACRE?

Facts in themselves don't solve the problem. Facts are only meaningful when they relate to a concept that you can grasp. If I say an acre is 43,560 square feet, that is factual but it doesn't tell you what an acre is. On the other hand, if I tell you that an acre is about the size of an American football field without the end zones, it is not as accurate, but I have made it understandable. I have made it infinitely more understandable to most Americans because it is as common a plot of ground as we have. We have a sense of that size. And you don't have to play football to know this.

You only understand information relative to what you already understand. You only understand the size of a building if there is a car or a person in front of it. You only understand facts and figures when they can be related to tangible, comprehensible elements.

Football is a mistake. It combines the two worst elements of American life. Violence and committee meetings.

– George Will

There is no safety in numbers, or in anything else.

– James Thurber

One Acre

THE NUMBERS GAME

The importance of setting information into a comprehensible context permeates any endeavor. In the business world, context should be the primary concern of anyone trying to sell a new product or idea. How can a new product or idea be related to something the market already understands?

Numbers, with their absolute value, are the easiest form of information to compare. However, many people suffer from innumeracy, an inability to comprehend numbers. According to **Douglas R. Hofstadter** in *Metamagical Themas*, the inability to make sense of numbers is a problem on par with illiteracy in this country. Numbers have the ability to summarize salient aspects of reality, yet the inability to comprehend numbers, large numbers in particular, is widespread. How many people know the difference between a million and a billion? How many people would understand the difference in defense spending in the billions versus the trillions of dollars? Yet these numbers affect all our lives.

For this very reason, we imbue them with an undeserved power. We live our lives by them, regarding them with awe—from scholastic aptitude tests to football scores. Sports fanatics expend energy memorizing the scores of games, yet the only important statistic is who won or lost. Numbers are often not as important as they seem.

SAY I DO, OR DIE

A set of numbers, without any reference or verification, can dramatically change our values, behavior, and emotions. We rarely question the figures quoted by the news because we assume them to be correct and valid, or at least important. But many times, these statistics are misinformation, disinformation, or just plain noninformation.

Anyone who disputes this probably didn't talk to any single women after the findings of a study regarding the marriageability of women over thirty were published. In its June 2, 1986 issue, *Newsweek* did a cover story based on a so-called, Harvard-Yale study on the marriage chances of women over thirty. Among the incendiary findings was that women over 45 were more likely to get assassinated by a terrorist than they were to walk down the aisle.

The article wreaked despair in the hearts of thousands of single women, inspired a flurry of media coverage worthy of Pearl Harbor, was the sole topic of conversation in certain circles for weeks afterward, probably increased revenues for dating services, and surprised schlubs everywhere when their proposals were accepted.

Few people, at the time, bothered to question the validity or accuracy of the findings because the ensuing turmoil was much more entertaining. Not only did the public not question the report's validity, but the media itself didn't.

Yet after the first volleys, the suspicions of statisticians were aroused, and some interesting facts about the findings were uncovered. Number one: The study was not conducted under the official aegis of either Harvard or Yale, but by two professors at the respective universities who were tinkering with some figures. Number two: They used a four-year-old census report that surveyed only around 1,500 college-educated women and based their conclusions on this, assuming that there were few subsequent changes in demographics and marriage patterns. Number three: They assumed that women always married men older than themselves.

The counterclaims started to surface. The U.S. Bureau of the Census report, more carefully done, although not infallible, found that 30-year-old women had a 58 to 66 percent chance of getting married, not a 20 percent chance as reported by the Two Tinkering Professors' Study.

What the professors came up with was highly suspect and could be shot full of holes by a high school freshman with a pocket calculator, but the aura of Harvard and Yale imbued these predictions with the patina of the absolute and the important.

The sensationalist aspects of the story eclipsed all questions of its accuracy. People didn't even ask themselves what it meant if the report were correct or why it mattered. The media went further to assume even more aspects that just weren't true, loaded their articles with personal examples of tales of woe, and in some cases even invented information that was never in the report.

And we didn't question it.

MAKING SENSE OF NUMBERS

The British-born Nigel Holmes, author of several books on the diagramming of information, suggests that the key to making sense of facts and figures is to "reduce them into bite-size chunks, which the reader can pick and choose."

He developed a delightful example of the problem of translating numbers into comprehensible information—using toothpaste. How much toothpaste is used in the United States every year? How would you go about understanding this? Multiply the population (240 million people), minus 50 million for the toothless or careless, by the average amount used, 1/2 inch per person twice a day. Then multiply by 365 days. You come up with a huge number: 1.1 million miles. This is a hard distance to comprehend. How far is that? Most people have no concept of this. It is over two round-trips to the moon, which is an average of 240,000 miles away. To translate figures they must be relative to what you can comprehend.

So let's look at toothpaste usage in a day. Divide 1.1 million miles by 365, and you come up with about 3,000 miles, which is about the distance from New York to Los Angeles, a distance most people can understand. As Holmes lectures, he actually squeezes out toothpaste on the floor. "The audience can suddenly see all these other relationships quickly. Not only are they laughing because someone who is supposed to be lecturing is instead squeezing toothpaste on the floor, but they are really seeing the numbers. It's a gimmick but it is another way of making people remember things," said Holmes.

What this implies is that constantly making comparisons and being open to new ways to chart and present information releases meaning.

Los Angeles

New York

Toothpaste usage for one day

SLICING THE PIE: THE NATURE OF RECREATION

In 1972 I was asked to develop a handbook on recreation for the National Gallery in Washington, D.C., which was presenting a show on **Frederick Law Olmsted**, one of the creators of Central Park in New York. The problem was how to break down the vast, complex, and ambiguous concept of recreation, which means something different to everyone.

You can't sum up the opportunities, problems, possibilities, physical and personal characteristics, age groups, desires, needs, and locations of recreation in a simple paragraph.

So I treated the subject as if it were a circle. Then I drew lines through the circle, the ends of which represented extremes on a continuum of the components of recreation—public and private, summer and winter activities, needs of the elderly and the very young. One line represented people. At one end of the line was a single person; at the other end of the line was a huge group of people.

Another line represented the contour of the land. One end of the line was flat; at the other end was a sheer cliff.

I drew another line and looked at the things people do and the equipment they use to do it. Some were very specific, e.g., a jungle gym. The line moved on to places that were less and less specific, until you had an open field on which you could do many things: picnic, run, play baseball or football, walk, or ride a bicycle.

The subject was divided into slices so I could deal with how landscape architecture performs to meet the varying needs that humans have for recreation—how physical places interact with personal desire.

Any larger subject can be broken down into slices. Each slice helps you understand what you cannot grasp as a whole. By breaking up a subject, you are less likely to be overwhelmed by it.

This can be applied to creating reports or to reading the reports of others. If the author hasn't broken down a subject, perhaps you could divide it in your own mind. By dividing a subject into manageable components, by experimenting with different ways of breaking it down, then comparing the components, you can really see the information.

THE NATURE OF RECREATION

Flat/Sloped

Cliffs, mountains, valleys, and rolling hills aren't just good to look at; they're good to use. If you live in a city (other than San Francisco and other hilly cities) and don't get much of a chance to wander over topographically interesting terrain, or if you strongly prefer games played on prepared flat surfaces, recreation to you is flat. But there are a great many interesting activities that can only be pursued on terrain that slopes: skiing, sledding, and

rolling down a hill, for example. There are also activities that can take place on several different kinds of topography, but which are made more enjoyable by stretching across a hill or two, such as hiking and golf.

The drawing below represents d topographies from absolutely ve absolutely horizontal, both abov below ground. Above the drawin of different activities. Draw a line each activity that needs a specifi topography to the appropriate te the drawing. Then, in the columr at the right, write in the activities take place on a variety of topogr

Bocce

Bocce originated in Italy and is considered one of the oldest sports. It can be played anywhere on a hard, level surface that measures 60 by 10 feet. The equipment consists of eight balls called bocce balls, having a diameter of 4½ inches, plus a smaller target ball 2¾ inches in diameter. The best balls are made of *lignum vitae*, said to be the heaviest wood in the world. However, less expensive composition balls similar to bowling balls can be used.

Two, four, or eight players are divided into two teams with a member of the lead team throwing out a target ball. The object of the game is to roll the bocce ball as close as possible to the target ball. Balls must be delivered underhanded. A round is won by the team placing a bocce ball nearest the target ball, and that team earns a point for every one of its balls closer to the target ball than the nearest ball of the opposing team. A game is won with twelve points, and a match consists of three games.

Lawn bowling · Back-packing · Making an echo · Catching a fish · Writing poetry · Playing baseball · Scaling a cliff · Picnicking · Surfing · King of the Mountain · Sailing · Exploring a cave · Building a sand castle · Skiing · Playing hide-and-seek · Playing croquet · Golfing · Skipping rocks · Rolling down a hill · Walking a dog · Sledding · Playing shuffleboard · Camping out · Skindiving · Throwing a frisbee · Playing tag · Riding a horse · Sightseeing · Finding seashells · Climbing a mountain · Painting a picture · Sleeping in the grass · Playing tennis · Daydreaming

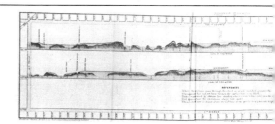

"*It is a mistake to suppose that a considerable extent of nearly flat ground is inadmissible or undesireable in a great park, or that it must be overcome, at any cost, by vast artificial elevations and depressions, or by covering all the surface with trivial objects of interest.*" *Chicago South Park Report*, 1871.

At right, profiles of Central Park south-to-north along Sixth and Seventh Avenues.

2¾"

4½"

32

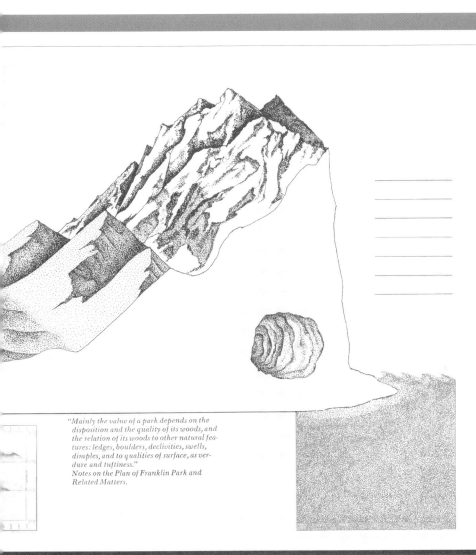

"*Mainly the value of a park depends on the disposition and the quality of its woods, and the relation of its woods to other natural features: ledges, boulders, declivities, swells, dimples, and to qualities of surface, as verdure and tuftiness.*"
Notes on the Plan of Franklin Park and Related Matters.

Skiing
The earliest ski edges were bones from large animals, strapped to the skis with leather thongs. The oldest pair of skis (purportedly 5000 years old) was found in Sweden.

Skis were first used in warfare in the Battle of Oslo in 1200 A.D. and proved so effective they became standard army equipment by the 1500's.

The bone ski had no standard size and was not turned up at the ends. Centuries later, when wood was substituted, the standard size became 7'6" long, about 2" thick, and 5" wide with about one foot of the front end of the ski turned up.

Skiing was introduced into Central Europe via Austria in 1590. It is not known how skis originated in North America, whether they were fashioned by native Indians or evolved out of the Canadian snowshoes. However, during the rush to the Pacific coast for gold in the 1850's, skis were in evidence in the Sierra Nevadas and in 1840 it was stated that "wooden blades, for use on ice and snow," were brought from Norway and were used by the immigrants along the north Atlantic coast.

33

THE NATURE OF RECREATION

Young/Old

An infant rocking contently in a baby carriage; a two-year old with pail and shovel in a sandbox; a young child testing his muscles and coordination on a jungle-gym; an older child learning how to shoot baskets; an old couple sitting on a bench talking.

If you are past childhood and not yet restricted in your activities by old age, you may have forgotten how many choices and limitations of recreational experience are determined on the basis of age. Age is a factor encouraging or discouraging *interest,* and a major factor in defining physical *capability*. Young children are not interested in sitting quietly on

Young

9½"

24

"Young children, when confined to the city during the summer, generally suffer in health. . . . When it is impracticable to make a visit of some length to the country with them, great advantage will be gained by spending the greater part of a day . . . in the open air, and under conditions otherwise favorable to health."
To Those Having the Care of Young Children, handbill, 1872.

ches; infants cannot climb jungle-
s; older children don't like to play in
dboxes; and older men and women
't have the stamina for basketball.
easy to forget, in thinking about the
eational profile of a neighborhood,
much people's age influences
need for particular recreational
ortunities.

There are, however, many activities that
are appropriate to several different age
groups. Camping, for example, can be
enjoyed by a two-year-old or a seventy-
year-old and by almost anyone in between.
A hike or bicycle ride appeals equally to
the young person and the middle-aged.

Finally there are activities that can be
enjoyed equally by all groups and in
which they can participate together. Sun-
bathing, people-watching, picnics, sports
events, outdoor plays and concerts, and
outings are activities which can bring all
the generations together.

ed age groups

Old

Shuffleboard

Shuffleboard, a derivative of
lawn bowling, began in England around the thirteenth
century. The earliest record
of the game in New England
was its denunciation as a
gambler's sport, and it was
outlawed in certain areas in
1845. The game appears to
have picked up again in the
1870's when it became a chief
feature of entertainment for
passengers on the ocean liner
voyage between England
and Australia.

It was reintroduced in Florida
after World War II and by
1951 it was estimated that
there were about 5000 public
courts in 455 cities. It is
played by all ages, although
it is especially popular among
older people.

The court is 52 by 6 feet with
a concrete or terrazzo surface. The composition disks
are one inch thick, six inches
in diameter, and weigh
between 11½ and 15 ounces.
The strategy of the game is
to knock a rival's disk out of
position in a scoring box,
replacing it with your own.
Each player or team shoots
eight disks each round.

*"Cultivate the habit of thoughtful atten-
tion to the feebler sort of folk—of asking, for
instance, can this or that be made easier and
more grateful to an old woman or a sick child,
without, on the whole, additional expense,
except in thoughtfulness? If so, ten to one, the
little improvement will simply be that refine-
ment of judgment which is the larger part of
the difference between good and poor art,
and the enjoyment of every man will be increased by it, though he may not know just
how."
Mount Royal.*

6"

25

COMPARING COMPONENTS

This is especially apparent when working with statistics. I was doing research for an urban atlas that I was developing and I discovered that most of the available information on income distribution consisted of dividing the total income by the number of residents. But this doesn't tell very much about disposable income. One person living on 10 acres who earned $1 million would have a higher average income than 10,000 people living on 10 acres sharing $1 million. But, if you were thinking of establishing a business, such as a shoe repair or grocery store, you would want to locate in an area of higher density. A very wealthy area with low density has much less disposable income than an area that has low income and very high density. One person can buy only so many groceries. To get this information, I multiplied the average income by the total number of people per block. I found out that the map of total income was quite different from the map of average income.

Comparing data can answer the question "where is the money?", but not how much disposable income there is, or where the rich people are. Those are different questions.

That is part of that information process; you have to build off things you understand. Comparisons enable recognition. We recognize night by its difference from day. We recognize all things by their relationship to other things, by the context in which they exist.

THE JOY OF DISCOVERY

Recognition is finding things. I am always delighted when I suggest an idea to someone, and they say, "That is obvious. I could have thought of that." That means that they have seen how one idea is connected to another.

New ideas are not so much discovered as uncovered by moving from what you already understand into the realm of what you would like to understand. Sometimes, simply by reorganizing the information you possess, by using and comparing what you already know, you can uncover other information. You also probably have some sense of how big a football field is. When you hear that a football field is about 43,560 square feet, you now can understand what an acre is—in a way that most likely you will remember.

These connections differentiate raw data from meaningful information.

I find this reassuring. I don't worry so much about discovering new information, but in connecting existing information in new ways. I think that all things are connected and that once you realize that, you will feel immediately justified to start your search at any place.

Those that know, do. Those that understand, teach.

– Aristotle

16 HAILING, FAILING, AND STILL SAILING

The winds of Puget Sound twisted, contorted, and destroyed the Tacoma Narrows Bridge, but also prompted urgent and exacting aerodynamic research that ultimately benefited all forms of steel construction. Beauvais Cathedral was built to the limit of the technology in its day, and it collapsed, but subsequent cathedrals made use of its failure.

Who's to know where any technology ends if its limits are not stretched? The machines of the world's greatest inventor, **Leonardo da Vinci**, were never built, and many wouldn't have worked anyway, but he was trying solutions where no man knew there were even problems. **Clarence Darrow** became a legend in the courtroom as he lost case after case, but he forced reevaluations of contemporary views of religion, labor relations, and social dilemmas.

Edwin Land's attempts at instant movies (Polarvision) absolutely failed. He described his attempts as trying to use an impossible chemistry and a nonexistent technology to make an un-manufacturable product for which there was no discernible demand. This created the optimum working conditions, he felt.

My play was a complete success. The audience was a failure.

– Ashleigh Brilliant

273

AN ODE TO ERROR

He's no failure. He's not dead yet.

– William Lloyd George

These people understood, tolerated, and even courted failure. They were alternately exhilarated, confident, and scared to death, but they didn't perceive failure as a stigma. They were able to say, "Sure, that didn't work, but watch this."

They saw failure not as a sign of defeat, but as a prelude to success. Failure to them was a stage or step to be understood and then used to best advantage—a delayed success. They embraced failure and manipulated it as a creative agent to drive their work. Their lives were failure-success cycles. Their submarines sank, their rockets exploded, their domes collapsed, their serums didn't work. But they documented their mistakes, they tried something else, then something else, and then something else again.

Failure is the condiment that gives success its flavor.

– Truman Capote

From the artist's studio to the scientist's laboratory, for the satisfaction of a problem solved or a fortune gained, those who seek to live their dreams and to conquer the new or simply to challenge the status quo all risk failure.

Buckminster Fuller built his geodesic domes by starting with a deliberately failed dome and making it "a little stronger and a little stronger…a little piece of wood here and a little piece of wood there, and suddenly it stood up." He edged from failure to success.

"There has never been a time in the industry where there are more opportunities but such a lack of human capital," laments high tech headhunter David Beirne. "The talent is not there to populate all the companies that have sprung up. So a lot of guys who have made mistakes are getting in on the opportunities. A lot of sins are being forgiven."

– *Forbes Magazine*, "Bouncing Back," (July, 1997)

A television program on "The Mystery of the Master Builders," part of the Nova series, made reference to how architects learned from mistakes to create some of the world's most beautiful Gothic cathedrals.

Builders of Notre Dame in Paris discovered that wind velocity increases with elevation, causing greater stress to taller buildings. "Pressures at the top of Notre Dame were much greater than anyone had foreseen," said the show's narrator. "The builders here had pushed into unknown territory. They faced new challenges, made mistakes, and devised new solutions. Notre Dame established the fashion for flying buttresses, but it was a fashion forged by necessity." And it was forged by trial and error. These discoveries led to the addition of flying buttresses to the cathedral at Bourges, France, which was not originally designed to have them.

But most of us equate failure with inadequacy or rejection. Failure suggests a shame to be borne in secret. Mistakes in school, on the job, or in social milieus are the switches with which we beat ourselves.

A major form of information anxiety exists because of the fear of failing to understand or of admitting a lack of understanding. Assimilating information means venturing into the realms of the new and unknown in order to come to understand them.

And with any new undertaking, the risk of failure increases. Some people shun new information and new technology to avoid the risk. Others persist despite their fears, but the burden of their fear of failure will make the acquisition of new information that much more difficult.

Perhaps if we kept in mind that many extraordinary people expect failure, we wouldn't fear it so much and could begin to learn how to use it.

PROPER MANAGEMENT OF FAILURE BREEDS SUCCESS

Success exploits the seeds that failure plants. Failure contains tremendous growth energy.

Human efforts that fail dramatize the nobility of inspired, persistent human endeavor. Great achievements have been built on foundations of inadequacy and error. The discovery of America was made when **Christopher Columbus** took a wrong turn en route (he thought) to the East Indies. **Charles Goodyear** bungled an experiment and discovered vulcanized rubber. **Sir Isaac Newton** failed geometry, and **Albert Einstein** lacked an aptitude for math. **Paul Gauguin** was a failed stockbroker, and **Alfred Butts** invented the game of SCRABBLE® after he lost his job as an architect during the Depression. **Robert Redford** wanted to be a painter.

If failing can be seen as a necessary prelude to impressive achievement, then the process of succeeding itself can be better understood.

The aspiration and determination of an athlete to succeed when his body is ruined, of an engineer to build again when his bridge falls down, of a nation to prosper after its economy has crashed,

---

Every strike brings me closer to the next home run.

– Babe Ruth

…in the high tech industry, failure is a prized, not a scorned, offense. Along Philadelphia's Main Line, on Wall Street, or in the Motor City, the executive who flops gets driven out and often becomes un-employable. But in Silicon Valley, failure is an everyday event. There's little (if any) stigma attached to a washout. Failing is even considered highly desir-able management experience.

This forgiving attitude is what makes the technology sector so dynamic. A failure is rarely a dead end; it's just another opportunity. The unemployment rate in Silicon Valley—consistently lower than the national average—reflects this entrepreneurial spirit. Currently just 3% of Silicon Valley residents are jobless, versus 5.3% nationally.

– *Forbes Magazine*, "Bouncing Back," (July, 1997)

or of a scientist to conduct years of unsuccessful experiments help us understand the origins of success. Their failures—sometimes quiet and interminable, sometimes quick and spectacular—define the foundations of success and the spirit it needs.

While thinking about how I was taught values, I realized I was taught to value the effort and the exploration that came before success. I have found that failure and the analysis of failure have always been more interesting to me, and I learn something from them. I don't learn anything by basking in success. When I can honestly say "I don't know," I begin to know. "I think of information as the oil in a piece of machinery," said **Nathan Felde**, the founding partner of Mezza. The information permits operation. There are a lot of systems now that are being designed by people who fail to notice that the exhaust pipe runs back into the passenger compartment. They are running along at quite a clip pouring exhaust into the cockpit or the passenger compartment; people are used to it; they have adjusted to a very high level of exhaust.

YOU WON'T BELIEVE WHAT WENT WRONG

In order to get to the bottom, in order to find what is there, you really do have to fail. We have a culture that sustains only the manifestation of success.

While many people probably aren't consciously aware of it, we all possess the capacity for endowing failure with more nobility— or at least with more humor and affection. When we look back on our lives, sometimes the things that we remember most fondly are the times when everything went wrong. I know a woman who could write a book about the terrible things that have happened to her on first days: the first day of school, the first day of a new job. Once she wore two different kinds of shoes and didn't discover it until the day was over. Another time she was beset by a case of static cling. After performing in what she thought was an exemplary manner during her first four hours at a new job, a coworker informed her that she had a pair of rainbow-colored panties clinging to the back of her white blouse.

When people talk about their vacations, invariably what they recount with the most delight are the misadventures. Long after

Flying is learning how to throw yourself at the ground and miss.

– Douglas Adams

they have forgotten the names of the cathedrals and museums, they will remember the time they went to California and their luggage went to Caracas, when the hotel in Hong Kong lost their reservations and they spent the night in the hotel sauna, when they rushed to the JFK Airport in New York to catch a plane that left from La Guardia.

In all my travels, one of my fondest memories was getting stuck on a hot runway in Jodhpur, India. I was en route to Jaipur and the plane had mechanical difficulties. Airport personnel told us that we would be there for seven hours and would have to wait on the plane. I was the only foreigner on the plane. After an hour, I started berating the airline personnel. I insisted that they find a bus and take us into town so at least we could see the place and have lunch. They did. After letting everyone else off the bus at a restaurant, the driver turned to me and said, "You stay on the bus. You're going to get a tour of Jodhpur." We returned to the restaurant to find everyone else still waiting for lunch. Someone from the airlines came and, glaring directly at me, made an announcement, "The plane is ready now, but you are going to eat first."

We all happily recount our misadventures when it comes to travel. We should be able to do more of this in our professional lives. When **John Naisbitt** was questioned for acting as a business consultant after his own company almost went bankrupt, he asserted that for this very reason, he was a better consultant. He understood from experience what could go wrong in a company.

In my company, I respect the person who can come to me and say, "I'm sorry. I tried something, and it didn't work." I know that the person has learned something.

THE BREAKING POINT

I am interested in failure because that is the moment of learning—the moment of jeopardy that is both interesting and enlightening. The fundamental means of teaching a course in structural engineering is to show the moment when a piece of wood breaks, when a piece of steel bends, when a piece of stone or concrete collapses. You learn by watching something fail to work. **William Lear**, who invented the jet that bears his name, invented a steam

---

Every exit is an entry somewhere else.

– Tom Stoppard

car and all sorts of other things that he was certain would fail. He felt that there was a cyclical relationship between failure and success, and that failure was the necessary first part of the cycle.

I often think one's life is molded more by inability than ability. When I visited the aerospace museum in Washington, D.C., as marvelous as it is, I missed the epiphany of things that failed. A few years ago, to celebrate the anniversary of the Wright airplane, there was an article in *Scientific American* about the **Wright brothers** and their inventions. It made me think about the beginning of that wonderful film, *Those Magnificent Men in Their Flying Machines*, in which you see a litany of failed aircraft. You laugh, but you also see how seriously involved everybody was in trying to fly. All the failures, all the things that didn't work, make you realize that the Wright brothers were really something. All the paths taken, all the good intentions, the logistics, the absurdities, all the hopes of people trying to fly testifying to the power we have when we refuse to quit.

> Because a fellow has failed once or twice, or a dozen times, you don't want to set him down as a failure till he's dead or loses his courage—and that's the same thing.
>
> – George Lorimer

MUSEUM OF FAILURE IS OVERNIGHT SUCCESS

There should be a museum dedicated to human inventive failure. The only problem it would face would be its overnight success. In almost any scientific field, it would add enormously to the understanding of what does work by showing what doesn't work. In developing the polio vaccine, **Jonas Salk** spent 98 percent of his time documenting the things that didn't work until he found the thing that did.

A scientist's notebook is basically a journal of negative results. Scientists try to disprove their ideas—that is the work they do. "Images become useful to scientists to the extent that they contain information that contradicts conventional wisdom, forming the basis of a polemical understanding of nature," according to **Chandra Mukerji** in a paper, "Imaginary Dialogues: The Practice of Picture-Making in Scientific Research," delivered at the International Sociological Association and published in 1986.

As economist **Kenneth Boulding** said, "The moral of evolution is that nothing fails like success because successful adaptation leads to the loss of adaptability.... This is why a purely technical education can be disastrous. It trains people only in thinking of things that have been thought of and this will eventually lead to disaster."

If you put a camera on the Golden Gate Bridge and photographed it for 20 years, you wouldn't learn very much because the bridge succeeded. You learn much more from the documentation of failure. So failure can be defined as delayed success.

The anxiety associated with failure inhibits us from exploiting our creativity, from taking the risks that might lead us into new territory, and from learning and thus assimilating new information. An acceptance of failure as a necessary prelude to success is imperative to reducing anxiety.

SOME OF MY FAILURES

For most of my career, I was not successful. I couldn't glue two nickels together. At best, I kind of failed sideways my whole life. Though to call some of what happened "sideways" would be to give it a pretty face.

I started an architecture firm with two partners, and for 13 years the firm never made it. My partners couldn't get clients, and I couldn't bear the idea of doing what somebody said to do; I was kind of an angry young man. Before the firm could go bankrupt, we closed it. I had no idea what I was going to do. That was not a trivial failure. I mean, 13 years of struggling is not a trivial amount of time. I've had lots of other failures.

Through the 1970s I lived thinly, although other people always thought I was rich, even when I was living in a third-floor garret over a restaurant kitchen in a bad part of Philadelphia and didn't own a car. People thought I was independently wealthy because I dressed badly and didn't care what I said at meetings. "You always must have had money," they'll say to me now. "I mean, you always did what you wanted to do." Yeah, and that's equated with money. It was the only way people could explain it to themselves. By 1981 all I owned was a used Honda. I didn't have a business.

Despite my subsequent success with Access Press, and the Smart Yellow Pages, then with *Information Anxiety*, and the **TED** conferences as they found an audience, I have continued with failures. I have a phrase, like a mantra, that I tell people all the time: "Most things don't work." This doesn't just refer to bad ideas. I have lots of ideas, more than that, I have lots of good ideas. Lots of my good ideas never happen for various reasons.

Apparent failure may hold in its rough shell the germs of a success that will blossom in time, and bear fruit throughout eternity.

– Frances Watkins Harper

MOMA ACCESS. One of the Access guides I always wanted to do, but that never happened, was MOMA Access. I knew all the right people for contributions. **Abbott Miller** and I worked on it for years, and we completed a fully-researched comp of the entire book. I have boxes of research, design, correspondence and plans. But it never happened.

On Time. This was a project I considered one of my best ideas: a clearer way of scanning airline schedules combined with the best features of the Access guides. *On Time* existed as a monthly publication for six months in 1991. Unfortunately, before it had a chance to catch on, we lost our funding, and it died.

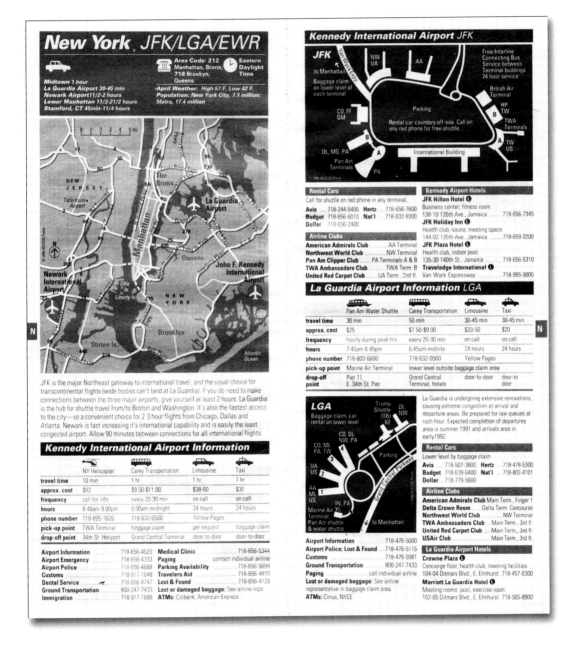

TEDMED & TEDMED2. One of my more-specifically focused **TED** conferences was **TED**MED in 1995. I had great contacts with a number of huge companies in related fields. I had the benefit of a large audience of **TED** regulars, who I thought would be as taken as I was with interest in learning more about their bodies.

I got an extraordinary group of presenters for **TED**MED. But only a few of the **TED** regulars registered. We even did a number of trade ads and a slick four-color mailing piece, but still very few people registered. I sucked it in, and went ahead with **TED**MED because I was confident it was compelling, it was important, and I had great speakers. The program came off well, but I didn't have the energy I wanted from a full auditorium. Somehow, we were in limbo—**TED** regulars didn't register, the theme didn't resonate for people hearing about **TED** for the first time, and **TED** is intrinsically so different than trade shows that the concept was lost on the healthcare community. I lost money on **TED**MED, and I've been spoiled over the years with the growing success of **TED**, so that hurt.

Based on that, you'd probably think I would never consider doing it again. I was determined not to, but a number of friends and acquaintances connected at the time with major players in related fields ponied up as general sponsors to underwrite **TED**MED**2** in 1998. I honestly believed that after **TED**MED had come off as a good experience, and with the growing buzz about **TED** in general, that it would take the second time just like **TED**2.

Once again, I got great presenters, but once again, it was a battle to get an audience. Our audience was larger than that of **TED**MED, but still we fell short in energy. I was very happy with the program, and it was certainly more successful financially because of the generous sponsors.

So, does that mean **TED**MED is dead? Maybe not. I've been approached by others more recently, but I'm not planning anything yet.

TEDNYC. I suppose I should have learned my lesson and just stuck with the growing success of the regular **TED**s in Monterey, but between the **TED**MEDs, I decided to go ahead and hold a special **TED** in New York. I decided that since I was holding this meeting

---

"Bricolage" is a French word which (loosely translated) can be taken to mean "trial-and-error," learning by poking around, trying this or that until you eventually figure it out. This is one of the best ways to approach learning on the computer. If you do something "wrong," the sky won't fall, you won't get shot. Just try again...

– Seymour Papert,
The Connected Family Web site

in New York, I would focus on learning as a new business, particularly with the involvement of the entertainment industry. I got major support from *Variety* to get the word out, along with trade ads with a number of other magazines. There was a definite built-in negative with New York because of holding **TED** in Monterey. For the most part, I have a captive audience, flying in for the intensive conference experience. Outside of making phone calls, or connected with others at **TED** on joint projects, everyone there is focused on the conference. New York City was a constant distraction to the **TED**NYC conferees, even though some of the best moments ever at **TED** took place during those four days.

TEDCITY. My latest effort at an overt variation on the classic **TED** experience was a joint venture with the brilliant and iconoclastic **Moses Znaimer** of CityTV in Toronto, the producer of the most innovative television programming in the world. We looked to bring together our expertise and connections to produce a Canadian **TED**, called **TED**CITY, in Toronto in June 2000.

Again we found ourselves with the seemingly perennial situation of non-Monterey **TED**s—failure to achieve sold-out registration before the event. Once again we had an impressive and eclectic list of presenters—some of whom we had tried and failed to get to **TED** in Monterey. We had a good crowd, but there were some gaps. Some sessions were better attended than others, for reasons similar to what happened at **TED**NYC—people from Toronto had business they could attend to, and visitors were drawn away by Toronto's attractions.

TEDCITY as a conference surpassed my expectations, but at the same time there were some disappointments, mostly because we didn't have a captive audience that would then have a collective memory of four days designed as a single piece. The image I use would be viewing the left half of DaVinci's Last Supper on Tuesday and Thursday, and then the right half on Monday and Wednesday. The **TED** conferences are designed to be experienced as a whole.

TED
TED2
TED3
TED4KOBE
TED5
TED6
TED7
TED8
TED9
TEDX
TED11
TEDCity
TEDMED
TEDMED2
TEDNYC
TEDSELL

MAGAZINETED. Even though I've discussed it with a number of parties over the years, it's never clicked. The concept is a magazine, split into two distinct sections: **TED**-related interviews, and sharp and probing editorial content, and then sponsor advertisements with each four pages long, each informing about a product or service in the depth possible with that much space. Between the two sections, there would be a series of perforated cards to mail in for more information on the advertisements.

My wife claims I warm up only upon rejection. I'm a welter of insecurities. I'm insecure about not understanding what the next person does, about not being as smart as the people listening to me, about teaching in schools that I could never get into, about running conferences where everybody is sharper and faster than I am.

When I was a child, I once saw someone in a wheelchair. My mother told me that the person in the wheelchair had been in an accident and would recover, but would need to learn to walk again. That was a revelation to me because it seemed that once we'd learned to walk, that we'd always know how to walk.

The notion of learning to walk has lingered in my mind, and I've contemplated the process of teaching someone to walk again. I realized that this process has a lot to do with thrusting a leg out into the terror of losing your balance, then regaining your equilibrium, moving you forward, then repeating with your other leg. Failure as loss of balance, the success of equilibrium, and you move forward. Terror of falling, confidence, regaining your balance—it's a fascinating metaphor for life. Risk is half of the process of moving forward. The risk of falling is inherent in achieving a goal.

My life has been marked by a continual series of failures, interspersed with successes. I am grateful for my failures—because of them I had nothing to lose, and could indulge my interests with occasional crucial successes, as well as more failures so I was able to design my life. By designing my life, I have been able to choose the projects I have worked on for my entire life.

17 DESIGNING YOUR LIFE

I was originally trained as an architect and my mentor was and is **Louis Kahn**. In 1959, I graduated first in my class in the School of Architecture at the University of Pennsylvania—then the best school in the country. I was the fair-haired boy, a protégé of the great Louis Kahn. Anything was possible. Even though Lou Kahn died years ago, he still lives with me every day.

I taught at a number of schools, from Cambridge University in England to Princeton to the City College of New York. Also at the University of North Carolina at Raleigh, and Washington University at St. Louis, where I did the *Urban Atlas* with **Joe Passonneau** for the MIT Press, the first comparative statistical atlas of major American cities. I taught as well at UCLA and USC. I always preferred to teach at the top or the bottom—graduate students or freshmen.

> If a man will begin with certainties, he shall end in doubts, but if he will be content to begin with doubts, he shall end in certainties.
>
> – Francis Bacon

DOING WHAT YOU WANT TO DO EACH DAY

My opening line to my students, and a recurring theme in my classes, was that the big design problem isn't designing a house for your parents or yourself, a museum, or a toaster, or a book, or whatever. The big design problem is designing your life. It's by the design of your life that you create the backboard off which you bounce all your thoughts and ideas and creativity. You have to decide what it is you want to do each day.

> Appetite comes with eating; the more one has, the more one would have.
>
> – French proverb

There's an **Eddie Murphy** movie in which he plays a soothsayer, and he makes the comment that you only have about 75 summers, 75 falls, 75 winters, and 75 springs. You only have 75 of everything, so you better make good use of them. Time is your only commodity—what else do you have?

If we are able to design our lives, wouldn't the best result—the best measure of success, ultimately—be that every day is interesting? Most people don't have enough interesting things in their lives, so in place of interest they try to accumulate money and power. But I think you're going to be a better businessperson if you look at your life as a collection of hobbies, a collection of interests, not a matter of things you do during the day and things you do in the evening—or what you do during the day and what you do during the weekend. Think of everything you do as driven by and connected to your real interests, and it will affect everything you do.

So, I really measure my life by what I want to do each day, which is a design problem that we have some control over. We can decide each day what our tradeoffs will be. Designing your life is not just a matter of deciding to be a suit or an artist. We have to decide if our object is power, fortune, and fame.

TERMINAL FAME

Fame is an interesting thing, and I've come up with a concept called terminal fame. If you were to fall from an airplane, you would reach a terminal velocity. You can only fall so fast —that's it, you will only reach a certain speed. So, if you're an accountant, no matter how good you are—even the best in the world—you can only reach a certain level of fame. If you're one of the best lawyers, you would be that much more famous. Of course, if you're a sports figure regarded as the very best, like Michael Jordan was, or Tiger Woods is now, almost everyone knows who you are.

As the creator of my own field of specialization—Information Architecture—I am as famous as I can be, which is marginally more than an accountant. No matter what I do, I cannot become more famous—unless I were to achieve widespread notoriety for doing something like killing someone universally famous, but not as an Information Architect.

BEYOND MONEY

If it takes X/2 dollars to live with comfort, then past the point of having X dollars, there is no value in having 2X, 10X, 20X. I think there are people who are starting to realize that they have more money than they can spend. After you get past the point of realizing there's no value in having more money, you realize there's value in doing what you want to do every day.

There is a certain generosity of spirit and ideas happening for people who have acquired a certain amount of wealth of really trying to think what it is they want to do with their lives. And that's happening more than ever before. Many people feel that too much money can actually be a deterrent to a good life.

So the classic goals of money, fame, and power perhaps should be reconfigured to achieving interesting days, and the two phases of well-being—physical and financial.

You have riches and freedom here but I feel no sense of faith or direction. You have so many computers, why don't you use them in the search for love?

– Lech Walesa

I'd like to live as a poor man with lots of money.

– Pablo Picasso

TOPS BOOKS

It's this simple. Everything that really matters boils down to just two things: Health & Wealth.

Finding helpful information is difficult: What questions do I ask? Why are the answers so hard to understand?

To help remedy these problems, I recently created a company called TOP, a new publishing venture in partnership with Ovations, a $4 billion UnitedHealth Group company.

TOPs book series and Internet content will cover a myriad of life topics. The key to TOPs formula is the design of understanding. Understanding comes from questions, not from answers. Based on the questions most asked by consumers, the books' answers are clear and informative.

DECIDING WHAT TO DO WITH YOUR LIFE

Man is free at the moment he wishes to be.

– Voltaire

The romance novelist, Barbara Cartland, was buried in a cardboard coffin in her garden in May 2000. The London-based National Death Centre encourages burial in cardboard coffins in woodland burial sites; more than 90 have been created in Britain since 1993, with 40 more now in development.

– Potter, Mitch
"Cardboard Coffins
Catching On in U.K.,"
Toronto Star, (6/4/00)

Read, every day, something no one else is reading. Think, every day, something no one else is thinking. Do, every day, something no one else would be silly enough to do. It is bad for the mind to continually be part of unanimity.

– Christopher Morley

I have come to the realization that what you choose to do should be a combination of what you like to do and what you do well. It's not realistic to expect to be successful, given just one or the other—it has to be a combination of both. Sometimes, people work at things they really want to do, but they aren't any good at them. But given both desire and capability, you can design your life.

It's not an issue of personally designing every minuscule feature of your surroundings, or of being in one of the design professions. You can, however, design your life in terms of decision-making, of making a series of choices versus alternatives (such as whether or not you work for someone else). You can do this and enjoy each day, consciously understanding your decisions and the trade-offs they involve with power, fame, and family.

I could never bear working for other people. My work has to do with overcoming the thoughts with which I have discomfort. My own understanding or lack of it is enough with which to begin. Committee meetings and market research are not part of this process. I don't believe in using such methods to determine what subjects to tackle for projects. Confidence in your own understanding, acceptance of your ignorance, and determination to pursue your interests are the weapons against anxiety.

There are sappy people on television and lecture circuits who feed unhappy and unfulfilled people pabulum—things they want to hear to make them feel better, but that doesn't change anything. We're not taught about designing our lives in school. Not learning this is an ethical issue, it's a moral issue, it's an issue of empowerment. You have to understand yourself—your life, your interests, your aptitudes—to empower yourself. This is not a multiple-step, pop-psychology solution. You can't begin to know how to specifically design your own life until you understand yourself and your situation. You have to be able to communicate this detailed understanding of yourself clearly in a form that your mother or a literate twelve-year-old would understand.

Honesty and understanding are critical to designing your own life. Telling the truth—the absolute truth—for 48 hours is a test that borders on the impossible. However, where and when you fail in that test is a telling profile of yourself.

OUR LIVES AND OUR TIMES

I think we are at a moment in history, perhaps the first time, when many people can start designing their lives. They can design where they work, what work they want to do, and when. This is design in a broader sense. Designing your life would be considered a concept outside of the boundaries of design. Designing your life has all kinds of well-being implications.

Because of the affluence in this country, there is a part of the population—not everybody, but more people than ever before—who can make a decision about what they want to do and what they don't want to do, when they want do it, and when they want to stop doing it.

It is stated that most people now change their careers 8–10 times in their lifetime, and that will go up. There is no longer an onus on being at a job for a year before going on to something else. The former concept of being at one job for your whole life or for most of your life—and the importance of that, the sociological ideal of that—is gone. In fact, one is suspect for being at a job for a long time. It's a point of strangeness, and it's considered something unusual. And in fact there's no great reward. The vesting of stock is a short-term thing, and even people on Wall Street have been fired but still get their bonuses and their stock vestments. So there's no huge financial gain for being at a job more than three or four years, and sometimes less.

This all has to do with work and design and the notion of how we can design our lives. You are no longer expected to go into your father's business, whether he owned it or not, or even your father's occupation. There are more and more people not doing anything that they were familiar with growing up, or what the people they came in contact with did. Television and movies allow you to see what everybody does. Television in particular allows you to have ideals outside of anything that you would have fantasized about before, or even that your high school counselors knew about.

So for example, as a result of Watergate, people went into journalism, and at other times they go into architecture, they go to Wall Street, they go into television, they go into various careers

We live in a moment of history where change is so speeded up that we begin to see the present only when it is already disappearing.

– R. D. Laing, *The Politics of Experience*

A specialist is a man who knows more and more about less and less.

– William James Mayo

When making a decision of minor importance, I have always found it advantageous to consider all the pros and cons. In vital matters, however, such as the choice of a mate or a profession, the decision should come from the unconscious, from somewhere within ourselves. In the important decisions of personal life, we should be governed, I think, by the deep inner needs of our nature.

– Sigmund Freud

on which they had no background, or on which anyone could advise them. This is a result of our new broader media environment of cable and satellite television and the Internet.

This will be the decade of empowerment, when people will make these choices about where they work, how long they stay at a job, and what interests them. The word interest will dominate not only your job, but your learning throughout your life. You will be freer to take courses that you are interested in as more and more parents are making the choice to home school, or have the ability to add to our education through the Internet. These choices will be based on what interests us, not what's given to us.

WHAT I DO ISN'T WORK

I believe work is joy, and when people ask me what kind of work I do, I tell them I don't do work—everything I do I enjoy. I choose what I want to do every day, and I don't work so I can have a weekend free, or two weeks free for a vacation. My whole life I really feel I'm on the vacation; this comes from doing what I really love to do—which is what a vacation is. My personal journey is the design of my life, so my work is joy.

I need to define freedom. Most people confuse freedom with permissiveness, but freedom has happy limitations within which you are free. Permissiveness is chaotic—there is nothing free about permissiveness because you have no boundaries, so you have anarchy. I believe I have happy limitations in my life which allow me to enjoy myself and my work. That's the way I live my life.

Happy limitations are the rules of the game. What would happen if we had a football game with no rules? Within those rules you have a better game, you have a lot of freedom to make plays. Happy limitations give you more freedom, give you a quality of freedom. Freedom in this country is based on happy limitations, and it is the greatest country in the world. We have happy limitations within which we have more freedom than anyone else in the world. Rules in themselves are not bad. As a concept, limitations are not bad, but specific rules can be terrible.

I don't think what I'm saying applies to everybody, because it's not possible for everybody, but it's the trend that more and more people can talk the way I'm talking. There's the difference between needs

> The more money an American accumulates, the less interesting he becomes.
>
> – Gore Vidal

> To laugh often and much; to win the respect of intelligent people and the affection of children; to earn the appreciation of honest critics and endure the betrayal of false friends; to appreciate beauty, to find the best in others; to leave the world a little better, whether by a healthy child, a garden patch or a redeemed social condition; to know even one life has breathed easier because you have lived. This is the meaning of success.
>
> – Ralph Waldo Emerson

and desires. A huge part of the world's population still doesn't have their needs taken care of, so for them what I'm saying is meaningless. In a more affluent world there is a trend towards what I'm saying.

DESIGN IN THE DRIVER'S SEAT

There are major companies where design is now in the driver's seat. More and more the automotive industry is run by designers rather than engineers, who did run it, as short a time as five years ago. And now people buy cars because of design. I have a Volkswagen Bug—I don't know what kind of engine it has. I don't know anything about its engineering. I bought it because it's a well-designed product.

Steve Jobs would be the first to admit that Apple Macintosh computers are driven by design. There is certainly great performance as well, but what's really taking them into the marketplace is design. It's not engineering that's just been packaged with design. The new Apple Cube is design and engineering locked together.

"Will & Still" is the theme for February 2001, where most of the presenters will be over 70 or under 30. Simply the greatest design conference that ever was. Everything from designing your life, designing your learning, designing your technology, designing your music and entertainment, designing your sensuality, your health, your chairs, your products, your cars. Design in the driver's seat in the new economy.

The physical design of offices, I must say, is slightly overplayed. In a recent *Business Week* there is a whole section on new fantasy offices, which I think strangely look like they came out of the Jetsons. Over the past few years, however, there has been a focus on really good chairs, which largely comes from trying to design your health, caring about your body, caring about your back, and not about aesthetics. The new chairs that people sit on in offices (the Aeron chair, and the Leap chair, and the Freedom chair— the three new wonderful, very comfortable chairs), don't fit in with any offices I know. So it has nothing to do with design as an aesthetic, but the design of your body, and you taking charge of what you want.

> Sometimes it is more important to discover what one cannot do, than what one can do.
>
> – Lin Yu-t'ang

> I think knowing what you cannot do is more important than knowing what you can do. In fact, that's good taste.
>
> – Lucille Ball

> The best way to have a good idea is to have lots of ideas.
>
> – Linus Pauling

EMPOWERING CONSUMERS

Corporations are responding to this by empowering people to make their own decisions. They are empowering people to find their way, to navigate through information, products, and comments about products. You can go to barnesandnoble.com and Amazon.com and write your own reviews. This gives you freedom to find out things.

This is why we created libraries. The Library of Alexandria was man's knowledge in one place—the core of civilization. And now we have it in everybody's home, at everybody's desk. We are empowered in an astonishing way, and certainly our economy is based now on that freedom of search, finding sources, the freedom of finding out.

More and more we'll be able to take vicarious vacations, if we can't afford the real ones. There will be a lot of empowering of people, and through the empowering of people a lot of products and a lot of industries will develop and grow. People are doing things they've never done before, in finding out the news, buying things on eBay, collecting things, understanding about antiques, buying clothes, and all kinds of things.

These new freedoms lead to even more freedom in our lives like the convenience of being able to buy almost anything on the Web (even cars) to a greater freedom to communicate (for example, by phone—the amazing invention of the past century, the more recent invention of the fax, which made people go back to writing letters and drawing little pictures in the margins, to email for being in touch with your family).

I have kids as well as grandkids in New York and Oklahoma, and I'm constantly getting photos emailed to me that are only a minute old. And I'm not high tech. We are becoming more of a community by being able to do things like that. This is an empowerment for everybody—more in control of our lives, more in control of our desires, and closer to our families, which is really quite wonderful. And it's not just for the wealthy.

Human history becomes more and more a race between education and catastrophe.

– H. G. Wells

The shepherd always tries to persuade the sheep that their interests and his own are the same.

– Stendhal

INDULGENCE VERSUS GUILT

We all probably subscribe to too many magazines, and bookmark a huge number of Web sites that we glance at a couple of times, then never go back. At times we might become anxious that we are not keeping up with important developments, and try to ingest much greater amounts of information from various sources. At other times, we might try to cut back, to simplify things, perhaps because of the guilt we're experiencing for falling behind.

Over the period of a week I receive a great number of emails, many times referring me to multiple URL addresses of Web sites recommended for my attention, which then of course point me to even more Web sites. All these, along with the many books and videotapes and CD-ROMs and magazine articles and newspaper clippings that people send me, leave me with the 21st-Century embodiment of a Jewish mother making me feel guilty for being behind on everything it seems I should know.

How do I handle this? I have to give myself permission to pursue only my own interests. This doesn't mean that my interests are unchanging and tightly limited, but that I have to direct my pursuit of information for it to be meaningful and manageable.

Our culture's puritanical origins have given the word *indulgence* a bad rap. It connotes the sybaritic or excessive. Yet, I am proud of how much I am able to make my life purely indulgent, to indulge my curiosity, my spirit, my ability to hear and see, to think up ideas, to see patterns.

My wife, **Gloria Nagy**, wrote a children's book about an evil wizard who can't stand it that people love Santa Claus, who has all these people helping him so he only has to work one day a year. That's an indulgent life. The capstone of my indulgence is the **TED** conferences.

I've modeled myself by that life. I work four days a year at the **TED** conference, and I get to hear and talk to the most interesting people who I've been able to find during the year. I've even gone one better than Santa: People pay me to come along for the ride. When we think of indulgence, we think of the salons in Paris, where people

Find something you're passionate about and keep tremendously interested in it.

– Julia Child

In order to live free and happily you must sacrifice boredom. It is not always an easy sacrifice.

– Richard Bach

Illustrations by Seymour Chwast

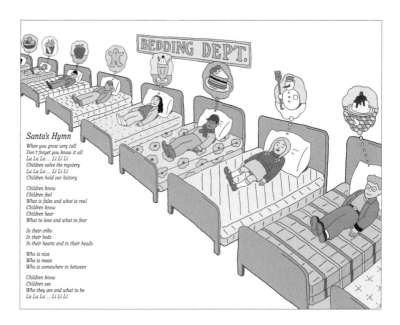

Santa's Hymn

When you grow very tall
Don't forget you know it all
La La La ... Li Li Li
Children solve the mystery
La La La ... Li Li Li
Children hold our history

Children know
Children feel
What is false and what is real
Children know
Children hear
What to love and what to fear

In their cribs
In their beds
In their hearts and in their heads

Who is nice
Who is mean
Who is somewhere in between

Children know
Children see
Who they are and what to be
La La La ... Li Li Li

drank absinthe, ate oysters, and traded stories in **Gertrude Stein**'s apartment, both egomaniacal and intelligent stories about themselves and their work. That's the model I use for **TED**—surrounding myself with the people, subjects, and issues that interest me.

So I literally program the **TED** conferences for myself. I invite presenters who are involved with things that I want to learn. While I am grateful for suggestions from my friends and acquaintances, as well as people pitching themselves, I use myself and the directions of my interests to filter all the possible presentations for **TED**.

For example, I invited **George Dyson** to come to **TED** a few years ago to make a presentation. I didn't invite him because his sister **Esther Dyson** suggested him, or because his speaking bureau encouraged me to have him join us, but because I read the review of his book *Darwin Among the Machines*, in the *New York Times Book Review*. He then spoke instead of his lifelong passion for building kayaks (about which he'd written another book). So, I make my plans, but then many things develop serendipitously.

Last year, I invited the **Raspyni Brothers**, a comedy juggling act. "No, we aren't brothers, and we aren't Italian either," they told us. Everyone loved them, and they loved being there. They juggled small maces on a stage decorated with $2 million worth of **Dale Chihuly**'s glass art. One of the maces flew apart and just missed a delicate piece of glass, as well as someone in the audience. They took out duct tape and wrapped the broken mace together, and they continued like it was part of the act. At dinner, they admitted it was a total mistake, but they didn't lose a beat. The audience was completely caught up in their amazing performance.

I believe I'm very normal. I'm hyper-normal. I'm more normal than anyone else I know. I think my thoughts, my indulgences, my desires, my pleasures may at first appear different, but that is only because they are more normal, not because they are more esoteric.

I believe I am bored when other people are bored, only faster. I am interested when others are interested, only more interested. But I also think I'm less, rather than more, intelligent than other people.

By indulging my interests throughout my life, and perhaps because of rather than despite many failures, I have been able to design my life.

My riches consist not in the extent of my possessions, but in the fewness of my wants.

– J. Brotherton

INDEX

A

abandoned Internet sales, 12
absolute instructions, 221
ACCESS© guides, 252
    personal failures, 278
accessibility, guide book examples, 21
accessing, importance, 21
ACCESSPRESS Ltd., 21
accuracy
    information, 13
    journalists, 31
    writers, 31
achieving goals, 185
acquiring information (Internet), 13
action, instructing, 199
adjectivitus (overuse of language), 57
adjusting Internet communication
  channels, 9
administering
    empowering employees, 195
    failure, 273
    flow of information, 180
    frustrations, 190
    improvement, 79
    instructions, 61-68, 185
    managers, 189
    no surprises, 182
    perception, 227
    temper tantrums, 182
    work environments, 179
administrating
    education, 238
    details, 59
    over administrating
      (administrativitis), 59
admitting
    ignorance, 25
    lack of understanding, 56

advertising
    attracting attention, 119
    audience, targeting, 84
    branding, 82
    classifieds, 104
    as communication, 81
    creating buzz, 117-118
    creating interest, 85
    customers, 81
    determining base, 90
    customization, 120
    data mining, 91
    designing, 93-94
      for Generation X, 99
    examples, *Understanding USA*, 142
    first question, 130
    fragmentation, media, 90
    Generation X, 99
    integrating, 82
    Internet, 83
      designing sites, 95
    maintaining interest, 86
    marketing, 90
    online shopping, 120
    overstimulation, 86
    patterns, 121
    quality of information, 94
    space, 81
    Super Bowl, 82
    technology solutions, 131
    Understanding USA examples, 142
    with instructions, 200
    word-of-mouth, 116
    younger audiences, 99
aesthetics as disease, 56
Age of Also, 3
agendas, meetings, 125

agreements
    communicating, 193
    inherent in listening, 192
    instruction by, 192
    obeying, 194
    at work, 192
Allen, T. Harrell, 226
alphabet
    LATCH, 41
    organizing information, 41
American Kennel Club, classifying
  breeds, 43
American Management Association,
  227
An Overview of Understanding, **Nathan
  Shedroff,** 27
Anders Gronstedt, *see* Gronstedt,
  Anders
animating transitions (interfaces), 167
answering phones, 123
answering questions, 152
    Becoming President example, 148
    buying lighting example, 153
    education, 239
    usability, 144
anxiety
    antidote to 21-22
    as learning technique, 241
    destructiveness, 242
    understanding instructions, 219
applying empowerment, 198
Architecturally Speaking, **Eugene
  Raskin**, 86
architecture
    information, 23, 99
    instructions example, 207
    learning, 260
Archimedes, 257
archives, 175
Arno Penzias, *see* Penzias, Arno
art of listening, 114